Max-Planck-Institut für ausländisches öffentliches Recht und Völkerrecht

Beiträge zum ausländischen öffentlichen Recht und Völkerrecht

Begründet von Viktor Bruns

Herausgegeben von
Armin von Bogdandy · Rüdiger Wolfrum

Band 193

Doris König · Peter-Tobias Stoll
Volker Röben · Nele Matz-Lück (eds.)

International Law Today: New Challenges and the Need for Reform?

Springer
the language of science

ISSN 0172-4770
ISBN 978-3-540-75204-2 Springer Berlin · Heidelberg · New York

Bibliografische Information der Deutschen Nationalbibliothek
Die Deutsche Nationalbibliothek verzeichnet diese Publikation in der Deutschen Nationalbibliografie; detaillierte bibliografische Daten sind im Internet über http://dnb.d-nb.de abrufbar.

Herstellung: LE-TEX Jelonek, Schmidt & Vöckler GbR, Leipzig
Umschlaggestaltung: WMX Design GmbH, Heidelberg

SPIN 12161621 64/3180YL - 5 4 3 2 1 0 Gedruckt auf säurefreiem Papier

Preface

Rüdiger Wolfrum celebrated his 65th birthday on 13 December 2006. On this special occasion, current and former members of the large circle of his PhD and post-doctorate students (Doktoranden und Habilitanden) organized a symposium on the subject of "International Law Today: New Challenges and the Need for Reform?" to honour him and his academic work as a teacher and researcher. The symposium took place at the Max Planck Institute for Comparative Public Law and International Law in Heidelberg on 15 and 16 December 2006.

Since Rüdiger Wolfrum is a renowned scholar in many different fields of public national and international law, the subjects covered by the speakers and commentators reflect the wide variety of issues he worked on in his long and impressive academic career. They extend from a critical evaluation of the new responsibility to protect and the role of the UN Security Council in post-conflict management, thoughts on the proliferation of international tribunals with regard to the unity or fragmentation of international law, marine genetic resources in the deep sea and environmental protection in Antarctica to human rights issues relating to intellectual property rights and the protection of minorities. All the presentations focused on new trends in international law and thus followed the lead of Rüdiger Wolfrum who has always been at the forefront of innovative legal developments.

The symposium and the publication of its proceedings would not have been possible without the support and commitment of many whom I want to thank *in toto*. Special thanks go to *Tono Eitel*, *Thomas Mensah* and *Fred Morrison* who did not hesitate to come to Heidelberg a week before Christmas to chair the sessions of the symposium. In addition, a great deal of gratitude is owed to *Dr. Anja Seibert-Fohr* and to *Yvonne Klein* who shouldered the major part of organizing the symposium in Heidelberg, as well as to *Dr. Nele Matz-Lück* who took on the task of collecting and preparing the papers for timely publication. The linguistic quality of the contributions profited enormously from the proficiency of *Kate Elliott* who performed the native speaker check.

Hamburg, July 2007 Doris König

Contents

Responsibility, Sovereignty and Cooperation – Reflections on the "Responsibility to Protect"

Tobias Stoll

I. Introduction

The international system and its legal structures are the subject of a broad discussion that probably dates back to the times of the fall of the Berlin wall. The turn of the millennium, the catastrophic terrorist attacks of September 11, 2001 and the attempts to reform the United Nations in 2005 have each furthered the debate. It takes place at political, diplomatic and academic level, and even includes concepts of a constitutionalisation. Due to its basic perspective, this discussion relates to a number of very fundamental concepts of international law. Among these are responsibility, sovereignty and cooperation.

Most observers agree that the 2005 UN reform attempt produced only some fairly limited results. The establishment of the Human Rights

Council and the Peacebuilding-Commission may be regarded as the most visible institutional outcome. In terms of concepts, the idea of a "responsibility to protect"[1] seems to be one of the few results. Although the set of arguments and observations which in total represent the concept of a "responsibility to protect" have not resulted in significant changes in existing or the explicit creation of new rules, the discussion is still relevant. It may importantly influence views on some fundamentals of the international legal order and have implications far beyond the issue of humanitarian intervention, which was originally the focus of the development of that concept.[2]

After a brief explanation of its origin and contents (II.), the concept of a responsibility to protect will be analysed in the light of three fundamental issues of international law, namely: responsibility (III.), sovereignty (IV.) and cooperation (V.). It will be submitted that the "responsibility to protect" in explicitly appealing to the notion of responsibility is dubious, whereas its implications for the concept of sovereignty are quite helpful. However, as will be shown, the "responsibility to protect" somehow fails adequately to take into account the dimension of cooperation.

II. "Responsibility to Protect" – The Career of a Concept

The notion of "responsibility to protect" was initially developed by an "International Commission for Intervention and State Sovereignty"

---

1 See P. Hilpold, "The Duty to Protect and the Reform of the United Nations – A New Step in the Development of International Law?", *Max Planck UNYB* 10 (2006), p. 35 et seq.; I. Winkelmann, "'Responsibility to Protect': Die Verantwortung der Internationalen Gemeinschaft zur Gewährung von Schutz", in: P.M. Dupuy/B. Fassbender/M.N. Shaw/K-P. Sommermann (eds.), *Völkerrecht als Wertordnung. Common Values in International Law – Essays in Honour of Christian Tomuschat*, 2006, p. 449 et seq.; A.M. Slaughter, "Security, Solidarity, and Sovereignty: The Grand Themes of UN Reform", *AJIL* 99 (2005), 619 et seq.; L. Feinstein/A.M. Slaughter, "A Duty to Prevent", *Foreign Affairs* 83 (2004), 136 et seq.; G. Molier, "Humanitarian Intervention and the Responsibility to Protect After 9/11", *NILR* 2006, 37 et seq.

2 See below, text preceding footnote 4.

(ICISS) established by the Canadian Government.[3] The latter thereby responded to an initiative of the UN Secretary General, who had asked the international community to clarify the issue of humanitarian intervention. He stated:

> "... if humanitarian intervention is, indeed, an unacceptable assault on sovereignty, how should we respond to a Rwanda, to a Srebrenica – to gross and systematic violations of human rights that affect every precept of our common humanity?"[4]

As is well known, the ICISS came back with the concept of "responsibility to protect". It basically envisages that

> "[s]tate sovereignty implies responsibility, and the primary responsibility for the protection of its people lies with the state itself ..."[5]

and that

> "[w]here a population is suffering serious harm, as a result of internal war, insurgency, repression or state failure, and the state in question is unwilling or unable to halt or avert it, the principle of non-intervention yields to the international responsibility to protect."[6]

Furthermore, the Commission has voiced a responsibility to prevent,[7] to react[8] and to rebuild,[9] and has specifically attributed duties in this regard to states and the international community.

---

[3] International Commission on Intervention and State Sovereignty, The Responsibility to Protect, Report of the International Commission on Intervention and State Sovereignty, Ottawa, 2001, www.iciss.ca.

[4] Report of the Secretary-General on the Work of the Organization, A/55/1 para. 37.

[5] ICISS report (footnote 3), at XI – "Principles" under A.

[6] *Ibid.* under B.

[7] According to the Commission report, Basic Principles, (3)(A) this includes "... to address both the root causes and direct causes of internal conflict and other man-made crises putting populations at risk."

[8] The responsibility to react is defined as follows: "... to respond to situations of compelling human need with appropriate measures, which may include coercive measures like sanctions and international prosecution, and in extreme cases military intervention.", *ibid.*, (3)(B).

[9] C. According to the Commission, the "responsibility to rebuild" means: "... to provide, particularly after a military intervention, full assistance with recovery, reconstruction and reconciliation, addressing the causes of the harm the intervention was designed to halt or avert.", *ibid.*, (3)(C).

At this stage, it has already become clear that the "responsibility to protect" is a two-tiered concept. It first reiterates that it is the most fundamental and genuine function of States to protect their citizens.[10] Secondly, in the sense of an "*international* responsibility to protect"[11] some sort of joint action is envisaged, which may include an international intervention. More or less explicitly, under specific circumstances, the ICISS envisaged the justification of intervention even in cases where there is no authorization by the United Nations Security Council.[12]

With some differences in wording and formulation, this responsibility to protect was endorsed by the so-called "High-level Panel on Threats, Challenges and Change" set up by the Secretary General later to develop concepts and ideas for the reform of the United Nations. The Panel stated:

> "We endorse the emerging norm that there is a collective international responsibility to protect, exercisable by the Security Council authorizing military intervention as a last resort, in the event of genocide and other large-scale killing, ethnic cleansing or serious violations of international humanitarian law which sovereign Governments have proved powerless or unwilling to prevent."[13]

As this statement may indicate, the Panel has importantly developed and altered the concept. It endorsed the concept by referring to an "emerging norm". However, it considerably diverged from the ICISS by emphasizing a "collective international responsibility" to be exercised by the Security Council.

---

[10] See for details below, text accompanying footnote 41.

[11] Emphasis added.

[12] The ICISS states: "If the Security Council rejects a proposal or fails to deal with it in a reasonable time, alternative options are: I. consideration of the matter by the General Assembly in Emergency Special Session under the "Uniting for Peace" procedure; and II. action within area of jurisdiction by regional or sub-regional organizations under Chapter VIII of the Charter, subject to their seeking subsequent authorization from the Security Council." It goes on in emphasizing: "The Security Council should take into account in all its deliberations that, if it fails to discharge its responsibility to protect in conscience-shocking situations crying out for action, concerned states may not rule out other means to meet the gravity and urgency of that situation – and that the stature and credibility of the United Nations may suffer thereby."

[13] A more secure world: our shared responsibility, Report of the High-level Panel on Threats, Challenges and Change, A/59/565, 2 December 2004, para. 203. For a general analysis of the report see, Slaughter (footnote 1), *passim*.

Finally, the Secretary General himself, in his 2005 report "On larger freedom", – although in somewhat more cautious words – endorsed those views by stating:

> "I believe that we must embrace the responsibility to protect, and, when necessary, we must act on it. This responsibility lies, first and foremost, with each individual State, whose primary raison d'être and duty is to protect its population. But if national authorities are unable or unwilling to protect their citizens, then the responsibility shifts to the international community to use diplomatic, humanitarian and other methods to help protect the human rights and well-being of civilian populations. When such methods appear insufficient, the Security Council may out of necessity decide to take action under the Charter of the United Nations, including enforcement action, if so required."[14]

Finally, the Heads of States attending the High level meeting of the General Assembly in 2005 addressed the issue in their closing document, the so-called 2005 World Summit Outcome as follows:[15]

> "Each individual State has the responsibility to protect its populations from genocide, war crimes, ethnic cleansing and crimes against humanity. This responsibility entails the prevention of such crimes, including their incitement, through appropriate and necessary means. We accept that responsibility and will act in accordance with it. The international community should, as appropriate, encourage and help States to exercise this responsibility and support the United Nations in establishing an early warning capability."

The document goes on to state:

> "The international community, through the United Nations, also has the responsibility to use appropriate diplomatic, humanitarian and other peaceful means, in accordance with Chapters VI and VIII of the Charter, to help protect populations from genocide, war crimes, ethnic cleansing and crimes against humanity. In this context, we are prepared to take collective action, in a timely and decisive manner, through the Security Council, in accordance with the Charter, including Chapter VII, on a case-by-case basis and in coop-

---

[14] In larger freedom: towards development, security and human rights for all, Report of the Secretary-General, A/59/2005, 21 March 2005, para. 135.

[15] 2005 World Summit Outcome, A/Res. 60/1, para. 138 et seq. The title of that section of the paper reads: "Responsibility to protect populations from genocide, war crimes, ethnic cleansing and crimes against humanity."

> eration with relevant regional organizations as appropriate, should peaceful means be inadequate and national authorities manifestly fail to protect their populations from genocide, war crimes, ethnic cleansing and crimes against humanity. ... We also intend to commit ourselves, as necessary and appropriate, to helping States build capacity to protect their populations from genocide, war crimes, ethnic cleansing and crimes against humanity and to assisting those which are under stress before crises and conflicts break out."[16]

In its resolution 1674 of 28 April 2006, the Security Council endorsed this statement.[17]

Taking all these statements together the concept of a "responsibility to protect" in substance deals with issues of humanitarian intervention. It spells out a responsibility of States to be backed up by an "international" responsibility, which – according to the more recent documents – will be exercised through the Security Council. The concept takes a broader view, which touches upon the fundamentals of the international legal order in the same way as responsibility and sovereignty. "Responsibility to protect" has been qualified as an "emerging norm of international law" by the High-level Panel[18] and the Secretary General.[19] Thus, it has some legal status.[20]

III. Taking a Closer Look at Responsibilities

As the "responsibility to protect" expressly incorporates it, an analysis may start with the notion of "responsibility". Responsibility is a term

---

16 *Ibid.*, at para 139.

17 Preambular para. 4 of the resolution states: "Reaffirms the provisions of paragraphs 138 and 139 of the 2005 World Summit Outcome Document regarding the responsibility to protect populations from genocide, war crimes, ethnic cleansing and crimes against humanity; ...".

18 See above, text preceding footnote 13.

19 Report of the Secretary General (footnote 14) at para. 135: "... recently the High-level Panel on Threats, Challenges and Change, with its 16 members from all around the world, endorsed what they described as an "emerging norm that there is a collective responsibility to protect" (see A/59/565, para. 203). While I am well aware of the sensitivities involved in this issue, I strongly agree with this approach. ..."

20 See Winkelmann (footnote 1), 459 et seq.

frequently used, for instance, in political debate.[21] It also has clear legal meaning, which is relevant here, as the "responsibility to protect" is considered to be a legal concept.

1. "Responsibility to Protect" and State Responsibility?

As all the statements referred to above highlight, the responsibility to protect is first considered a responsibility of the relevant State. It is thus open to comparison with the well-established and long-standing law of state responsibility, which has recently been incorporated into Draft Articles by the International Law Commission.[22]

One of the cornerstones of the law of State responsibility is a two-tiered structure, where responsibility relates to an underlying obligation and arises where the latter is breached.[23] As is often observed, state responsibility at this point comes close to the concept of a law of torts. This structure aims at defining obligations and the consequences that their breach may entail. It thereby serves an important function within a legal system, the fundamental objective of which is clearly to delineate rights and duties and to provide for their enforceability.[24]

The concept of a "responsibility to protect" hardly fits this pattern, as it does not precisely define the kinds of obligations which are at stake and the potential consequences of their breach. Drawing from the debates and documents, one could expect a State to provide for safety, security, well-being, the rule of law, democracy and human rights.[25] However,

---

21 The term has also moral and ethical connotation, see P. Cane, *Responsibility in Law and Morality*, 2002; P. Warner, *An Ethic of Responsibility in International Relations*, 1991.

22 Draft articles on Responsibility of States for internationally wrongful acts, adopted by the International Law Commission at its fifty-third session (2001), A/56/10; See also GA res. 59/35 of 2 December 2004. See J. Crawford, *The International Law Commission's Articles on State Responsibility*, 2002.

23 See Draft Articles 1 and 2 and Crawford (footnote 22), 14 et seq.

24 See K. Zemanek, "Responsibility of States: General Principles", in: R. Bernhardt (ed.), *Encyclopedia of Public International Law,* Vol. IV (2000), p. 219; G. Dahm/J. Delbrück/R. Wolfrum, *Völkerrecht*, Vol. I/3, 2nd. ed., 2002 at p. 864 et seq. As regards environmental law see R. Wolfrum, "Means of Ensuring Compliance with and Enforcement of International Environmental Law", *Recueil des Cours*, Vol. 272, 1999, p. 13 et seq.

25 See text accompanying footnote 45, referring to "Welfare".

there is a critical lack of precision at this point, which raises concerns. Speaking about responsibility without clear reference to obligations may be considered rhetoric amounting to covertly claiming new obligations by implication. It may also, and possibly even worse, make the alarm function of the concept of State responsibility less compelling.

At a first glance, such ambiguities appear to have been eliminated largely by the changes made in the course of the 2005 high level meeting of the General Assembly. In the Summit outcome document, responsibility to protect was clarified and narrowed down by the formulation: "[r]esponsibility to protect populations from genocide, war crimes, ethnic cleansing and crimes against humanity".[26] Now, the "responsibility" can be considered to rest firmly on the basis of peremptory norms of international law. Taken to such narrow confines, however, the disconnect to the existing and proposed rules on state responsibility becomes even more apparent when one looks at Chapter III of the Draft Articles, which specifically addresses the issue of "serious breaches of obligations under peremptory norms of general international law". Such serious breaches are defined as "a gross or systematic failure by the responsible State to fulfil an obligation" (Draft Art. 40 para. 2) "arising under a peremptory norm of general international law" (para. 1).[27] This is not to say that both aspects could not or should not coexist. To the contrary the relevant ILC draft articles even expressly refer to "... further consequences that a breach ... may entail under international law".[28] However, without clarification the interrelationship between these Draft Articles and a "responsibility to protect" remain doubtful. In sum, a responsibility to protect can hardly be considered properly to fit the structures of state responsibility in conceptual terms.

2. "Responsibility to Protect" as an "Institutional" Responsibility?

"Responsibility to protect" might better comply with a distinctly different understanding of responsibility, which can be found in the UN Charter and many other instruments. Art. 24 para. 1 of the UN Charter may be cited as an example, where it refers to "[t]he primary *responsi-*

---

[26] See above, text accompanying footnote 15.

[27] See Crawford (footnote 22), at p. 242 et seq.

[28] Draft Art. 41 para. 3, see Crawford, *ibid.*, at p. 252 et seq.

bility"[29] of the Security Council for the maintenance of international peace and security.[30] Responsibility in this sense comes close to the German "Zuständigkeit" and basically is supposed to attribute and distribute power and authority within institutions and organizations. Apparently, this sort of responsibility differs importantly from the aforementioned understanding of state responsibility. Responsibility in such institutional terms does not carry with it the judgment of the breach of an international obligation in the way that state responsibility does. Moreover, it is debatable whether it carries any substantial legal authority at all.

"Responsibility" in this institutional sense has an important meaning regarding the attribution of functions within the United Nations. The famous 1950 "uniting for peace" resolution already referred to the notion in order to emphasize the role and explicitly: the responsibility of the General Assembly in the case of a "blockade" of the Security Council by the veto powers of the permanent members.[31] Thus, the notion of "responsibility" in our case might have been used to signify a proposal for some institutional or procedural change. Indeed, initially, the ICISS understood the concept of "responsibility to protect" as embracing an option for action even without the explicit consent of the Security Council.[32] However, neither the Panel nor the Secretary General nor the Summit Outcome document endorsed the proposal, but on the contrary pointed out the exclusive powers of the Security Council.[33] If the use of the term "responsibility" was ever intended to signify a proposal for change of the institutional setting, this purpose has become obsolete.

---

29 Emphasis added.

30 See J. Delbrück, Art. 24 in: B. Simma (ed.), *The Charter of the United Nations*, 2nd. ed., Vol. I, 2002, p. 442.

31 A/RES/377(V) of 3 November 1950. Preambular para. 9 reads: "Conscious that failure of the Security Council to discharge its responsibilities on behalf of all the Member States, particularly those responsibilities referred to in the two preceding paragraphs, does not relieve Member States of their obligations or the United Nations of its responsibility under the Charter to maintain international peace and security, ...". It has to be emphasised, that the wording refers to "responsibilities" in view of the UN and their organs, whereas it uses the term "obligations" to mark the commitment of States.

32 See above, at footnote 12.

33 See above, at footnote 16.

Moreover, the use of the term "responsibility" raises concerns even if considered to be used in "institutional" mode. The "responsibility to protect" addresses States and institutions alike without much explanation regarding the proper delineation between such "responsibilities" and without stating, whether a member State's responsibility arises out of its sovereignty or its membership of the UN.

3. Responsibility to Protect and the International Criminal Responsibility

A closer look reveals that such a narrow understanding of a "responsibility to protect" would basically mirror international individual criminal responsibility under the Rome Statute.[34] It may be recalled that under Art. 5 of its statute the International Criminal Court has jurisdiction with respect to the "... crime of genocide, ... crimes against humanity, ... war crimes and the crime of aggression ...". In view of the state of development of the international legal order, it is quite telling that individual responsibility can be secured, while the respect of States for these fundamental values is so difficult to achieve.[35]

IV. Taking Sovereignty Seriously

Apparently, putting forward a "responsibility to protect" has earned some merits in the context of sovereignty.[36] Interestingly, the two commissions as well as the report of the Secretary General begin with an appraisal of sovereignty and its place within international law and the

---

[34] Rome Statute of the International Criminal Court, 2187 U.N.T.S. 90, entry into force: July 1, 2002.

[35] As for the interrelationship between state responsibility and international criminal responsibility see H. Gros Espiell, "International responsibility of the State and Individual Criminal Responsibility in the International Protection of Human Rights", in: M. Ragazzi (ed.), *International Responsibility Today. Essays in Memory of Oscar Schachter*, 2005, p. 151 et seq. and A. A. Concado Trinidade, "Complementarity Between State Responsibility and Individual Responsibility for Grave Violations of Human Rights: The Crime of State Revisited", *ibid.*, at 253 et seq.; see also N. Jørgensen, *The Responsibility of States for International Crimes,* 2000 at p. 151 et seq.

[36] See Slaughter (footnote 1), 627 et seq.

United Nations.[37] Two achievements can be seen in this regard. First: the discussion helped to find ways to define an inherent limitation of sovereignty in the context of UN membership. Secondly, the discussion supported an understanding where sovereignty relates to people living in a State and their well-being.

1. Promotion and Inherent Limitation of Sovereignty in the United Nations

For a long time, sovereignty has been referred to as some sort of pre-constitutional autonomy status of an absolute nature. This kind of sovereignty defence has been extensively and successfully used within the UN, although it often neglected the state of international commitments of States.

The discussion on "responsibility to protect" has brought about a decisive turnaround in this regard. The ICISS is especially explicit in pointing out that the United Nations is not an institution for reducing or limiting sovereignty but that it, on the contrary, contributes to its promotion. Such promotion, it is understood, rests on the appreciation and acknowledgement of sovereign States through their membership and also includes a guarantee of security and non-intervention. In the words of the ICISS: "Membership of the United Nations was a final symbol of independent sovereign status and thus the seal of acceptance into the community of nations".[38] It goes on to state that the UN is the "main arena for the jealous protection, not the casual abrogation of State sovereignty".[39]

On the understanding that the United Nations importantly serves the interest in sovereignty, the ICISS concludes that it is a legitimate right of the United Nations to ask that such sovereignty be exercised in accordance with the general objectives and needs of that organization.

In its own words, the high-level panel indeed uses a similar line of argument:

> "In signing the Charter of the United Nations, States not only benefit from the privileges of sovereignty but also accept its responsibili-

---

[37] See above, text accompanying footnote 5 and 13.

[38] See report of the ICISS (footnote 3), Para. 2.11.

[39] *Ibid.*

ties. Whatever perceptions may have prevailed when the Westphalian system first gave rise to the notion of State sovereignty, today it clearly carries with it the obligation of a State to protect the welfare of its own peoples and meet its obligations to the wider international community."

2. Linking Sovereignty to the People

Even more far reaching than the concept outlined above, a second line of argument addresses the link between a State and its people. The ICISS highlighted that providing security is the most fundament task of sovereign States,[40] and the panel noted that the UN protects sovereign nation states because of what they do for their people:

> "What we seek to protect reflects what we value. The Charter of the United Nations seeks to protect all States, not because they are intrinsically good but because they are necessary to achieve the dignity, justice, worth and safety of their citizens."[41]

Similarly, the Secretary General stated in his report:

> "I believe that we must embrace the responsibility to protect ... This responsibility lies, first and foremost, with each individual State, whose primary *raison d'être* and duty is to protect its population."[42]

In this statement, he appealed to what has been considered a core function of States ever since Thomas Hobbes' writings.[43] Of course, this kind of protection includes effective protection against other groups or individuals as well as against unlawful acts of the State authorities themselves. Security for individuals always comprises both: security against threats from others as well as from the State and its forces. In this vein, the High-level Panel used an even more imaginative formula in stating:

> "State sovereignty ... clearly carries with it the obligation of a State to protect the welfare of its own peoples ...".[44]

---

40 See above, text accompanying footnote 5, see also below, at footnote 44.

41 *Ibid.*, at para. 30.

42 "In larger freedom", footnote 14 at para. 135.

43 See Stoll, *Sicherheit als Aufgabe von Staat und Gesellschaft*, 2003, at 2 et seq.

44 Footnote 13, at para. 29.

It has to be emphasised that the task of providing for security and well-being is not just derived from existing human-rights obligations but understood to be related to security: As has been stressed more than once, international security under the United Nations relies on its sovereign Member States and their contribution, and thus represents a sort of a shared responsibility. In this regard, it is stated that States whose stability is put into question cannot always readily fulfil their commitments and duties. It is further pointed out that this can best be prevented if progress, welfare, security, stability and justice are effectively furthered and maintained by the government in question.

Asking what States do to their people automatically implies addressing the issue of governance. Indeed, governments and responsible officials are addressed in particular in the High-level Panel's document. In this regard, one needs to stress that the responsibility of States has been given considerable backing by the individual criminal responsibility brought about by the establishment of the International Criminal Court.[45]

3. Conclusion

In sum, these developments have had an enormous impact on our view of sovereignty, which can basically be understood to be based on an understanding whereby firstly, the United Nations system is regarded as an important device for noting and securing sovereignty, secondly, sovereignty is linked via the internal order of a State to the needs and interests of its people, and thirdly, the responsibility of individuals comes into play.

V. Cooperation

An assessment of the responsibility to protect and its conceptual implications would be incomplete without addressing the issue of cooperation. That issue has not played much of a role in the debate. However, the kind of changes implied by the concept of a responsibility to protect can hardly be considered without reference to cooperation. Indeed, assuming responsibilities on the part of particular States and the State

---

45 See above, text accompanying footnote 34 et seq.

community and heading for an understanding of sovereignty as just outlined imply and require a state of the international order, which includes an element of cooperation.

Cooperation can basically be understood to mean an "effort of states to accomplish an object by joint action".[46] It is an inherent element of the United Nations system, as, for instance, Arts. 55 and 56 of the Charter may show.[47]

Also, cooperation is said to be key to altering the quality of the international legal order. As is often stated, the international legal order was initially structured in a way which has been referred to as "the law of coordination".[48] The rules of international law at that time, it is stated, served as a means of bringing into accordance the interests and concerns of States in particular areas. In contrast, the "international law of cooperation" has sought to delineate an advanced stage of development, where States define common interests and determine ways and means of achieving them. Cooperation also involves an element of solidarity.[49]

Obviously, it has become clear over the last few years that international security is importantly and seriously put into question and that contributions from a wide range of different States are urgently required to maintain it. Thus, cooperation is key in responding to such new challenges. Developing new legal concepts to cope with such challenges obviously has to take this aspect into account.

Furthermore, the development of structures and means of cooperation may facilitate the attribution of more meaningful obligations and – eventually – of elements of responsibility, as, for instance, the emergence of international environmental law may show.

---

[46] R. Wolfrum, "International Law of Cooperation", in: R. Bernhardt (ed.), *Encyclopedia of Public International Law*, Vol. II, 1995, p. 1242

[47] R. Wolfrum, "Art. 55 (a) and (b)", "Art. 56", in: B. Simma (ed.), *The Charter of the United Nations*, 2nd. ed., Vol. I, 2002, p. 759 et seq.

[48] R. Wolfrum, "Entwicklung des Völkerrechts von einem Koordinations- zu einem Kooperationsrecht", in: P. C. Müller-Graff/H. Roth (eds.), *Recht und Staatswissenschaft. Signaturen und Herausforderungen zum Jahrtausendbeginn*, 2001, p. 421 et seq.

[49] See R. Wolfrum, "Solidarity amongst States: An Emerging Structural Principle in International Law", in: P.M. Dupuy et. al. (eds), *Essays in Honor of Christian Tomuschat*, 2006, 1087 at p. 1090 et seq. and Slaughter (footnote 1) 623.

In sum, it appears that a meaningful debate on "responsibility to protect" would have duly to consider the aspect of cooperation. It is well understood that such consideration does not automatically imply a claim for more resources and particularly financial contributions. Also, it should not be allowed to result in an excuse for failure to act. However, a concept which altogether neglects the issue of cooperation can hardly be considered to be conclusive.

VI. Outlook

The merits of the emerging "responsibility to protect" as a norm of international law are few at the moment. The concept lacks precision and substance. It is highly questionable whether it can contribute to a new understanding of the legality of interventions – which have hitherto been called "humanitarian" ones. According to the Report of the Secretary General and the Summit Outcome, the concept implies hardly any change. Also, it has to be emphasised that there is a considerable disconnect between "responsibility to protect" and other developments in international law. The international legal order has recently seen encouraging developments concerning the promotion of an effective responsibility of States and individuals. Both the 2004 ILC Draft Articles and the establishment of the International Criminal Court can be considered important steps in this direction. There is a need to uphold the clear-cut structure of a responsibility based on obligations and their breach. Such structure is the basis for important achievements in the direction of a rule-based international order that we fortunately see developing in other areas of international law, including, for instance, the law of the sea and trade. It has to be emphasised that for international security to be provided for by law requires legal certainty and thus a legal order which effectively attributes responsibility to others and likewise precisely delineates the limits of such responsibility.

Establishing a "responsibility to protect" without a clear message is not helpful in this regard. The damage done to the normative value of fundamental international law principles in order to promote the laudable and urgent endeavour to provide for safe legal grounds for humanitarian interventions is considerable. Also, it does not seem to be required, as a number of other political and normative concepts, including inter alia the *ius cogens* and *erga omnes* approaches, are available to achieve the same result.[50]

The "responsibility to protect" has had its merits in initiating an important debate heading for a more differentiated understanding of sovereignty. It has become clear that such status has inherent limits and derives its justification from the protection that is provided to the people by a sovereign State.

Voicing a responsibility to protect can be read as a claim to make progress with a view to a more accountable international order. In order to make this claim a sound one, it will very likely be necessary to complement it by elements taking account of the necessary cooperation between States with different strengths, capabilities and resources.

---

[50] See Molier (footnote 1), at 47 et seq: "Old Wine in New Bottles?" at 44, who also discusses a justification of a humanitarian intervention by reference to the principle of necessity, p. 52 et seq.

Sovereignty and the Responsibility to Protect in International Criminal Law

Markus Benzing[*]

---

[*] This paper is an extended version of a comment on Professor *Stoll's* presentation. I would like to thank *Jakob Pichon* for valuable comments.

I. Introduction

Ever since the notion of "sovereignty" has entered the vocabulary of international law, it has suffered from considerable vagueness and has undergone significant changes. In the traditional perspective (often referred to as: Westphalian[1]), its meaning is restricted to the independence of a state both from other states and from international legal obligations not freely entered into. Its main function is that of the monopolization of the exercise of power or political authority within a certain territory. States are under no international obligation unless they have freely consented to it.[2] Needless to say, such absolute monopolization is fictitious.[3] Nevertheless, this understanding of sovereignty is the capstone for a positivist understanding of international law.[4]

Particularly in recent decades, and increasingly so due to processes such as globalization, the emergence of new actors on the international plane and a growing interdependence in the international legal system, this

---

1 But see: S. Krasner, "Justice & Sovereignty: Implications of the International Criminal Court", *UCLA J. Int'l L. & Foreign Aff.* 8 (2003), 61 et seq. (62-2).

2 See PCIJ, *The Case of the S.S. Lotus*, Judgment of 7 September 1927, PCIJ Series A No. 10; C. Hillgruber, "Souveränität – Verteidigung eines Rechtsbegriffs", *Juristenzeitung* 57 (2002), 1072 et seq. (1075) who stresses the consensual character of international law and refers to state sovereignty as a "constitutional principle" of international law (p. 1076).

3 J. H. Jackson, "Sovereignty-Modern: A New Approach to an Outdated Concept", *AJIL* 97 (2003), 782 et seq. (794): "sovereignty fiction".

4 See S. Oeter, "Souveränität – ein überholtes Konzept?", in: H.-J. Cremer *et al.* (eds), *Tradition und Weltoffenheit des Rechts, Festschrift für Helmut Steinberger*, 2002, 259 et seq. (273).

absolute concept of sovereignty has been under attack; some have even called it "organized hypocrisy".[5] Given its uncertainties and problems, it may be understandable that some international legal scholars want to do away with the notion altogether, arguing that it fails to explain the realities of international relations.[6] More and more international lawyers see sovereignty as a collective noun for the competences and duties of states accorded to them by international law.[7] Instead of defining "sovereignty" as such, many international lawyers rather specify different aspects of sovereignty, such as "autonomy", "equality", "participation" (also: "cooperation"), and "responsibility". These aspects comprise what can be said to be a modern international law understanding of "sovereignty". Seeing sovereignty as a product of international law also make its contents flexible, allowing it to adjust to the developing nature of international law.[8]

II. Sovereignty as responsibility to protect

The responsibility aspect of sovereignty essentially means that sovereignty must not be considered as a purely "negative" rule declaring that no duties are involved (in Hohfeldian terms: a privilege), but as one that also, or even mainly, entails "positive" duties. As opposed to a purely formal conception of "sovereignty" that served as an ordering principle of international relations in an era where formality and (formal) equality were the main guarantors of international peace and security, this new understanding reflects the increasing recognition of substantive values by the international legal system.

While the responsibility aspect of sovereignty has been in the limelight of academic discussion in particular since the publication of the ICISS

---

[5] S. D. Krasner, *Sovereignty: Organized Hypocrisy*, 1999.

[6] L. Henkin, *International Law: Politics and Values*, 1995, 8-10.

[7] Henkin, see note 6, 10; B. Fassbender, "Die Souveränität des Staates als Autonomie im Rahmen der völkerrechtlichen Verfassung", in: H.-P. Mansel *et al.* (eds), *Festschrift für Erik Jayme*, Vol. 2, 2004, 1089 et seq. (1095); Oeter, see note 4, 276

[8] A. Clapham, "National Action Challenged: Sovereignty, Immunity and Universal Jurisdiction before the International Court of Justice", in: M. Lattimer/P. Sands (eds), *Justice for Crimes against Humanity*, 2003, 303 et seq. (305).

Report ("The Responsibility to Protect"),[9] the High Level Panel Report on Threats, Challenges and Change,[10] and the Report of the Secretary-General ("In larger freedom"),[11] the underlying idea that sovereignty entails duties is not new to international legal thinking. The ICJ emphasized the responsibility aspect of (territorial) sovereignty as early as in the *Corfu Channel* case.[12] Many "newer" areas of international law, in particular human rights law and international environmental law,[13] have also promoted the perception that sovereignty necessarily entails responsibility.

As defined by the ICISS and the High Level Panel, the obligations imposed on states by reason of the responsibility aspect of sovereignty are twofold: First, to respect the welfare, dignity and human rights of people within the state, and secondly to meet their obligations to the international community.[14] Furthermore, sovereignty as responsibility to protect means that, in principle, both states *individually* and the international community *collectively* are responsible.[15] The ICISS Report

---

9 International Commission on Intervention and State Sovereignty (ICISS), *The Responsibility to Protect*, 2001.

10 Report of the High-level Panel on Threats, Challenges and Change, *A more secure world: our shared responsibility*, UN Doc. A/59/565, 2 December 2004.

11 Report of the Secretary-General, *In larger freedom: towards development, security and human rights for all*, UN Doc. A/59/2005, 21 March 2005.

12 ICJ, *The Corfu Channel Case* (United Kingdom v. Albania), Merits, Judgment of 9 April 1949, ICJ Reports 1949, 4 et seq. (22): obligation of every state not knowingly to allow its territory to be used for acts contrary to the rights of other states.

13 See K. Odendahl, *Die Umweltpflichtigkeit der Souveränität*, 1998.

14 ICISS, see note 9, para. 2.15; Report of the High-level Panel on Threats, Challenges and Change, see note 10, para. 29.

15 Report of the Secretary-General, see note 11, para. 135; 2005 World Summit Outcome, A/RES/60/1, 16 September 2005, paras 138-139: "Each individual State has the responsibility to protect its populations from genocide, war crimes, ethnic cleansing and crimes against humanity. This responsibility entails the prevention of such crimes, including their incitement, through appropriate and necessary means. We accept that responsibility and will act in accordance with it. The international community should, as appropriate, encourage and help States to exercise this responsibility and support the United Nations in establishing an early warning capability. ... The international community, through the United Nations, also has the responsibility to use appropriate diplomatic, humanitarian and other peaceful means, in accordance with Chapters

further distinguishes between the responsibility to prevent, the responsibility to react, and the responsibility to re-build.

Even though the concept of sovereignty as the "responsibility to protect" has been mainly developed with regard to "humanitarian intervention" (where it remains contentious),[16] it may be useful in understanding and explaining the purpose and function of international criminal law. Accordingly, this paper will elaborate on this point by analysing some of the fundamental tenets of international criminal law. To this end, the concept of the "responsibility to protect" will be applied to international criminal law from the perspective of both international institutions (mainly the ICC, III.1.) and states (III.2.). The paper will then look at the differences between state and individual responsibility (IV.) before offering some concluding thoughts (V.).

VI and VIII of the Charter, to help to protect populations from genocide, war crimes, ethnic cleansing and crimes against humanity."

This generally acceptable statement, however, raises several important questions: First, it is unclear whether, or under which circumstances, one state, or a group of states, may rely on its sovereign responsibility in acting *unilaterally* in order to set right another state's failure to discharge its responsibility to protect. Another major question is the conditions upon which *collective responsibility* is transformed into a *right*, or even a *duty*, to act against the will – and territorial integrity – of one state and to intervene. See Report of the High-level Panel on Threats, Challenges and Change, see note 10, para. 203: "We endorse the *emerging* norm that there is a *collective international responsibility* to protect, exercisable by the Security Council authorizing military intervention as a last resort, in the event of genocide and other large scale killing, ethnic cleansing or serious violations of international humanitarian law which sovereign Governments have proved powerless or unwilling to prevent." (my emphasis).

16 For a sceptical view see P. Hilpold, "The Duty to Protect and the Reform of the United Nations – A New Step in the Development of International Law?", *Max Planck UNYB* 10 (2006), 35 et seq. (39 et seq.). Approving, however: G. Molier, "Humanitarian Intervention and the Responsibility to Protect after 9/11", *NILR* 53 (2006), 37 et seq. (47-52); on p. 52, she concludes that "the concept of the responsibility to protect replaces the doctrine of humanitarian intervention".

III. International criminal law and state sovereignty as responsibility to protect

The purposes of international criminal law comprise the three main aspects of the responsibility to protect as identified by the ICISS: the responsibilities to prevent, to react and to rebuild. International criminal law, just like its national counterpart, primarily has a preventive function.[17] Enforcing international criminal law may also contribute to putting an end to a continuing conflict (responsibility to react). Finally, under the heading of "post-conflict justice", international criminal law may help in efforts to rebuild states and societies shattered by war.[18]

International criminal law proceeds from the basis that sovereign states are still – and will remain so even after the establishment of the ICC – the main actors in preventing and punishing international crimes. This is in line with the general structure of the international system, the "basic and indispensable building blocks"[19] of which are sovereign states.

However, this statement must not be misunderstood as a conservative or even anachronistic characterization of the international system, which increasingly includes important actors other than states. On the contrary, the statement makes clear that states must fulfil the role assigned to them by the international legal system. State sovereignty is not an end in itself; but states are obliged to discharge the duties imposed on them by sovereignty. In the words of the Secretary-General, "[i]t is their job to guarantee the rights of their citizens, to protect them from crime, violence and aggression, and to provide the framework of freedom under law".[20] States thus have a protective role to play.

---

[17] G. Dahm/ J. Delbrück/ R. Wolfrum, *Völkerrecht*, 2nd ed., Vol. I/3, 2002, 994. See also: H.-H. Jescheck, *Die Verantwortlichkeit der Staatsorgane nach Völkerrecht, Eine Studie zu den Nürnberger Prozessen*, 1952, 194: general prevention (*Generalprävention*). Jescheck also points out that as long as violations of international criminal law are not prosecuted by international institutions, political action will not be subject to the pressure exerted by the international criminalization of core human rights violations. But compare the sceptical remarks by Krasner, see note 1, 65, arguing that international criminal law may not have a deterrent, but the opposite effect on international leaders.

[18] See generally: A. Seibert-Fohr, "Reconstruction through Accountability", *Max Planck UNYB* 9 (2005), 555 et seq.

[19] Report of the Secretary-General, see note 11, para. 19.

[20] Report of the Secretary-General, see note 11, para. 19.

1. International criminal courts and the responsibility to protect

If sovereignty comprises the responsibility to protect, then states, by creating international criminal courts, transfer their protective responsibility to an international institution tasked with discharging this responsibility.[21] This insight has several consequences for the relationship between the ICC and states.

a. Do international criminal courts challenge state sovereignty?

It is often argued that the ICC is a challenge to state sovereignty. A classic understanding of sovereignty was – and still is – often used to explain why there is doubt about the effectiveness of an international criminal jurisdiction: "The territoriality of national criminal law [which is nothing more than an aspect of state sovereignty] accords to every national order of criminal law a massive defence position *vis-à-vis* an international criminal law order."[22] Under this approach, international criminal law and national sovereignty are necessarily in conflict.

If one follows the definition of sovereignty as the responsibility to protect, however, international institutions do not challenge state sovereignty. On the contrary, their establishment is a logical consequence of sovereignty. If the responsibility to protect cannot be discharged at the national level, state sovereignty requires that states provide for other means. It is this aspect that makes clear that the Westphalian model of international law is outdated:[23] Sovereignty as responsibility to protect takes away the option of inaction.[24] By ensuring collective action, inter-

---

[21] See R. Cryer, "International Criminal Law vs State Sovereignty: Another Round?", *EJIL* 16 (2005), 979 et seq. (986): "[S]tates parties ... have locked themselves into a regime that can take over part of the protective role of the state, by prosecuting offences if the state later becomes unwilling or unable to do so."

[22] K. Ipsen, in: *id.*, *Völkerrecht*, 5th ed., 2004, § 42, MN 2 (my translation).

[23] But see R. E. Fife, "The International Criminal Court", *NJIL* 69 (2000), 63 et seq. (75): "The [ICC] Statute does not challenge the basic Westphalian system of international law."

[24] It is this curtailment of discretion to remain inactive for political reasons that is sometimes described as one of the "major concessions" in terms of sovereignty that states make to the international community: F. Mégret, "Why would States want to join the ICC? A theoretical exploration based on the legal

national criminal courts thus complete the deterrent (i.e. preventive) effect of international criminal law:[25] potential perpetrators will know that even their own state will not be able to shield them from accountability.

There is another aspect that reinforces this paradigm shift. In accordance with the insight that international crimes protect legal interests of the international community as a whole, and that, in relation to international crimes, states only exercise jurisdiction on its behalf, it can be argued that by the creation of an international criminal court states do not *delegate* jurisdiction to that institution.[26] Rather, the state's own jurisdiction in these matters is only derivative,[27] which means that the ICC, as the "institutionalized international community" in fact exercises *original* criminal competence over international crimes which – before its creation – was latent or dormant for lack of institutional organization.[28] If that is the case, then all claims that the Court – for reasons of sovereignty – must not investigate crimes committed by nation-

nature of complementarity", in: J. K. Kleffner/ G. Kor (eds), *Complementary Views on Complementarity*, 2006, 1 et seq. (10).

25 See the remark already cited from Jescheck, see note 17, 194-5.

26 For a delegation: J. Verhoeven, "Vers un ordre répressif universel? Quelques observations", *A.F.D.I.* 45 (1999), 55 et seq. (64); M. P. Scharf, "The ICC's Jurisdiction over the Nationals of Non-Party States: A Critique of the U.S. Position", *Law & Contemp. Probs* 64 (2001), 67 et seq. (98 et seq.); Mégret, see note 24, 42; O. Bekou/ R. Cryer, "The International Criminal Court and Universal Jurisdiction: A Close Encounter?", *ICLQ* 56 (2007), 49 et seq. (50-1).

27 For the derivative character of universal jurisdiction exercised by states see Dahm/ Delbrück/ Wolfrum, see note 17, 999; K. Oellers-Frahm, "Das Statut des internationalen Strafgerichtshofs zur Verfolgung von Kriegsverbrechen im ehemaligen Jugoslawien", *ZaöRV* 54 (1994), 416 et seq. (417).

28 O. Lagodny, "Legitimation und Bedeutung des Ständigen Internationalen Strafgerichtshofs", *Zeitschrift für die gesamte Strafrechtswissenschaft* 113 (2001), 800 et seq. (805); A. Eser, "Völkermord und deutsche Strafgewalt: Zum Spannungsverhältnis von Weltrechtsprinzip und legitimierendem Inlandsbezug", in: A. Eser *et al.* (eds), *Strafverfahrensrecht in Theorie und Praxis, Festschrift für Meyer-Goßner*, 2001, 3 et seq. (17-18). But see D. M. Amann, "The International Criminal Court and the Sovereign State", in: I. F. Dekker/ W. G. Werner (eds), *Governance and International Legal Theory*, 2004, 185 et seq. (198), who points out that this may not be true with respect to all offences contained in the Rome Statute.

als of non-State Parties are unfounded.[29] In other words, notwithstanding its establishment by treaty as an international organization and thus its character as a creation of states, the ICC could potentially exercise "universal" jurisdiction. Even though its establishment is consensual, it could also exercise non-consensual jurisdiction – a novel phenomenon in the law of international dispute resolution that is still firmly rooted in the principle of consent.[30]

It is therefore regrettable that article 12 of the ICC Statute – for political or diplomatic reasons – does not provide for universal jurisdiction.[31] Instead, it relies on the territoriality and nationality principles. The only way to extend the jurisdiction to crimes committed on the territory of non-State Parties by persons who do not have the nationality of one the States Parties is by a Security Council referral.[32]

b. The complementary character of the ICC: deference to state sovereignty?

The ICTY (and the ICTR) are the result of collective state action through the UN, i.e. the Security Council. Their jurisdiction is concurrent with that of national courts, but both courts have primacy over na-

---

[29] For these claims see R. Wegdwood, "The International Criminal Court: An American View", *EJIL* 10 (1999), 93 et seq. (99 et seq.); D. Scheffer, "The United States and the International Criminal Court", *AJIL* 93 (1999), 12 et seq. (18).

[30] See Dahm/ Delbrück/ Wolfrum, see note 17, 1151. To the aspect of non-consensual jurisdiction of the ICC see: Amann, see note 28, 189 et seq.

[31] For the reasons for the limited scope of article 12 ICC Statute see H.-P. Kaul, "Der IStGH: Das Ringen um seine Zuständigkeit und Reichweite", *Humanitäres Völkerrecht* 11 (1998), 138 et seq. (140 et seq.); H.-P. Kaul/ C. Kress, "Jurisdiction and cooperation in the Statute of the International Criminal Court: principles and compromises", *Yearbook of International Humanitarian Law* 2 (1999), 143 et seq. See also Dahm/ Delbrück/ Wolfrum, see note 17, 1005, 1152, who state that the restrictive scope of article 12 ICC Statute is not convincing both from a point of view of legal doctrine and legal policy.

[32] L. Arbour/ M. Bergsmo, "Conspicuous Absence of Jurisdictional Overreach", *International Law Forum* 1 (1999), 13 et seq. (19); I. Prezas, "La justice pénale internationale à l'épreuve du maintien de la paix: À propos de la relation entre la Cour pénale internationale et le Conseil de sécurité", *RBDI* 39 (2006), 57 et seq. (68).

tional jurisdictions.[33] In contrast, the ICC's jurisdiction is complementary to those of national courts. The principle of complementarity is a central feature of the ICC.[34] Complementarity is a condition of the exercise of jurisdiction by the ICC designed to "protect" sovereignty.[35] Often, this generally accepted statement has pejorative overtones, meaning that the fact that the ICC has only complementary jurisdiction will make it less effective.[36] It is submitted, however, that complementarity is not necessarily to be seen as a feature hampering the operation of the court. Rather, it can be explained by reference to the concept of "responsibility to protect" to accord with principles of general international law.

aa. Complementarity as shared responsibility

In line with the general thrust of "sovereignty as responsibility", complementarity recognizes that the prevention and repression of international crimes is most effectively implemented by states themselves. By creating the ICC, they have not completely discharged the protective component of state sovereignty; they retain concurrent responsibility. Only in cases where states are unable or unwilling to investigate or prosecute, may the Court – as an organ of collective enforcement of international law[37] – take action. The principle of complementarity thus ensures that sovereignty as responsibility to protect is exercised even where states are not in a position to act. In this way, overlapping responsibilities are created in a multilevel system; taking up the equation "sovereignty = responsibility", one can thus legitimately speak, not of one single sovereignty, but of "overlapping sovereignties"[38] or "shared

---

[33] Article 9 (2) ICTY Statute; Article 8 (2) ICTR-Statute. See Dahm/ Delbrück/ Wolfrum, see note 17, 1137.

[34] R. Wolfrum, "Internationale Verbrechen vor internationalen und nationalen Gerichten: Die Verfolgungskompetenzen des Internationalen Strafgerichtshofs – ein Fortschritt oder ein Rückschritt in der Entwicklung?", in: J. Arnold *et al.* (eds), *Menschengerechtes Strafrecht, Festschrift für Albin Eser zum 70. Geburtstag*, 2005, 977.

[35] Cryer, see note 21, 986; Fife, see note 23, 72.

[36] For a critique see Wolfrum, see note 34, 977.

[37] Wolfrum, see note 34, 979.

[38] See (with respect to the EU): P. G. Carozza, "Subsidiarity as a Structural Principle of International Human Rights Law", *AJIL* 97 (2003), 38 et seq. (52).

sovereignty".[39] The system so established can be characterized as the "international criminal justice system".[40] This system is based on the objective of avoiding impunity, *i.e.* of ensuring that the protective aspect of sovereignty is fulfilled under all circumstances.

It is decisive to see in this context that complementarity is not a "self-judging reservation" of national sovereignty. It will be the Court itself that determines whether the conditions of article 17 are met.[41] It is hard to see in this competence of the Court "one of the worst assaults on sovereignty",[42] since, for reasons of efficiency, it is hardly imaginable that states themselves could decide when they were willing or able to prosecute. The ultimate decision on power allocation, the *compétence de la compétence*, is thus put in the hands of the international institution, the ICC.[43]

bb. Complementarity as an instrument of international governance

Complementarity is also an instrument of international governance, in that states will try to avoid being declared "unable" or "unwilling" by the Court.[44] In consequence, complementarity creates an incentive for states to act. It can be characterized as a non-confrontational enforcement mechanism for duties of states to exercise jurisdiction over international crimes.[45] It may also be the beginning of a system of oversight

---

[39] S. D. Krasner, "The Hole in the Whole: Sovereignty, Shared Sovereignty, and International law", *Mich. J. Int'l L.* 25 (2004) 1075 et seq. (1091), who restricts the term "shared sovereignty" to shared *territorial* sovereignty in the context of the international administration of territories. It is submitted, however, that its meaning may be extended to comprise all instances where governance is exercised by different actors on various levels.

[40] K. Ambos, "Völkerrechtliche Kernverbrechen, Weltrechtsprinzip und § 153f StPO – Zugleich Anmerkung zu GBA, JZ 2005, 311 und OLG Stuttgart, NStZ 2006, 117", *Neue Zeitschrift für Strafrecht* 26 (2006), 434 et seq. (435).

[41] J. Meißner, *Die Zusammenarbeit mit dem internationalen Strafgerichtshof nach dem Römischen Statut*, 2003, 69.

[42] But see: Mégret, see note 24, 11.

[43] See Jackson, see note 3, 796.

[44] As to the difference between *global governance* and *global government* in relation to the ICC see: R. Jensen, "Globalization and the International Criminal Court: Accountability and a New Conception of the State", in: Dekker/Werner, see note 28, 159 et seq. (182).

[45] See Jensen, see note 44, 180.

over the activity of national courts and agencies in the prosecution of international crimes; until the establishment of the ICC, such a system did not exist.[46] One should, however, not expect too much of the Court: Due to its limited resources, the exercise of a supervisory function may be seriously hampered.

cc. Complementarity as subsidiarity and solidarity

The principle of complementarity has rightly been compared to subsidiarity.[47] The idea of subsidiarity harmonizes (international) intervention with non-interference in a state's internal affairs and serves as a constitutional ordering principle between the two levels:[48] Where a lower (political or social) level can effectively undertake a task, the higher level has to abstain from acting; where lower forms of organization cannot achieve these ends, the higher level may (or: must) intervene. The reason for this is that the exercise of decision-making authority closer to the constituents can better reflect the subtleties, necessary complexity and detail of the decision.[49] The rationale of subsidiarity thus captures a major underlying reason for the principle of complementarity: International crimes are best prosecuted where they occur, as local prosecution will best serve the interests of deterrence and reconciliation.

Even though it is not entirely clear whether subsidiarity is already a general principle of international law,[50] article 17 ICC Statute may be pointing to its emergence and, at the same time, clarifying the parameters of its operation. In this context, it is interesting to note that the threshold for action of the (organized) international community, instead of state action, is the "inability" or "unwillingness" of states to investigate or prosecute international crimes in a genuine manner. It is the ex-

---

46 Dahm/ Delbrück/ Wolfrum, see note 17, 996.

47 Fife, see note 23, 81; B. Fassbender, "Comment", in: Kleffner/ Kor, see note 24, 73.

48 Carozza, see note 38, 44, 49.

49 Jackson, see note 3, 792.

50 Fassbender, see note 47, 74; M. Kumm, "The Legitimacy of International Law: A Constitutionalist Framework of Analysis", *EJIL* 15 (2004), 906 et seq. (921): "[Subsidiarity] ought to be an integral feature of international law." With respect to the WTO: R. Howse/ K. Nicolaidis, "Enhancing WTO Legitimacy: Constitutionalization or Global Subsidiarity?", *Governance* 16 (2003), 73 et seq. (86 et seq.).

act same test that is proposed by the UN Secretary-General and the ICISS in their respective reports for the general switching from *individual* to *collective* responsibility to protect, e.g. for Security Council action in the face of international crises.[51] It is important to stress in this respect that the principle of subsidiarity does not generally envisage a unilateral right to intervene; the complementary notion of sovereignty may be pictured as open at the top, but closed at the sides,[52] permitting the intervention of the (organized) international community (e.g. the Security Council, the ICC or another international institution within its mandate), but not of individual states.[53]

A corollary of the principle of subsidiarity is solidarity, *i.e.* the idea that the international community needs first to assist individual states to achieve what they cannot do on their own before intervening by assuming the task itself.[54] If one accepts that complementarity is a form of subsidiarity, then the ICC can play an active role in assisting states in the prosecution of international crimes. Such assistance as part of the complementarity principle is in fact envisaged by the Policy Paper of the ICC Office of the Prosecutor, published in the first months of its operation.[55] In a later Report, the Office of the Prosecutor has explicitly confirmed this "positive approach" to complementarity, stating that it "encourages genuine national proceedings where possible".[56] In fact, the Statute itself provides for forms of cooperation by the Court with

---

[51] Report of the Secretary-General, see note 11, para. 135; ICISS, see note 9, Basic Principle (1) B. (p. XI), paras 2.25, 2.29 (second recital), 2.31.

[52] See G. Nolte, "Zum Wandel des Souveränitätsbegriffs", *Frankfurter Allgemeine Zeitung*, 6 April 2005, p. 6.

[53] This is the reason why subsidiarity is not entirely capable of substituting for sovereignty (but see Kumm, see note 50, 920-1).

[54] I. Feichtner, "Subsidiarity", in: R. Wolfrum (ed.), *Max Planck Encyclopedia of Public International Law*, 2007, in preparation.

[55] See ICC-OTP, *Paper on some policy issues before the Office of the Prosecutor*, September 2003, available at <http://www.icc-cpi.int/library/organs/otp/030905_Policy_Paper.pdf>, p. 5.

[56] ICC-OTP, *Report on the activities performed during the first three years (June 2003 – June 2006)*, 12 September 2006, available at <http://www.icc-cpi.int/library/organs/otp/OTP_3-year-report-20060914_English.pdf>, p. 22.

states aimed at making national prosecutions more effective (article 93 (10) ICC Statute).[57]

dd. Complementarity in the early operation of the ICC

In an early decision, a Pre-Trial Chamber of the ICC took a rather cautious stance on the interpretation of the principle of complementarity. Even where states, by way of a so-called "self-referral" under article 13 (a) of the Statute,[58] have implicitly renounced or waived their right to challenge the exercise of jurisdiction by the court, the Court has stated that it still must positively establish that the case is admissible.[59]

While it is true that the Court is competent to decide on the complementarity regime, it is doubtful whether article 17 really requires that its conditions be reviewed by the Pre-Trial Chamber even where a state explicitly articulates that it is not able to prosecute. "Waivers" of complementarity are generally possible,[60] as they are in line with the object and purpose of the complementarity regime.[61] An interpretation of complementarity as "shared responsibility" and "subsidiarity" allows for states to renounce their "right" to prosecute where they are aware of the fact that they cannot fulfil their responsibility to protect by way of criminal prosecutions. One can think of an acute political controversy that would taint the impartiality of national trials and/or undermine national reconciliatory processes; moreover, it is possible that the

57 F. Gioia, "State Sovereignty, Jurisdiction, and 'Modern' International Law: The Principle of Complementarity in the International Criminal Court", *LJIL* 19 (2006), 1095 et seq. (1117 et seq.).

58 C. Kress, "'Self-referrals' and 'Waivers of Complementarity' – Some Considerations in Law and Policy", *JICJ* 2 (2004), 944.

59 Pre-Trial Chamber I, *Prosecutor v. Thomas Lubanga Dyilo*, Decision on the Prosecutor's Application for a Warrant of Arrest, Article 58, ICC-01/04-01/06, 10 February 2006, paras 18, 29 et seq.

60 Fife, see note 23, 83; Kress, see note 58, 946; M. Benzing, "The Complementarity Regime of the International Criminal Court: International Criminal Justice between State Sovereignty and the Fight against Impunity", *Max Planck UNYB* 7 (2003), 591 et seq. (629-631).

61 Gioia, see note 57, 1112.

prosecution of a particularly powerful accused before national courts could destabilize a newly formed democratic government.[62]

Given the rationale of the complementarity principle as a safeguard of sovereignty as "responsibility to protect", only where states used self-referrals to *mala fide* circumvent their own responsibilities could the Court hold the case inadmissible. Such situation can, however, hardly be imagined, especially if the criteria set out above are present. At the same time, complementarity does not only envisage primary jurisdiction of the territorial state, but also of other states having jurisdiction over the crimes concerned. In this respect, the ICC has to consider whether there are other states exercising jurisdiction, e.g. on the basis of the universality principle.[63]

c. Prosecutorial discretion and the collective responsibility to protect

Another pressing question is whether there is a duty on the ICC to intervene, i.e. to investigate or prosecute, if states are unwilling and unable to do so themselves. If one takes the concept of a "shared responsibility to protect" seriously, i.e. regards states and the ICC as "jointly and severally liable", the answer seems to be in the affirmative.[64] Nevertheless, it is widely recognized that the ICC Prosecutor enjoys considerable discretion under the Statute in initiating investigations and prosecutions.[65] This discretion is justifiable by reason of practical con-

---

62 To these scenarios see: P. Akhavan, "The *Lord's Resistance Army* Case: Uganda's Submission of the First State Referral to the International Criminal Court", *AJIL* 99 (2005), 403 et seq. (414).

63 Kress, see note 58, at fn. 15.

64 Carozza, see note 38, 57-8, stating that subsidiarity creates a responsibility on the international community to intervene. It is true that the ICC Statute envisages abstaining from investigation or prosecution in certain circumstances, i.e. when crimes do not reach a certain gravity threshold, when other interests of justice mandate that the Court not intervene, or when the Security Council decides that prosecution would endanger peace and security (article 16). But these are instances of an international weighing of goods (*Güterabwägung*) and cannot serve as calling into question the general principle.

65 A. M. Danner, "Enhancing the legitimacy and accountability of prosecutorial discretion at the International Criminal Court", *AJIL* 97 (2003), 510 et seq. (519); V. Röben, "The Procedure of the ICC: Status and Function of the Prosecutor", *Max Planck UNYB* 7 (2003), 513 et seq. (523): "system of prosecution ... based on the legality maxim tempered by substantial opportunity elements"; Wolfrum, see note 34, 986.

straints, as the ICC will not realistically be able to enforce international criminal law in all situations where states fail to do so. However, if a duty to act is accepted in principle (as a result of and subject to the principle of subsidiarity), the exercise of the discretion is not unfettered, but must be guided by legal criteria. The decision to abstain from investigation or prosecution is thus reviewable by the Pre-Trial Chamber at the request of a State Party which had referred a situation to the Court under article 14 or the Security Council under article 13 (b) of the Statute (article 53 (3) (a) ICC Statute). If such decision is based solely on the ground that an investigation or prosecution would not serve the interests of justice, the Pre-Trial Chamber may even review this decision *proprio motu* (article 53 (3) (b) ICC Statute).

d. Duty to cooperate with the ICC even for non-State Parties?

As a consequence of the *pacta tertiis* rule, states not party to the Rome State are not under any obligation to cooperate with the Court.[66] The rule is essentially a safeguard of sovereignty preventing states – all independent and equally sovereign – from becoming bound by a (treaty) rule without their consent. If, however, sovereignty is (re-)interpreted as a responsibility to protect, and this responsibility is exercised by the (organized) international community in the form of the ICC, it is indeed arguable that *all* States, to a certain extent, retain a "residual responsibility to protect" in the form of cooperating with the Court. Even states not parties to the ICC Statute could thus be obliged to cooperate with the Court at least in some basic form (i.e. not subject to the terms of Part 9 of the Statute).

This approach would require a modification of Article 34 VCLT. This is possible as the *pacta tertiis* rule serves to protect state sovereignty, and is thus open to modification induced by changes to the content of sovereignty. Of course, one must be careful not to abolish the principle by the back door by a semantic trick. However, in an area where community interests are affected in such a direct and fundamental way, and if it is accepted that a rule of international law can serve an interest of the international community as a whole even though it only binds a group

---

[66] Dahm/ Delbrück/ Wolfrum, see note 17, 1132, 1146; M. Benzing, "U.S. Bilateral Non-Surrender Agreements and Article 98 of the Statute of the International Criminal Court: An Exercise of the Law of Treaties", *Max Planck UNYB* 8 (2004), 181 et seq. (196).

of states,[67] certain modifications of the principle may be necessary and permissible.[68]

In this specific instance, it is thus arguable that non-States Parties at least will have seriously to consider a request for cooperation by the Court, even where they have not entered into an *ad hoc* arrangement or other formal agreement under article 87 (5) (a) ICC Statute.

2. The meaning of responsibility to protect for states in the area of international criminal law

a. Universal jurisdiction

Universal jurisdiction has in recent years become one of the buzz words of the discussion on how effectively to enforce substantive international criminal law. Asserting jurisdiction means exercising sovereignty, and to do so against a non-national who has allegedly committed a crime abroad potentially infringes the sovereignty of other states in the form of the principle of non-intervention. However, it is now accepted that the principle of non-intervention extends only so far as universal jurisdiction may be exercised.[69] As a consequence, the principle of non-intervention – as a corollary of state sovereignty – cannot in principle restrict the exercise of universal jurisdiction.[70] While this gen-

---

[67] J. d'Aspremont, "Contemporary International Rulemaking and the Public Character of International Law", International Law and Justice Working Paper 2006/12, p. 21, with specific reference to the ICC Statute.

[68] In consequence, it has been suggested that treaties protecting basic interests of the international community could, as a result of their addressing global concerns, more easily transform into customary international law. (C. Tomuschat, "Obligations arising for states without or against their will", *RdC* 241 (1993-IV), 195 et seq. (269-70)). In the same vein, it has been argued that the objective element of customary international law, i.e. state practice, could diminish in significance where community interests are concerned. (A. Seibert-Fohr, "Unity and Diversity in the Formation and Relevance of Customary International Law", in: A. Zimmermann/ R. Hofmann (eds), *Unity and Diversity in International Law*, 2006, 257. In the same direction: J. I. Charney, "Universal International Law", *AJIL* 87 (1993), 529.

[69] Dahm/ Delbrück/ Wolfrum, see note 17, 1000.

[70] See A. Eser, "Harmonisierte Universalität nationaler Strafgewalt: ein Desiderat internationaler Komplementarität bei Verfolgung von Völkerrechtsverbrechen", in: A. Donatsch/ M. Forster/ C. Schwarzenegger (eds), *Strafrecht,*

eral statement is easy to agree with, it begs the question where the line between the two principles is to be drawn.[71]

aa. The nature of universal jurisdiction

Investigating and prosecuting international crimes under the form of *universal jurisdiction* means that a single state steps in for the international community as a whole. The state is entitled, "pursuant to the principle of universal jurisdiction and in the capacity of a guardian of international law and an agent for its enforcement", to try the person accused of international crimes.[72] As international crimes protect legal interests or values of the international community as a whole, states only exercise criminal jurisdiction on behalf of the international community[73] and engage in the "decentralized prosecution of international offences".[74] National courts act instead of – in line with the theory of *dédoublement fonctionnel*[75] one may even say: as – international organs. To apply the changed notion of sovereignty to this phenomenon, one could say that states have a responsibility to protect not only towards their own citizens, but also towards humanity in general.[76]

Nevertheless, the exercise of universal jurisdiction is a form of *unilateral* enforcement of international (criminal) law. Its general permissibility may be deduced from the fact that it normally constitutes a relatively minor interference with the autonomy of a state (*e.g.* that of the nationality of the alleged perpetrator), while it serves the enforcement of very important values of the international community. It is this clear preponderance in favour of the interests of the international community that sets it apart from other, more serious, forms of unilateral interna-

---

Strafprozessrecht und Menschenrechte, Festschrift für Stefan Trechsel, 2002, 219 et seq. (229).

[71] T. Weigend, "Grund und Grenzen universaler Gerichtsbarkeit", in: Arnold, see note 34, 955 et seq. (963).

[72] Supreme Court of Israel, *Attorney-General of the Government of Israel v. Adolf Eichmann*, 29 May 1962, *ILR* 36 (1968), 277 et seq. (304).

[73] Lagodny, see note 28, 803.

[74] R. Wolfrum, "The Decentralized Prosecution of International Offences through National Courts", *Isr. Y. B. Hum. Rts* 24 (1994/1995), 183 et seq. (186).

[75] G. Scelle, *Précis de droit des gens; principes et systématique, vol. 2 (Droit constitutionnel international)*, 1934, 10-12.

[76] Amann, see note 28, 208.

tional law enforcement by states, such as military humanitarian intervention. In the latter case, article 2 (4) of the UN Charter, a *ius cogens* norm, weighs in heavily on the side of the non-permissibility of unilateral action, if one considers that the prohibition of the use of force is susceptible to an interest-balancing exercise at all.

bb. Limits to the exercise of universal jurisdiction?

It is a hotly debated question whether there are limits to the exercise of universal jurisdiction when it comes to the prosecution of international crimes, in particular, whether universal jurisdiction is subject to the principle of subsidiary. The German *Generalbundesanwalt* (Federal Prosecutor) has recently made clear that such exercise (under section 1 of the German Code of International Crimes (GCIC) and section 153f (2) 4 German Code of Criminal Procedure (GCCP)) will only occur under conditions similar to those set out in article 17 ICC Statute, *i.e.* when another state fails to exercise its jurisdiction for reasons of unwillingness or inability to do so.[77] It is important to note that the decision

[77] German Federal Prosecutor (*Generalbundesanwalt*), "Keine deutschen Ermittlungen wegen der angezeigten Vorfälle von Abu Ghraib/Irak", *Juristenzeitung* 60 (2005), 311. He reasoned: "It is the objective of the German Code of International Crimes to close the gaps in the criminalization and prosecution of international crimes. However, this needs to be done against the backdrop of the principle of non-intervention. This follows also from article 17 of the ICC Statute, which needs to be considered in normative context with the German Code of International Crimes. Following article 17, the jurisdiction of the ICC is subsidiary to the competence of the state where the crime occurred or the state of nationality; the ICC can only take action where the states primarily called upon to prosecute are unwilling or unable to do so. On the same reasoning, a third state may not examine the practice of other states against its own standards, correct it in individual cases or even supplant it. The German legislator has allowed for subsidiarity not by going back on the fundamental decision in favour of the principle of universal jurisdiction, but by providing for a differentiated procedural regulation in section 153 f of the German Code of Criminal Procedure." (my translation).

The decision not to prosecute was upheld by the Higher Regional Court (*OLG*) *Stuttgart*, *Neue Zeitschrift für Strafrecht* 26 (2006), 117. For a similar reasoning by the Spanish *Tribunal Constitucional* see H. Ascensio, "The Spanish Constitutional Tribunal's Decision in *Guatemalan Generals*: Unconditional Universality is Back", *JICJ* 4 (2006), 586 et seq. (591). See also: C. Tomuschat, "Issues of Universal Jurisdiction in the *Scilingo* Case", *JICJ* 3 (2005), 1074 et seq. (1080-1081).

was based on the Code of Criminal Procedure and thus was strictly procedural in character. As a matter of legal doctrine it did not distract from the full applicability of the universality principle; in practice, however, it constitutes a clear limitation of the universality principle. It may thus be justified to speak of two components of the universality principle under German law: a jurisdictional (section 1 GCIC) and a procedural (section 153f GCCP) one, both of which define its contents.

In fact, even though the decision and its reasoning have been criticized,[78] it is clear that the extension of universal jurisdiction will increase the number of jurisdictional conflicts between states, conflicts which in the long run could destabilize the international legal order.[79] Rules for the coordination of its exercise thus seem necessary.[80]

From this point of view, the reasoning of the Federal Prosecutor does not seem to be unjustifiable from a viewpoint of legal doctrine. In fact, considerations of complementarity or subsidiarity similar to those underlying article 17 of the ICC Statute and the reasoning of the Federal Prosecutor have also been put forward in literature.[81] Admittedly, the

---

[78] A. Fischer-Lescano, "Torture in Abu Ghraib: The Complaint against Donald Rumsfeld under the German Code of Crimes against International Law", *German Law Journal* 6 (2005), 689 et seq. (709 et seq.).

[79] See ICJ, *Case Concerning the Arrest Warrant of 11 April 2000* (Democratic Republic of the Congo v. Belgium), Judgment of 14 February 2002, Joint Sep. Op. By Judges *Higgins*, *Kooijmans* and *Buergenthal*, ICJ Rep. 2002, 63 et seq. (80, para. 59, 85, paras 73-75). On the potential for inter-state tensions see also: S. R. Ratner, "Belgium's War Crimes Statute: A Postmortem", *AJIL* 97 (2003), 888 et seq. (893); B. Broomhall, *International Criminal Justice and the International Criminal Court*, 2003, 125: "irreducible element of friction".

[80] See M. Rau, "Das Ende der Weltrechtspflege? Zur Abschaffung des belgischen Gesetzes über die universelle Verfolgung völkerrechtlicher Verbrechen", *Humanitäres Völkerrecht* 16 (2003), 212 et seq. (216).

[81] Eser, see note 70, 236; Ratner, see note 79, 895: "The complementarity theme of the ICC should thus apply to decisions by individual states as well."; J. K. Kleffner, "The Impact of Complementarity on National Implementation of Substantive International Criminal Law", *JICJ* 1 (2003), 86 et seq. (109), who refers to this concept as "horizontal complementarity/subsidiary universal jurisdiction"); Weigend, see note 71, 973; C. Kress, "Universal Jurisdiction over International Crimes and the *Institut de droit international*", *JICJ* 4 (2006), 561 et seq. (580). Also see Princeton Project on Universal Jurisdiction, *Princeton Principles on Universal Jurisdiction*, Principle 8 ("Resolution of Competing National Jurisdiction"), p. 38, and commentary on p. 53; ILA, London Conference (2000), Committee on International Human Rights Law and Practice, *Final Report on the Exercise of Universal Jurisdiction in Respect of Gross Human Rights*

argument that complementarity (article 17) governs only the relationship between two different levels of political power, i.e. the national and the international, and not the horizontal distribution of competences between states is compelling at first sight,[82] as it reflects what has been said about complementarity as subsidiarity.[83] If, however, one accepts that the principle of subsidiarity governs the exercise of jurisdiction by the (organized) international community in the form of the ICC, then it is arguable that states, when prosecuting international crimes, are under the exact same constraints, as they act only on behalf of the international community when exercising universal jurisdiction.[84] If they exercise only "delegated" jurisdiction, their competencies cannot extend further than that of the delegator, the international community.[85]

The principle of complementarity would then, in essence, have modified the procedural aspect of the universality principle also inasmuch as

---

Offences, 20-1: "Gross human rights offenders should be brought to justice in the state in which they committed their offences. In the absence of such proceedings, full advantage should be taken of the possibility to bring perpetrators to trial on the basis of universal jurisdiction." For limitations on (a possibly emerging rule of) universal *civil* jurisdiction along the lines of complementarity see: D. F. Donovan/ A. Roberts, "The Emerging Recognition of Universal Civil Jurisdiction", *AJIL* 100 (2006), 142 et seq. (159).

82 M. Bothe/ A. Fischer-Lescano, "Die Bedeutung völkerrechtlicher Bestrafungspflichten und der völkergewohnheitsrechtlichen Jurisdiktions- und Immunitätsregeln für Verfahren nach dem Völkerstrafgesetzbuch", Kurzgutachten (November 2006), available at <http://www.rav.de/download/Gutachten_Bothe_Fischer_Lescano_dt.pdf>, p. 9, arguing that article 17 ICC Statute cannot serve as a standard for the (horizontal) coordination of the exercise of jurisdiction, since it regulates only the (vertical) relationship between states and an international institution (the ICC).

83 See above at III. 1. b. cc.

84 One can, of course, argue that this conclusion is tenuous given that the ICC Statute – which serves as the agent for a "transformation" of the universality principle – does not even provide for universal jurisdiction (article 12 ICC Statute), so that it would be impermissible to conclude from its article 17 on a restriction of the principle. See F. Jessberger, "Universality, Complementarity, and the Duty to Prosecute Crimes Under International Law in Germany", in: W. Kaleck *et al.* (eds), *International Prosecution of Human Rights Crimes*, 2006, 213 et seq. (219-220). What is important, however, is that the Court *could* exercise its (dormant) universal jurisdiction but for article 12, which constitutes a political compromise.

85 Ambos, see note 40, 437 also takes this approach, though with a different reasoning (sovereign equality of states).

its application by states as a jurisdictional title is concerned. This restriction of the principle may also accommodate concerns of an "international vigilantism"[86], "humanitarian imperialism"[87] or "jurisdictional imperialism"[88] resulting from the *mala fide* exercise of states' competences granted by international law in relation to *erga omnes* obligations.[89]

It is another question whether the subsidiary nature of the principle of universal jurisdiction was correctly interpreted by the Federal Prosecutor in the case at hand. In other words, if one accepts the conclusion drawn above, the exercise of national jurisdiction under the universality principle is subsidiary to other national jurisdictions *only* if and when a state *is* in fact investigating or prosecuting. In particular, it is not sufficient to block the exercise of jurisdiction under article 17 ICC Statute that another state – or several states – has jurisdiction over the crimes in question. That it does is a necessary, but not a sufficient condition. The same has to go for the procedural aspect of the universality principle governing the exercise of jurisdiction of national courts. Taking this into account, the reasoning of the Higher Regional Court (*OLG*) of *Stuttgart* that the fact that the persons accused of international crimes were at all relevant times subject to the jurisdiction of US courts and

---

86 B. Simma, "Bilateralism and Community Interest in the Law of State Responsibility", in: Y. Dinstein/ M. Tabory (eds), *International Law at a Time of Perplexity: Essays in Honour of Shabtai Rosenne*, 1989, 821 et seq. (832); C. Tomuschat, "The Duty to Prosecute International Crimes Committed by Individuals", in: Cremer et al., see note 4, 315 et seq. (342).

87 A. Cassese, *International Criminal Law*, 2003, 9.

88 ILA, London Conference (2000), Committee on International Human Rights Law and Practice, *Final Report on the Exercise of Universal Jurisdiction in Respect of Gross Human Rights Offences*, 19.

89 It is, however, questionable whether the universality principle is subject to a further restriction, i.e. "reversed vertical complementarity" (see Kleffner, see note 81, 109). This would mean that states may exercise universal jurisdiction only if the ICC does not exercise its jurisdiction. Such restriction arguably takes the influence of complementarity on the universality principle one step too far, as it poses a requirement that in fact turns the idea of complementarity on its head (primary international jurisdiction). The same is suggested for universal *civil* jurisdiction by Donovan/ Roberts, see note 81, 160.

Nevertheless, as a matter of legal policy, the jurisdiction of an international criminal court is generally to be preferred to (random and sometimes arbitrary) prosecution by a state on the basis of the universality principle with no connection to the crime (see Weigend, see note 71, 976).

that in consequence there was no risk of impunity[90] seems to be based on a misunderstanding of complementarity.[91] In particular, it is not conceivable that it is sufficient for a state to commence some individual investigations or prosecutions with regard to a "situation" (e.g. the incidents in *Abu Ghraib*) to block the jurisdiction of other states with regard to other individuals in respect of which the territorial state or state of nationality has remained inactive.[92]

b. Duty to prevent and prosecute

States are generally under a duty to prevent the commission of international crimes, at least within their territorial jurisdiction.[93] This follows from specific treaty obligations (*e.g.* article I of the Genocide Convention) which explicitly provide for a duty to prevent, but more generally also from human rights law which requires states to take positive action to prevent breaches of fundamental human rights.[94]

Whereas a duty to prevent is rather unproblematic, the same is not true for the duty to punish. Normally, international law leaves states a wide

---

90 OLG Stuttgart, see note 77, 118, para. 14.

91 In the same direction: Ambos, see note 38, 436.

92 See Jessberger, see note 84, 219, pointing out that article 17 refers to "cases" instead of "situations" and Pre-Trial Chamber I , *Decision on the Application for Participation in the Proceedings of VPRS 1, VPRS 2, VPRS 3, VPRS 4, VPRS 5 and VPRS 6*, 17 January 2006, ICC 01/04-101, para. 65: "Situations, which are generally defined in terms of temporal, territorial and in some cases personal parameters [...] entail the proceedings envisaged in the Statute to determine whether a particular situation should give rise to a criminal investigation as well as the investigation as such. Cases, which comprise specific incidents during which one or more crimes within the jurisdiction of the Court seem to have been committed by one or more identified suspects, entail proceedings that take place after the issuance of a warrant of arrest or a summons to appear."

93 Significantly, the ICJ, *Case Concerning the Application of the Convention on the Prevention and Punishment of the Crime of Genocide* (Bosnia and Herzegovina v. Serbia and Montenegro), Judgment of 26 February 2007, para. 434 did not limit the duty to prevent to the territorial state, arguing that the FRY "was in a position of influence ... unlike that of any of the other States parties to the Genocide Convention" with respect to the situation in Bosnia-Herzegovina.

94 The ICJ, see note 93, para. 429 shied away from supporting such a general preventive duty.

discretion on how to enforce international law nationally. Domestic courts generally thus do not necessarily have to have jurisdiction to enforce international law.[95] In line with this general tendency, there are few explicit instances where international law establishes a duty to prosecute international crimes. These are, above all, treaty obligations established in the Genocide Convention (article I), the four Geneva Conventions[96] and the Torture Convention. Where customary international law establishes criminal sanctions or allows for prosecution under the principle of universal jurisdiction, it normally provides for a right, not a duty to prosecute;[97] thus, there is – at least as a matter of *lex lata* – no general duty to prosecute under international law.[98]

The ICC Statute itself neither contains an express duty for states to implement the substantive crimes of articles 5 to 8 into national law,[99] nor does it establish a duty to prosecute.[100] This is significant, as the Statute penalizes crimes with respect to which no clear duty to prosecute exists under international law, such as crimes against humanity or war crimes committed in internal armed conflict.[101]

In the search for a general duty to prosecute, international lawyers have turned to human rights law. It is accepted that states are under a positive obligation actively to prevent individuals from being deprived of the enjoyment of fundamental human rights by other individuals.[102] If violations have occurred, and the state has incurred responsibility by reason of a dereliction of its duty to prevent human rights violations, a response is mandated by human rights law. However, a general duty to

---

[95] Kumm, see note 50, 911.

[96] GC I: articles 49, 50; GC II: articles 50, 51; GC III: articles 129, 130; GC IV: articles 146, 147. See also articles 11; 85 Additional Protocol I.

[97] See Donovan/ Roberts, see note 81, 143.

[98] Cassese, see note 87, 302; Dahm/ Delbrück/ Wolfrum, see note 17, 1000.

[99] Fife, see note 23, 83.

[100] Dahm/ Delbrück/ Wolfrum, see note 17, 1018; A. Zimmermann, "Auf dem Weg zu einem deutschen Völkerstrafgesetzbuch: Entstehung, völkerrechtlicher Rahmen und wesentliche Inhalte", *Zeitschrift für Rechtspolitik* 35 (2002), 97 et seq. (98); Tomuschat, see note 86, 338. The Statute does, however, contain explicit duties for States Parties to have legislation in place enabling the state to cooperate with the Court.

[101] There is no explicit duty to prosecute in Additional Protocol II.

[102] See Tomuschat, see note 86, 317.

prosecute international crimes is not uncontroversial.[103] It is doubtful whether human rights generally require states to impose criminal sanctions for breaches by private actors. While it is agreed that some process of individual accountability needs to be established,[104] the proposition that there was a duty to prosecute would make it impossible to have recourse to alternative justice mechanisms, in particular in post-conflict situations.

However, many authors argue that under customary international law there is a duty on states to penalize and prosecute international crimes as particularly grave forms of human rights violations.[105] Perceiving sovereignty as "responsibility to protect" adds an additional argument in favour of such a general duty. If such a duty arising from human rights law is accepted, it is limited to crimes that have taken place under the territorial jurisdiction of the state concerned.[106]

3. Preliminary conclusion: A system of shared responsibility

Taking account of the interplay between the exercise of international and national jurisdiction over international crimes, it is reasonable to speak of responsibilities to protect being shared between the (organized) international community and states. The principle of a "responsibility to protect" can explain how the two levels – the international and the national – work together to achieve the underlying objective of the international criminal justice system: effective prosecution of international crimes and the prevention of impunity. The principle of subsidi-

---

[103] Dahm/ Delbrück/ Wolfrum, see note 17, 1014 et seq.

[104] S. R. Ratner/ J. S. Abrams, *Accountability for Human Rights Atrocities in International Law*, 2nd ed., 2001, 154.

[105] Lagodny, see note 28, 803; Tomuschat, see note 86, 325; K. Ambos, "Völkerrechtliche Bestrafungspflichten bei schweren Menschenrechtsverletzungen", *AVR* 37 (1999), 318 et seq. (327, 353).

[106] Tomuschat, see note 86, 326, 332. In relation to the crime of genocide see, on the one hand, ICJ, *Application of the Convention on the Prevention and Punishment of the Crime of Genocide* (Bosnia and Herzegovina v. Yugoslavia), Preliminary Objections, Judgment of 11 July 1996, ICJ Reports 1996 (II), 595 et seq. (616, para. 31): "the obligation each State ... has to prevent and to punish the crime of genocide is not territorially limited by the Convention", and, on the other hand, ICJ, see note 93, para. 442: "Article VI only obliges the Contracting Parties to institute and exercise territorial criminal jurisdiction."

arity, of which the complementarity principle is but one example, can serve to organize the exercise of authority within this multilevel international legal system.

IV. The relationship between individual criminal responsibility and state responsibility for international crimes

State responsibility in relation to the commission of international crimes can arise in different situations:[107]

1. Where an international crime is committed by an individual acting in an official capacity or is in any other manner attributable to the state (see articles 4-11 ILC Articles), dual responsibility will arise: (direct) individual and state responsibility (by attribution).[108] In this area, for state responsibility to be triggered, all elements of the crime (which are the relevant primary rules) need to be present, including the requirements of fault for individual criminal responsibility.[109]

2. A state further engages responsibility where it fails to discharge its positive duty to protect or prevent.[110] Specific obligations to prevent (such as article I of the Genocide Convention) are but examples of responsibility for omission or failure to act.[111] In cases where an individual acts in a private capacity (and does not fall within article 8, 9 or 11 of the ILC Articles), direct individual responsibility of the person acting in a private capacity and state responsibility for *omission* to intervene and stop the crimes that are occurring may run in parallel. Article 2 of the ILC Articles also comprises omission as a *modus* for incurring state responsibility. Under certain circumstances, the organ (or rather: a member of the organ) of the state responsible for the omission may also be individually liable under the doctrine of command responsibility.

---

[107] But see Mégret, see note 24, 38, who restricts state responsibility to breaches of the "*aut dedere aut iudicare*" principle.

[108] Cassese, see note 87, 19.

[109] See M. Milanović, "State Responsibility for Genocide", *EJIL* 17 (2006), 553 et seq. (595, 507).

[110] Dahm/ Delbrück/ Wolfrum, see note 17, 1012; Wolfrum, see note 74, 198.

[111] ICJ, see note 93, para. 432.

3. A third possibility for incurring state responsibility is where a state fails to punish crimes in those cases where it is under a duty to investigate and prosecute.[112] The ICJ has recently clarified that, while a state cannot at once incur responsibility both for the commission of international crimes and the failure to prevent them, such parallel liability may well be possible with respect to the commission of crimes and breach of its obligation to punish them.[113]

In principle, individual and state responsibility for international crimes are thus complementary and not exclusive.[114] This is also shown by article 58 of the ILC Articles on State Responsibility, providing that the articles are "without prejudice to any question of the individual responsibility under international law of any person acting on behalf of the state", whereas article 25 (4) of the ICC Statute states that "[n]o provision in this Statute relating to individual criminal responsibility shall affect the responsibility of States under international law". However, it almost seems as if both texts, which belong to the most important developments in international law in recent years, shy away from any clear statement on the relationship between the two regimes. This is to be regretted, given that the difference or even tension between state and individual responsibility for international crimes has been identified as "one of the central challenges for the future of international criminal law".[115]

1. The rise of individual criminal responsibility

It may be argued that the rise of international *individual* criminal responsibility has done more – and will continue to contribute more in the future – to implement the responsibility to protect in the field of international criminal law than *state* responsibility. The recent judgment of the ICJ in the *Application of the Genocide Convention Case* clearly

---

[112] Dahm/ Delbrück/ Wolfrum, see note 17, 1012; Wolfrum, see note 74, 198.

[113] ICJ, see note 93, para. 380-383.

[114] ICJ, see note 93, para. 173; N. L. Reid, "Bridging the Conceptual Chasm: Superior Responsibility as the Missing Link between State and Individual Responsibility under International Law", *LJIL* 18 (2005), 795 et seq. (797); A. Nollkaemper, "Concurrence between individual responsibility and state responsibility in international law", *ICLQ* 52 (2003), 615 et seq. (619-20).

[115] Ratner, see note 79, 893.

shows the jurisdictional restrictions that inter-state litigation with respect to state responsibility in international criminal law is subject to: The ICJ could only exercise jurisdiction on the basis of article IX of the Genocide Convention, making it impossible to look into Serbia's state responsibility as regards crimes against humanity or war crimes.[116] While sound as a matter of legal reasoning, this outcome is hardly easily explained to the victims of the crimes in the territory concerned. While the Court, anticipating their frustration, draws attention to the "fundamental distinction between the existence and binding force of obligations arising under international law and the existence of a court or tribunal with jurisdiction to resolve disputes about compliance with these obligations",[117] the judgment is a painful reminder of the lack of compulsory jurisdiction in inter-state disputes.

It is, however, a sign of maturity of the international legal system that the reality that "crimes against international law are committed by men, not by abstract entities", is reflected by mechanisms for the enforcement of individual responsibility.[118] As a political, though not legal, assessment, it is correct to say that "unless responsibility is imputed and attached to persons of flesh and blood, it rests with no one."[119] It is a necessary part of the "individualization" of international law, i.e. the progressive recognition of the individual as a bearer of rights and duties under international law and thus a turning away from one of the fundamental tenets of classical legal positivism.[120] The traditional focus of international law on *state* responsibility by shielding the individual (e.g., through the mechanism of diplomatic or state immunity) arguably rather undermined the efficacy of international law.[121]

---

116 ICJ, see note 93, para. 277.

117 ICJ, see note 93, para. 148.

118 See Nuremberg Judgment of 1 October 1946, in: Trial of the Major War Criminals before the International Military Tribunal, 1947, vol. 1, 171 (223).

119 H. Lauterpacht, *International Law and Human Rights*, 1950, 40.

120 Dahm/ Delbrück/ Wolfrum, see note 17, 995; Wolfrum, see note 74, 188.

121 Nollkaemper, see note 114, 617-8.

2. What role for state responsibility for international crimes?

If the increasing role of individual criminal responsibility is a sign of a maturing international legal system, what then is the state in current international law of state responsibility for international crimes?

a. Conceptual differences between state and individual responsibility

There are several conceptual differences between state and individual responsibility. First, and most obviously, the first is an enforcement of international law against the state as such, the second against individuals. Secondly, state and individual responsibility follow different purposes: state responsibility is essentially comparable to the classical concept of civil liability. It has a compensatory or reparatory function (*Ausgleichsfunktion*).[122] Individual responsibility is penal responsibility, i.e. punitive in character. Thirdly, generally speaking, the rules on state responsibility as secondary rules do not require fault (*culpa*) on the part of the state.[123] Strictly speaking, the fault requirement is relevant only for individual criminal responsibility.[124]

b. Loss of significance of state responsibility in international criminal law

aa. The general distrust in state responsibility in international criminal law

As described above, state and individual criminal responsibility can arise simultaneously. It is certainly not correct to see individual responsibility as the only, or even always the preferable, viable way of enforcing international criminal law.[125] At present, however, there is a ten-

---

[122] Dahm/ Delbrück/ Wolfrum, see note 17, 995; P.-M. Dupuy, "International Criminal Responsibility of the Individual and International Responsibility of the State", in: A. Cassese/P. Gaeta/ J.R.W.D. Jones (eds), *The Rome Statute of the International Criminal Court: A Commentary*, Vol. 2, 2002, 1085 et seq. (1097).

[123] Milanović, see note 109, 560.

[124] Dupuy, see note 122, 1095-6.

[125] In this direction: Nuremberg Judgment of 1 October 1946, in: Trial of the Major War Criminals before the International Military Tribunal (1947), vol. 1, 171 (223): "[O]nly by punishing individuals who commit ... crimes [against international law] can the provisions of international law be enforced." ICJ, *Ap-*

dency to focus more on individual criminal responsibility than on state responsibility for international crimes.[126] Commentators even speak of a "profound distrust of State responsibility".[127]

Some of this distrust may hark back to the confusion concerning the term "crimes of states" in the discussion leading up the ILC Articles on State Responsibility. The proposal to include international crimes of states within the Articles on State Responsibility failed in the end, and the Articles in their final version explicitly refrain from dealing with individual responsibility (article 58). In the drafting process, some members of the ILC in fact felt uneasy about this incongruence, stating that "it would be illogical to punish such acts solely at the individual level".[128] The institutions implementing individual responsibility, such as the *ad hoc* tribunals and the ICC, make even more apparent the lack of collective enforcement mechanisms for state responsibility.[129]

bb. Problems with the judicial enforcement of state responsibility

One reason for the relatively insignificant role of state responsibility for international crimes may be the legal and political complexity of interstate litigation. Establishing state responsibility in the ICJ may take a long time,[130] as proved by the *Genocide Case* which began in 1993, with a final judgment delivered only in 2007. A second difficulty may be that the responsibility of the state for international crimes is necessarily a heightened or aggravated one that implies serious moral condemnation (see articles 40, 41 of the ILC Articles on State Responsibility). States may thus think that political costs are significantly lower for judicial determination of individual than state responsibility, at least when mid-level and lower-level perpetrators are concerned. Thirdly, procedural, in

---

plication of the Convention on the Prevention and Punishment of the Crime of Genocide (Bosnia and Herzegovina v. Yugoslavia), Preliminary Objections, Judgment of 11 July 1996, Joint Decl. Judges *Shi* and *Vereshetin*, ICJ Rep. 1996 (II), 631 et seq. (632).

[126] Cassese, see note 87, 19.

[127] Mégret, see note 24, 39.

[128] Report of the International Law Commission on the work of its fiftieth session (20 April-12 June and 27 July-14 August 1998) UN Doc. A/53/10, *ILCYB* 1988 II(2), 1 (69, para. 276).

[129] Nollkaemper, see note 114, 627.

[130] See Mégret, see note 24, 39.

particular evidentiary, mechanisms of the ICJ and other international courts dealing with inter-state disputes are not particularly suited to the task of establishing the complex factual background of such cases.[131] A final reason is that complementarity, at least for breaches by states of their duty to prosecute, may be a far more effective means for the enforcement of international criminal law than the establishment of state responsibility. The (organized) international community steps in and takes prosecution into its own hands by way of substitution, thereby ensuring that the responsibility to protect is honoured.

c. *Reasons for reviving interest in state responsibility*

There are, however, several reasons for re-focusing on state responsibility for international crimes, the main one being that it can help to close *lacunae* in the protection of the international public goods protected by the prohibition of international crimes. This is mainly due to the fact that the obligations of states are more far-reaching than those of individuals with respect to international criminal law, and to the differentiated means of enforcing state responsibility on the international plane.

aa. Wider scope of state obligations

State responsibility is more comprehensive than individual responsibility as it covers a wider range of situations. State responsibility may arise not only with respect to the commission proper of international crimes (by attribution or omission), but also in relation to duties applying before and after the actual commission. To make clear their supplemental function, one may speak of "ancillary duties"[132] without, however, distracting from their importance.

For instance, the duty to prevent may be breached where international law requires states to criminalize certain behaviour and the state fails to do so. In addition, a state's responsibility is also engaged where it fails to take action if it is under a duty to investigate and prosecute.[133] Via the

---

131 Ratner/ Abrams, see note 104, 227.

132 Milanović, see note 109, 570.

133 Interestingly, Serbia argued before the ICJ that state responsibility as provided for in article IX of the Genocide Convention was limited to these preventive and repressive obligations to the exclusion of liability for the actual commission of genocide. The ICJ rejected this argument: ICJ (1996), see note 106,

principle of universality, combined with a duty to prosecute, state responsibility may thus be incurred even by third states that have no link with the crime committed.[134]

Potentially, the notion of sovereignty as responsibility could lead to an even larger field of application for state responsibility if it contributed to a further extension of "ancillary duties", such as the duties to criminalize and punish conduct. The same goes for responsibility for omissions, if sovereignty as responsibility leads to intensification of the duty to react, i.e. to intervene in the continued commission of international crimes.

bb. Range of enforcement mechanisms

Another major reason for reviving interest in state responsibility is the range of mechanisms available to enforce it. The enforcement of individual criminal responsibility largely focuses on judicial procedures; these may be very complicated and politically costly with regard to state responsibility, as is shown by the *Genocide* case. State responsibility can be enforced by other means, in particular countermeasures. Under the ILC Articles on State responsibility, breaches of states' duties with relation to international criminal law are addressed in articles 40, 41, 48 and 54. In particular, *any* state may take lawful measures against a state breaching an *erga omnes* obligation to ensure the cessation of the breach and reparation in the interests of the beneficiaries of the obligation (article 54, so called "solidarity measures"), always subject to the prohibition on the use of force.

These mechanisms may at times avoid the problems of individual criminal prosecution, especially by national jurisdictions under the principle of universal jurisdiction. Even though nothing should distract from the seminal importance of both the national and international prosecution of international crimes as part of sovereign responsibility, it is true that, in the reality of the international legal system, individual prosecutions may sometimes cause significant tensions. "[W]hen justice becomes personal, so does foreign policy".[135] Thus, traditional state-to-

---

616, para. 32. But see Mégret, see note 24, 38, who restricts state responsibility to breaches of the "*aut dedere aut iudicare*" principle.

[134] But see ICJ, see note 93, para. 184, holding that the obligation to prosecute imposed by Article VI of the Genocide Convention is territorially limited.

[135] Ratner, see note 79, 893-4.

state mechanisms may play a significant role in the enforcement of international criminal law, such as diplomatic isolation, economic sanctions, or the suspension of foreign aid. In extreme cases, state responsibility can be enforced by military intervention under a Security Council mandate.

It is in particular with respect to the crime of aggression that state responsibility has a potentially greater role to play than individual criminal responsibility. There is, as yet, no internationally accepted definition on the crime of aggression. While article 5 (1) (d) of the ICC Statute mentions aggression as a crime under the jurisdiction of the ICC, para. 2 specifies that the actual exercise of that jurisdiction will only be possible after the amendment of the Statute. This provision has been called a "diplomatic smoke screen" and doubts have been raised whether it is realistic that a crime of aggression will ever be prosecutable by an international criminal court, let alone by individual states by way of universal jurisdiction.[136] It may be more successful to rely on traditional conceptions of state responsibility for a breach of article 2 (4) of the UN Charter.[137]

V. Conclusion

The following conclusions can be drawn from the above analysis:

1. One important aspect of the notion of "sovereignty" in modern international law is responsibility.
2. The fundamentals of the international criminal law system can be explained by reference to "sovereignty as responsibility": the duty to prevent, duty to act, and duty to rebuild.
3. The (organized) international community and individual states have a shared responsibility. One can thus speak of "shared sovereignty" in a multilayered international system.
4. A fundamental principle of coordination between the international (collective) plane and the individual state is the (emerging) princi-

---

[136] Tomuschat, see note 86, 341. See also: Ratner/ Abrams, see note 104, 124 et seq.

[137] See the recent decision of the Eritrea Ethiopia Claims Commission, *Partial Award,* Jus Ad Bellum, *Ethiopia's Claims 1-8*, 19 December 2005 and the critique by C. Gray, "The Eritrea/Ethiopia Claims Commission Oversteps Its Boundaries: A Partial Award?", *EJIL* 17 (2006), 699.

ple of subsidiarity, in international criminal law termed "complementarity".

5. Subsidiarity not only regulates the allocation of competences between national and international criminal jurisdictions (vertical subsidiarity), but also informs the application of competences in relations between states when they exercise universal jurisdiction (horizontal subsidiarity).
6. The "international criminal justice system" comprises not only individual criminal responsibility (enforced by international and national institutions), but also state responsibility, enforced collectively (judicially by international courts like the ICJ, and executively by the Security Council), as well as individually or decentralized, *e.g.* by countermeasures. Both branches, state and individual responsibility, complement each other.

Managing Risks to Global Stability: the UN Security Council's New-found Role Post Iraq

Volker Röben

Introduction

The events in Iraq in 2003 were the result of the Security Council's inability to live up to its task of maintaining international peace and security. That failure, however, should not mask the fact that since then and in its recent practice the Council has made ample use of its powers under Chapter VII UN Charter. In so doing, it has changed the focus of its activity and retooled its working methods pursuant to a broad reading of Chapter VII and its own powers thereunder.

The Council's focus of activity has shifted from the classic inter-state wars to certain categories of risks to regional and global stability. Risk (management) in this sense is not a normative notion such as "threat to international peace and security" within the meaning of Art. 39 UN Charter. It is a concept that highlights legal and practical developments and problems common to diverse areas of Security Council Chapter VII-based activity. It is the reference point of a new function of the collective security system and an indicator of problems for the law of the UN Charter.

The common feature of risk management, compared to classic ad hoc conflict intervention, is cognitive uncertainty or the remoteness of the connexion between certain circumstances and an actual international crisis including a potential military confrontation between states. In that respect, the Iraq situation of 2003 at least in its official version is a case in point. As such it was about the risk presented by alleged weapons of mass destruction. That distinguishes it fundamentally from Iraq 1990. And it illustrates the consequences of botched risk management.

The plan of this paper is as follows: it will flesh out this analytical framework distinguishing four elements of such management: the enunciation of strong principles and standards, ensuring that they are complied with, while leaving space for negotiated solutions, and subsidiarity (A). It will then use the proliferation of weapons of mass destruction and precarious states marred by national (state-internal) violence as categories of risks to global stability that call for management by the Security Council along the above identified lines. This paper will look at recent Council action under Chapter VII in the cases of Iran and North Korea to illustrate that the Council addresses the risk of nuclear proliferation (B). In the case of Lebanon and Sudan, as diverse as they may seem, there is the overarching concern for the risks to global stability presented by precarious states with national (and international) violence necessitating the Council's early and constant involvement and important standard-setting by the Council (C). As will be shown, using the Sudan, where all of these elements are present, as an example, decentralization is a constituent part of the Council's risk management. Finally, the paper will turn to the broader consequences of risk management for the proper understanding of Chapter VII and the role and powers of the Security Council thereunder in an increasingly globalising world (D).

A. Risk management: a typology

I. From conflict to risk

Art. 24 UN Charter states that the UN Security Council has primary responsibility for the maintenance of international peace and security. For that purpose, Art. 25 confers special powers on the Council, chiefly, but of course not exclusively, those under Chapter VII. For the Council to act under Chapter VII, it needs to determine that there is a breach of, or at least a threat to, international peace and security. The Charter's focus here is thought to be on inter-state violence, which has happened (breach) or is about to happen (threat). An international conflict of this kind warrants action by the Council uniting the powerful states of the world that have presumably put troops at its disposal (Art. 43). Overall, the crucial concept of "international" peace remains firmly in place if the Council intervenes in such a situation not with its own troops but by authorizing certain of its member states, as happened in the second Gulf War. It matters little, for that matter, whether the legal basis of that empowerment is Art. 42 or Art. 42 in conjunction with Art. 48.

From that basis of Council intervention in actual inter-state conflicts, the current practice of the Council marks a major departure. The Council's activity focuses now on risks to global stability, i.e. developments that may, in the future, trigger inter-state violence. Such risks are not internal affairs of states but per se concern the collective international security system and transcend the individual instance where they occur.

In its approach to these risks the Council has been shaping a common "horizontal" approach. The central idea of this approach is that risks need to be managed, i.e. they need to be addressed preventively before there is an actual crisis, receive responsive action when a crisis nevertheless breaks out and, eventually, post-crisis attention. The Security Council starts monitoring such risks at a fairly early point in time. That is to say, encompassing *prevention*, Council involvement deliberately sets in before an *acute* international crisis erupts creating a threat to international peace and security. Prevention also encompasses the Council obligating the states to monitor certain private activities. All of this gives the impression of the Council supervising situations that appear to fall under certain more or less well-defined categories of risks to global stability.

The Council then uses a cadenced approach comprising a number of finely tuned steps that allow for the calibrated escalation of the collective action in a concrete situation that falls under one of these categories. Whether the Council is officially seised of the situation constitutes a first pressure point. Once seised of the matter, the Council may act through presidential statements and only later through Council action pursuant to its powers under Chapter VII, which presupposes that the Council determines that the situation now constitutes a threat (to international peace and security). Under Chapter VII and on the basis of Art. 40, the Council may take *provisional* measures.[1] Hence, the focus of the Council is on the *preservation of the status quo*, including requiring a state to abstain from any acts that might aggravate the situation. Often and to a large extent, this very continuous supervision by itself has a considerable effect on the situation. Suffice it to mention that for a

---

[1] On the binding effect of an order under Art. 40 see J.A. Frowein/N. Krisch, "Art. 40, para. 14-17", in: B. Simma et al. (eds.), *UN Charter*, 2nd ed., 2002.

state to be put under Council supervision will often have a strong deterrent effect on foreign capital and (direct) investment in it.

II. Applicable standards

While the Charter conceives the Security Council first and foremost as a political body, under its current practice which is of interest here, the Security Council carries out *genuinely legal action*. The Council's risk management action (even if provisional but still mandatory) crucially relies on the definition of legal entitlements, rights and obligations of states and other actors; in short the legal framework of the crisis. In so doing the Security Council bases itself on certain *generally* accepted relevant legal standards found in international treaty law and customary international law, but it strengthens them.

III. Negotiated solutions

All the while, the Council consistently emphasizes the need for a peaceful and – thus – negotiated solution to crises and crisis-prone situations.[2] However, the Council does not purport to conduct these negotiations itself, preferring to task informal groups with a negotiating mandate while reserving for itself the power to frame the possible negotiations and to enforce their eventual results.

IV. Compliance

Notwithstanding the room for manoeuvre created by the emphasis placed on negotiated solutions, compliance with the Security Council's standards is crucial. Not content with setting the relevant standard and

---

[2] See, e.g., the presidential statement on the situation in the Middle East (S/PRST/2006/26, para 12): "... the situation in the Middle East is very tense and is likely to remain so, unless and until a comprehensive settlement covering all aspects of the Middle East problem can be reached". That statement of the Secretary-General reflects the view of the Security Council. This puts the current crisis in Lebanon and in Iraq in the context of the disputes involving Israel and the Palestinians.

deciding on steps for a state to meet it, the Council will actively seek to ensure compliance by targeted states and other actors. That has several aspects: enabling, controlling and enforcing compliance. The UN Charter envisages a straightforward system, in which the Council is given a range of powers under Chapter VII with which to force a recalcitrant state to comply with the Council's decisions to curtail any threat to peace and security.[3] Essentially, managing risks squares with this. The basic structure is still that compliance with Security Council demands on risk is to be achieved by way of escalating the pressure on a target state. However, a much broader panoply of instruments designed to ensure compliance is being developed. While sanctions do play a role, they are not the first resort. Rather, a collective enabling effort is required: risk management may require a permanent international presence within states, by means of international expertise, military presence – an international peacekeeping force with a robust mandate –, or an international tribunal. If compliance with its demands is nevertheless not forthcoming, the Security Council may resolve to take enforcement action. The upshot of the Council's initial emphasis on the status quo is that the Council may *escalate* its response to an evolving crisis from provisional measures under Art. 40 UN Charter[4] to non-forcible sanctions (Art. 41 UN Charter) and forcible measures (Art. 42, 48 UN Charter). Both Arts. 41 and 42 focus essentially on international reaction to a conflict that has erupted and now needs to be contained by cross-border action. The legal basis for peaceful (non-military, non-forcible) coercive measures is Art. 41 UN Charter. But such sanctions need to be tailored effectively to be commensurate with the demands posed. As these become more sophisticated and individualized, so do the sanctions required. Non-forcible sanctions are targeted towards furthering a concrete objective: concrete demands of the Security Council including, generally, the return of the state concerned to the negotiating table and making the negotiation process work.[5] Through increasingly

---

[3] See R. Higgins, "Peace and Security Achievements and Failures", *EJIL* 6 (1995), 1.

[4] This may come close to classic sanctions, as in the case of the de facto embargo on nuclear technological material against Iran pronounced by the Security Council pursuant to Art. 40 UN Charter.

[5] See the Security Council president statement on strengthening international law: rule of law and maintenance of international peace and security (S/PRST/2006/28): "The Security Council considers sanctions an important tool in the maintenance and restoration of international peace and security. The Council resolves to ensure that sanctions are carefully targeted in support of

routine use of its powers pursuant to Art. 41 UN Charter, the Council pierces the state's veil, reaching individuals held to be responsible for the failure to fulfil the Council's demands.[6] The choice of non-forcible sanctions comprises targeted embargoes of certain material, individualized sanctions such as asset freezing and travel bans, often administered by Security Council committees benefiting from independent expert advice. However, this objective of reaching the individual decision-maker may increasingly also be pursued on other legal grounds, namely the Rome Statute of the International Criminal Court. Beyond the physical effect that Art. 41 measures may have, the desired effect is that they make visible the isolation of the targeted state. As a last step, the Council may take enforcement mechanisms under Chapter VII short of authorizing military measures.[7] The Council makes it clear that Arts. 39 (i.e. Chapter VII unspecified)[8], Arts. 40, 41 and 42 UN Charter are *normatively clearly distinguishable* allowing for a escalation of *Council action* by referring to the specific legal basis in a resolution; it thereby also reasserts its authority over the military enforcement of any of its demands expressed under Chapter VII UN Charter preventing any uni-

---

clear objectives and are implemented in ways that balance effectiveness against possible adverse consequences. The Council is committed to ensuring that fair and clear procedures exist for placing individuals and entities on sanctions lists and for removing them, as well as for granting humanitarian exemptions. The Council reiterates its request to the 1267 Committee to continue its work on the Committee's guidelines, including on listing and delisting procedures, and on the implementation of its exemption procedures contained in resolution 1452 (2002)".

6 See C. Schaller, *Internationales Sanktionsmanagement im Rahmen von Art. 41 UN Charta*, 2003.

7 See A. Cassese, *International Law*, 2nd ed., 2004, 339 note 1, distinguishing collective countermeasures, sanctions stricto sensu, i.e. countermeasures decided upon or recommended by an organ of an international organization, and political sanctions, i.e. measures imposing hardship which do not involve a breach of international law and which are taken by an international organization in reaction to the deviant conduct of a member state regardless of whether or not such conduct contravenes international norms.

8 As well as any action just short of these provisions. If the Council does not cite Art. 39 or 40, the mandatory nature of the Council's demands needs to be ascertained mainly on the basis of the particular choice of words. Thus, "calls for" may lack the full mandatory effect of "demands" but, if accompanied by a determination that a threat to international peace exists, carries much the same weight. See, for an illustration; Israel's compliance with the ceasefire "called for" in resolution 1701 (2006).

lateral enforcement action by a single state or a group of states without explicit prior authorization by the Council.

V. Decentralisation

Decentralization refers first to peaceful negotiations being sought through internal processes of a state. Alternatively or complementarily to such domestic processes, relevant negotiations are conducted through informal groups.[9] Special interests and capabilities represented by such groups are relevant at the negotiation stage *and* at the – potential – enforcement stage through sanctions which, in turn, will reinforce the negotiating power of the group. The range of actors to be considered for inclusion in such a group is not limited to states, but extends to the UN itself and other international organizations. The Security Council is not directly involved in the negotiations as such, which are conducted by the informal group, although the group may comprise States that are also (permanent) members of the Security Council.[10] The Security Council will endorse existing plans for resolving the crisis put forward in the course of decentralized negotiations. While such groups do not operate under a formal mandate from the Security Council or the General Assembly,[11] the Security Council may *defer to them and back them up* directly or indirectly. The Council will endorse informal groups and their specific plans, if any, turning them effectively into representatives of the international community, in whose name the Council

[9] Cf. UN Secretary-General Boutros-Ghali, "The increasing complexity of operations has led, on the political side to the intensification of peacemaking efforts. Thus, a new concept, that of "Friends of the Secretary General", "International Conferences", or "Contact Groups" means that, while the UN peacekeepers are on the ground, intense diplomatic efforts continue with many parties to a conflict in order to reach a political settlement" (SG/SM/5624), 1 May 1995. See J. Prantl, *The UN Security Council and Informal Groups of States, Complementing or Competing for Governance*, 2006, analysing the role of such groups in the cases of Namibia, El Salvador and Kosovo.

[10] Lebanon is an exception insofar as the Council defined substantive principles for the negotiations between the parties to the conflict. But even here, the Council left the actual negotiations to the Secretary-General and it did not prevent other actors from joining in such talks or even carrying them through by themselves.

[11] Prantl, *supra*, note 9, at 5.

will claim to speak. The relevant informal group thus shares the legitimacy of the international community, which in turn will enhance its negotiating power. The Council will then require all the parties to the crisis further to cooperate with a view to the success of the negotiations, sign up to their outcomes and to implement them. If need be, the Council will resort to enforcing its demands using its Chapter VII powers. And, consistent with the general reliance on decentralization respectively subsidiary action by the UN, the Council will support peacekeeping forces manned by a regional organization to the extent that that force is effective.

B. Proliferation of weapons of mass destruction

Proliferation of weapons of mass destruction in particular nuclear weapons of mass destruction presents a risk to global stability. Proliferation per se makes it more probable that such weapons end up in the hands of irresponsible non-state actors such as terrorists that would feel little restraint using them. Possibly even greater harm may result from certain states acquiring such weapons causing more states to also seek such weapons making a nuclear war much more likely. The Security Council has moved in two directions in order to manage this risk created by the very proliferation of weapons of mass destruction: States need to cooperate in preventing non-state actors from obtaining such weapons (I). And certain states should not produce them in the first place (II).

I. Weapons of mass destruction in the hands of non-state actors – res. 1540 (2004) and 1673 (2006)

The Security Council has said as much in general terms in two resolutions adopted under Chapter VII resolution 1540 (2004) "affirmed" that the proliferation of nuclear, chemical and biological weapons, as well as their means of delivery, constitutes a threat to international peace and security.[12] It is particularly concerned by the "risk" that a terrorist non-

[12] Res. 1540 (2004), preamb para. 1. Means of delivery are defined, for the purpose of the resolution, as: missiles, rockets and other unmanned systems capable of delivering nuclear, chemical, or biological weapons that are specially designed for such use.

state actor may obtain such weapons. In its operative part the Resolution sets out the legislative measures that states need to take and establishes the 1540-Committee to oversee their implementation. Resolution 1607 (2006) "reaffirmed" the first part. Breaking with tradition, these resolutions are not addressed to individual states, concrete situations or crises. Rather, they are abstract, in the sense that they designate the proliferation of nuclear weapons of mass destructions as such as requiring action by states consistent with Council-legislation made mandatory pursuant to Chapter VII UN Chapter.

II. States in control of nuclear weapons of mass destruction: the cases of North Korea and Iran

The Council has not bound itself in a legal sense to step in every time a proliferation case presents itself (and it did not do so in the cases of India and Pakistan).[13] However, the Iranian and North Korean nuclear programmes increase the risk of the proliferation of nuclear weapons, and the Security Council has addressed them for precisely that reason, using a cadenced approach aiming at supervision of the situation under Chapter VII UN Charter.

1. Escalation: From presidential statements to Chapter VII resolutions

Council action in both cases starts out with so-called presidential statements containing an early warning addressed to Iran and North Korea but not yet triggering Chapter VII.

a) The Iranian nuclear enrichment programme

The Iran scenario is an illustration of this type of supervision of risk, which came into effect before Iran actually produced a nuclear weapon. Council action in the case of Iran was triggered by a report by the International Atomic Energy Agency, a specialized UN body with a

---

[13] Res. 1540 (2004), preamb para. 3 provides: "Affirming its resolve to take appropriate and effective actions against any threat to international peace and security caused by the proliferation of nuclear, chemical and biological weapons and their means of delivery, in conformity with its primary responsibilities, as provided for in the United Nations Charter".

mandate to verify the compliance by States Parties with the Non-Proliferation Treaty regime. As in the North Korean case to be discussed infra, Security Council action with regard to Iran began with a presidential statement that already contains all the elements of the Security Council's future approach to this situation. In its presidential statement of 29 March 2006 the Security Council noted with "serious concern" the many International Atomic Energy Agency (IAEA) reports and resolutions relating to Iran's nuclear programme that had been "reported" to it.[14] The statement also noted with such concern that that Agency's report of 27 February 2006[15] listed a number of outstanding issues and concerns, including topics which could have a military nuclear dimension, and that the Agency was unable to conclude that there were no undeclared nuclear materials or activities in Iran. The presidential statement "called upon" Iran to take the steps required by the IAEA, notably in the first operative paragraph of its resolution GOV/2006/14, which the Council deemed essential to build confidence in the exclusively peaceful purpose of its nuclear programme and it underlined, in this regard, the particular importance of re-establishing full and sustained suspension of all enrichment-related and reprocessing activities, including research and development, to be verified by the IAEA. The Security Council expressed the conviction that such suspension and full, verified Iranian compliance with the requirements set out by the IAEA would contribute to a *diplomatic, negotiated solution* that guaranteed that Iran's nuclear programme was for exclusively peaceful purposes, and underlined the willingness of the international community to work positively towards such a solution, which would also benefit nuclear non-proliferation elsewhere. The presidential statement requested a report from the Director General of the IAEA to the IAEA Board of Governors and to the Security Council within 30 days on the process of Iranian compliance with the steps required by the IAEA.[16]

Resolution 1696 (2006) under Art. 40 of Chapter VII of the Charter of the United Nations recalled that preceding presidential statement and "demanded" in this context, that Iran shall suspend all enrichment-related and reprocessing activities, including research and development, to be verified by the IAEA.[17] It also reaffirmed that Iran must take the

---

[14] S/PRST/2006/15.

[15] IAEA doc GOV/2006/15.

[16] That reporting mandate has been continued.

[17] The Council's intention is to make this a mandatory demand, see last preamb para. of res. 1696 (2006).

steps required by the IAEA's Board, which called for a full and sustained suspension of all enrichment-related and reprocessing activities. Resolution 1737 (2006), this time under Art. 41, definitively decided on Iran having to suspend specific proliferation sensitive nuclear activities. Additionally, the March 2007 resolution 1747, again citing Art. 41, said that Iran must ratify and implement the Nuclear Non-Proliferation Treaty's (NPT) Additional Protocol which grants the IAEA expanded rights of access to information and sites, as well. Resolution 1747 (2007) clearly stated that the Iranian case is of such concern to the Council because of the risk of general proliferation that it presents. Thus it is the general category of threat that triggers the Council's action, not just, and maybe not even, primarily the specific case of Iran.

b) North Korea's tests

Under the impression that North Korea had launched ballistic missiles on 5 July 2006, Security Council resolution 1695 (2006) of 15 July 2006 with the Council "acting under its special responsibility for the maintenance of international peace and security" but not further specified "condemned" the multiple launches by the DPRK of ballistic missiles.[18] It also "demanded" that the DPRK suspend all activities related to its ballistic missile programme and re-establish its previous commitments to a moratorium on missile launching. It also "required" all Member States to exercise vigilance and prevent missile and missile-related items, materials, goods and technology being transferred to DPRK's missile or weapons of mass destruction programmes. Furthermore, resolution 1695 (2006) strongly urged the DPRK to return immediately to the so-called Six-Party Talks without preconditions, to work towards the expeditious implementation of the 19 September 2005 Joint Statement, in particular to abandon all nuclear weapons and existing nuclear programmes, and to return at an early date to the NPT and International Atomic Energy Agency safeguards.

However, North Korea did in fact continue its programme and announced the testing of a nuclear bomb on 3 October 2006. The Council reacted swiftly to this announcement, and through the *presidential statement* of 6 October 2006 urged the DPRK not to undertake such a test and to refrain from any action that might aggravate tension, to work on the resolution of non-proliferation concerns and to facilitate a

---

[18] Reaffirming res. 825 (1993) and 1540 (2004).

peaceful and comprehensive solution through political and diplomatic efforts. It also warned North Korea that the carrying out of a test as announced would meet with condemnation *and* that it would represent a clear threat to international peace and security.[19] The Security Council reiterated the need for the DPRK to comply fully with all the provisions of Security Council resolution 1695 (2006).

Further to North Korea's claimed testing of a nuclear bomb on 9 October 2006, the Council adopted resolution 1718 on 14 October 2006 under Chapter VII UN Charter. The resolution "condemned" this testing. The Council thereby implemented its earlier presidential statement. Further, resolution 1718 (2006) "decided" that the DPRK was to abandon all nuclear weapons and existing nuclear programmes in a complete, verifiable and irreversible manner, act strictly in accordance with the obligations applicable to parties under the NPT and the terms and conditions of its IAEA Safeguards agreement[20] and was to provide the IAEA with transparency measures extending beyond these requirements, including such access to individuals, documentation, equipments and facilities as might be required and deemed necessary by the IAEA.

2. *The Nuclear Non-Proliferation Treaty as controlling standard*

a) The Nuclear Non-Proliferation Treaty

The Nuclear Non-Proliferation Treaty in its constituent elements becomes the standard for resolving cases brought about by the proliferation of nuclear weapons. Under the NPT, States Parties renouncing the production or acquisition of nuclear weapons have the right to develop the research, production and use of nuclear energy for peaceful purposes without discrimination and are entitled to technical assistance to

---

[19] S/PRST/2006/41: "The Security Council underlines that such a test would bring universal condemnation by the international community and would not help the DPRK to address the stated concerns particularly with regard to strengthening its security. The Security Council urges the DPRK not to undertake such a test and to refrain from any action that might aggravate tension, to work on the resolution of non-proliferation concerns and to facilitate a peaceful and comprehensive solution through political and diplomatic efforts. The Security Council reiterates the need for the DPRK to comply fully with all the provisions of Security Council resolution 1695 (2006)".

[20] IAEA doc INFCIRC/403.

that effect (Art. I, II, IV NPT).[21] In its relevant resolutions on both Iran and North Korea, the Council refers to the NPT, mentioning both the right of every state to use nuclear energy for peaceful purposes *and* the closed circle of the nuclear power states under that treaty. This core provision of the NPT has become the standard that the Council expects states to comply with and that will guide its own course of action. Normatively, this standard is mandatory by forced of Chapter VII UN Charter, not treaty law. For, unlike Iran, North Korea was not bound by the NPT after it withdrew from it in 2002. However, resolution 1718 (2006) concerning North Korea treats the NPT as the centre of the international effort[s] to control the proliferation of weapons of nuclear mass destruction.[22] Notwithstanding the fact that North Korea was not a party to that treaty, it was to act strictly in accordance with the obligations applicable to parties under it and the terms and conditions of its IAEA Safeguards Agreement[23] and was to provide the IAEA transparency measures extending beyond these requirements, including such ac-

---

[21] Art. IV reads as follows: "(1) Nothing in this Treaty shall be interpreted as affecting the inalienable right of all the Parties to the Treaty to develop research, production and use of nuclear energy for peaceful purposes without discrimination and in conformity with Articles I and II of this Treaty. (2) All the Parties to the Treaty undertake to facilitate, and have the right to participate in, the fullest possible exchange of equipment, materials and scientific and technological information for the peaceful uses of nuclear energy. Parties to the Treaty in a position to do so shall also co-operate in contributing alone or together with other States or international organizations to the further development of the applications of nuclear energy for peaceful purposes, especially in the territories of non-nuclear-weapon States Party to the Treaty, with due consideration for the needs of the developing areas of the world". It should be added that the NPT also contains the obligation for the nuclear powers to disarm that may be part of the original bargain struck by the nuclear powers and the non-nuclear powers party to the NPT.

[22] Preamb. para. 3 and 4: "*Expressing the gravest concern* at the claim by the Democratic People's Republic of Korea (DPRK) that it has conducted a test of a nuclear weapon on 9 October 2006, and at the challenge such a test constitutes to the Treaty on the Non-Proliferation of Nuclear Weapons and to international efforts aimed at strengthening the global regime of non-proliferation of nuclear weapons, and the danger it poses to peace and stability in the region and beyond; *Expressing* its firm conviction that the international regime on the non-proliferation of nuclear weapons should be maintained and recalling that the DPRK *cannot have the status of a nuclear-weapon state in accordance with the Treaty on the Non-Proliferation of Nuclear Weapons*" (emphasis added).

[23] IAEA doc INFCIRC/403.

cess to individuals, documentation, equipments and facilities as might be required and deemed necessary by the IAEA.[24] Resolution 1718 (2006) also "demanded" in mandatory language that North Korea retract its withdrawal from the treaty and return to the treaty and the IAEA safeguards.[25] While the Council sought to ensure that North Korea become a party to the treaty, it held North Korea to the same Chapter VII-based standard as Iran.

b) Applying the NPT

The Council will also *concretize* the relevant standard if the need arises. As we saw, the Council did so when it decided that Iran was to suspend its enrichment activities, which are therefore no longer covered by Art. IV NPT. In fact, given the lack of any reaction from Iran, the Security Council adopted resolution 1696 specifically under Art. 40 of Chapter VII UN Charter on 31 July 2006.[26] While resolution 1696 (2006) reaffirmed the Council's commitment to the NPT and recalled the right of states parties, in conformity with Arts. I and II of that treaty, to develop the research, production and use of nuclear energy for peaceful purposes without discrimination, this resolution "requested" Iran to *suspend* its uranium enrichment activities, including research and development.[27] Iran had asserted its sovereign right to close the nuclear enrichment circle. *Provisional* in nature, the Security Council's mandatory suspension decision nevertheless changed the relevant legal entitlements precluding Iran from arguing that its uranium enrichment activities were covered by its rights as a sovereign nation consistent with the NPT. And it decided the steps the state concerned had to take to be in compliance with the standard thus concretized by the Council. Given the legal entitlement of that state to continue its uranium enrichment activities (short of using them to produce nuclear weapons), this is con-

---

[24] Res. 1718 (2006), para. 6.

[25] Para. 3 and 4.

[26] Art. 40 UN Charter provides: "In order to prevent an aggravation of the situation, the Security Council may, before making the recommendations or deciding upon the measures provided for in Article 39, call upon the parties concerned to comply with such provisional measures as it deems necessary or desirable. Such provisional measures shall be without prejudice to the rights, claims, or position of the parties concerned. The Security Council shall duly take account of failure to comply with such provisional measures".

[27] Para. 2.

sistent with the NPT, which assumes that it is for the Security Council to determine the point at which the use of nuclear technology stops being for peaceful purposes.[28]

3. Negotiated solutions

a) The P5+Germany negotiations with Iran (Res. 1696 (2006))

Resolution 1696 (2006) also backed negotiations between Iran and a group of States consisting of those States that had strong interests in the matter and/or an effective and working diplomatic relationship with Iran. Emphasizing the importance of political and diplomatic efforts to find a negotiated solution, and underlining the willingness of the international community to work positively for such a solution, the resolution "endorsed" the proposals of China, France, Germany, the Russian Federation, the United Kingdom and the United States, with the support of the European Union's High Representative,[29] for a long-term comprehensive arrangement which would allow for the development of relations and cooperation with Iran based on mutual respect and the establishment of international confidence in the exclusively peaceful nature of Iran's nuclear programme.[30]

b) The Six-party negotiations with North Korea

In much similar fashion, resolution 1695 (2006) had encouraged the efforts by all States concerned to intensify their diplomatic efforts to refrain from any actions that might aggravate tension and to facilitate the early resumption of the so-called Six-Party Talks, with a view to the expeditious implementation of the Joint Statement issued on 19 September 2005 by China, the DPRK, Japan, the Republic of Korea, the Russian Federation and the United States, to achieve the verifiable denuclearization of the Korean Peninsula and to maintain peace and stability on the Korean Peninsula and in north-east Asia.[31] Resolution 1718 (2006) "endorsed" the so-called Joint Statement issued on 19 September

---

28 In 2005, Governments failed to strengthen the NPT in May at the NPT review conference, and again at the UN World Summit in September.

29 In particular the presidential statement of 12 July 2006, S/2006/521.

30 Res. 1696 (2006), para. 5.

31 Res. 1695 (2006), para. 4.

2005 by China, the DPRK, Japan, the Republic of Korea, the Russian Federation and the United States in that forum.[32] And it "called upon" the DPRK to return immediately to the Six-Party Talks without precondition and to work towards the expeditious implementation of the Joint Statement.[33] In the North Korean case, this approach bore fruit leading to the settlement reached in February 2007.

4. Compliance

a) Verification by IAEA-expertise

Compliance with the standards set forth by the Security Council needs to be controlled. In highly technical matters such as uranium enrichment activity, expert advice will be indispensable in such compliance control. The International Atomic Energy Agency (IAEA) fulfils this role in the non-proliferation area. It will then be the Security Council's task to ensure IAEA access to both Iranian and North Korean nuclear facilities and the compliance of those States with the verification steps requested by that agency. The Security Council will explicitly demand compliance with the verification requirements originally formulated by the agency, giving them legally binding force under Chapter VII UN Charter. Thus, in February 2006, the IAEA Board of Governors passed resolution GOV/2006/14 outlining steps to restore international confidence in the peaceful nature of the Iranian programme.[34] However, Iran decided to resume enrichment-related activities, including research and

---

32 Res. 1718 (2006), preamb. para. 7.

33 Res. 1718 (2006), para. 14.

34 The subsequent steps taken by the IAEA are set out in the preamble to [of] resolution 1696. The IAEA Director General's report of 27 February 2006 (GOV/2006/15) listed a number of outstanding issues and concerns on Iran's nuclear programme, including topics which could have a military nuclear dimension, and that the IAEA was unable to conclude that there were no undeclared nuclear materials or activities in Iran. The IAEA Director General's report of 28 April 2006 (GOV/2006/27) found that, after more than three years of Agency efforts to seek clarity on about all aspects of Iran's nuclear programme, the existing gaps in knowledge continued to be a matter of concern, and that the IAEA was unable to make progress in its efforts to provide assurances about the absence of undeclared nuclear material and activities in Iran. And the IAEA Director General's report of 8 June 2006 (GOV/2006/38) confirmed that Iran had not taken the steps required of it by the IAEA Board of Governors, reiterated by the Council in its statement of 29 March 2006.

development, and to suspend cooperation with the IAEA on its nuclear programme under the Additional Protocol.[35] As a consequence of Iranian non-cooperation, the IAEA decided to "report" the case of Iran to the Security Council, which then took action under Chapter VII UN Charter, giving legal force to the demands of the IAEA.[36] Resolution 1696 (2006) on Iran also aimed at any suspension by Iran of its nuclear activities being verifiable through Iran taking the steps required by the IAEA Board of Governors in its resolution GOV/2006/14.[37] Additionally, the Council's March resolution said that Iran must ratify and implement the Nuclear Non-Proliferation Treaty's (NPT) Additional Protocol which grants the IAEA expanded rights of access to information and sites, as well

b) Sanctions on North Korea

By way of resolution 1718 (2006), the Security Council finally decided on sanctions referring specifically to Art. 41 UN Charter. Essentially, this was an embargo on relevant material. However, this sanctions regime looks weak.[38] In particular it provides for wide, albeit Committee-controlled, exceptions to be decided on by "relevant states".[39] This may

---

[35] Iran has been and still is party to the NPT. It has also concluded so-called safeguards that define the verification rights of the IAEA in each State party. Iran has not ratified the 1997 Additional Protocol to the NPT designed to strengthen and expand existing IAEA safeguards for verifying that non-nuclear-weapon States-parties use nuclear materials and facilities only for peaceful purposes. But Iran had unilaterally pledged to work with the IAEA under the terms of the protocol with the IAEA.

[36] IAEA Board Resolution, IAEA doc GOV/2006/14, Feb. 2006.

[37] As well as making this specific IAEA resolution effectively mandatory for Iran, the Council generally expressed its confidence in the IAEA and its governing organs, thereby strengthening the authority of the IAEA in the process of solving this crisis brought about by Iran's enrichment-related and reprocessing activities; resolution 1696 (2006), para. 6.

[38] Res. 1718 (2006), para. 8 (f): "In order to ensure compliance with the requirements of this paragraph, and thereby preventing illicit trafficking in nuclear, chemical or biological weapons, their means of delivery and related materials, all Member States are called upon to take, in accordance with their national authorities and legislation, and consistent with international law, cooperative action including through inspection of cargo to and from the DPRK, as necessary".

[39] Res. 1718 (2006), para. 9.

be interpreted as signalling a lack of political will. Alternatively, it may also be interpreted as the Security Council giving the States most interested in a negotiated solution, such as neighbouring China, room to continue to maintain their negotiating stance with North Korea.

c) Sanctions on Iran

Finally, the resolution set a deadline for Iran to comply with its demands[40] and threatened action under Art. 41 UN Charter[41] if Iran did not do so.[42] In resolution 1696 (2006), the Security Council was careful not to take any enforcement action under Chapter VII or even to threaten to impose such sanctions as a next step. The Council made this quite clear by explicitly referring to Art. 40 UN Charter as the legal basis of the resolution. In conformity with the limited nature of the Council's powers under this provision, the Council only "calls upon all States, in accordance with their national legal authorities and legislation and consistent with international law, to exercise vigilance and prevent the transfer of any items, materials, goods and technology that could contribute to Iran's enrichment-related and reprocessing activities and ballistic missile programmes."[43] The deadline set in resolution 1696 (2006) expired on 31 August 2006, without reaction.

---

40 Res. 1696 (2006), para 7: "Requests by 31 August a report from the Director General of the IAEA primarily on whether Iran has established full and sustained suspension of all activities mentioned in this resolution, as well as on the process of Iranian compliance with all the steps required by the IAEA Board and with the above provisions of this resolution, to the IAEA Board of Governors and in parallel to the Security Council for its consideration".

41 Art. 41 UN Charter provides: "The Security Council may decide what measures not involving the use of armed force are to be employed to give effect to its decisions, and it may call upon the Members of the United Nations to apply such measures. These may include complete or partial interruption of economic relations and of rail, sea, air, postal, telegraphic, radio, and other means of communication, and the severance of diplomatic relations".

42 Res. 1696 (2006), para. 8: "Expresses its intention, in the event that Iran has not by that date complied with this resolution, then to adopt appropriate measures under Article 41 of Chapter VII of the Charter of the United Nations *to persuade Iran to comply with this resolution and the requirements of the IAEA*" (emphasis added).

43 Res. 1696 (2006), para. 5.

Resolution 1737 (2006) of 27 December 2006 "noted" that Iran had not complied with the Council's demands as set out in resolution 1696 (2006). It decided that Iran shall without further delay suspend its proliferation-sensitive nuclear activities. And it decided on a range of very specific sanctions. By its resolution 1737 (2006) of 23 December 2006, the Council imposed certain measures on Iran. These measures included an embargo on nuclear and ballistic missile programmes and individual targeted measures – namely an asset[s] freeze and measures concerning travel – on persons and entities designated in an Annex to the resolution as well as on any additional persons and entities designated by the Security Council or the Committee, based on the criteria set out in the resolution. In addition, the Council called upon all States to prevent the specialized teaching or training of Iranian nationals in disciplines which would contribute to Iran's proliferation sensitive nuclear activities and development of nuclear weapon delivery systems.

Relying on the same grounds, resolution 1747 of 24 March 2007 imposed further sanctions, this time individual travel restrictions and the freezing of individual accounts. Subsequently, by its resolution 1747 (2007), the Council imposed a ban on exports of arms from Iran. It also designated additional persons and entities, in an Annex to the resolution, subject to the asset[s] freeze and the measures concerning travel. In addition, the Council called upon all States to exercise vigilance and restraint in the provision of heavy weapons and related services to Iran, and called upon all States and international financial institutions not to enter into new commitments with regard to grants, financial assistance and concessional loans to the Government of Iran, except for humanitarian and developmental purposes.

III. Managing the risk of nuclear proliferation: conclusions

Security Council action vis-à-vis North Korea and Iran is of risk-management type. The Council assessed the risk of proliferation of nuclear weapons of mass destruction present in these cases and then undertook to manage this risk. It did so using finely tuned, cadenced approach. Managing the risk of proliferation, it can be shown, will be based on the NPT as a Chapter VII-based standards, compliance with which will be ensured, ultimately by sanctions under Article 41, while leaving room for negotiated solutions to be found between the targeted state and an informal groups of states identified by the Security Council. Effectively managing the proliferation risk, however, has a much farther reach involving the regulation of non-state actor behaviour, an area in which the Council has taken the first but probably not conclusive steps.

C. Precarious states

The second fairly well-defined category of risks is precarious states.

I. Precarious states with national conflicts and violence as risk: the cases of Lebanon and Sudan

Precarious or fragile States, i.e. States that are unstable either because they are emerging from civil war, are oppressing parts of their population or have exceptionally weak institutions. Such states will sooner or later often also be involved in international conflicts with other countries. Sudan and Lebanon have provided recent examples of this scenario.[44] Council action on this type of risk can be well analysed using the examples of Lebanon and Sudan. The Security Council had been involved with Lebanon for some time,[45] supporting its nation-building efforts long before the Israeli invasion. And in Sudan, there has been international involvement for a long time, with Darfur just being added.

II. Standard-setting

The standard for dealing with the proliferation of nuclear weapons is relatively straightforward. It suffices to turn to a quasi-universal treaty for inspiration. Dealing with precarious states is, by contrast, more difficult in this respect. No ready-made treaty standard is available. Rather

---

44 Council action vis-à-vis the states of the former Yugoslavia and other cases may also belong here but cannot be examined in any detail.

45 See, in particular, resolution 425 (1978), 426 (1978), 520 (1982), 1559 (2004), 1655 (2006) 1680 (2006) and 1697 (2006), as well as the presidential statements on the situation in Lebanon, in particular the statements of 18 June 2000 (S/PRST/2000/21), of 19 October 2004 (S/PRST/2004/36), of 4 May 2005 (S/PRST/2005/17), of 23 January 2006 (S/PRST/2006/3) and of 30 July 2006 (S/PRST/2006/35).

the Council has to devise them incrementally. But the contours of at least two such standards have emerged in the Council's practice.

1. The legitimate government

Standard-setting revolves around the central idea that a state's legitimate government enjoys protection. That involves the election of such a government, its protection against violent overthrow, and its effective control over its territory.

In Lebanon, the full control of the legitimate government over its territory is declared the controlling legal standard.[46] In fact, the sovereign state of Lebanon has enormous internal problems. Its legitimate government has no control over large swathes of its own territory and thus does not exercise the most central of a state's functions: ensuring the monopoly of power, and thus public order and peace equally.[47] On top of this came external intervention mostly from Syria and, additionally, the international armed conflict in the wake of Israel's invasion of Southern Lebanon, which was triggered by Hezbollah forces capturing three Israeli soldiers inside Israel.

Resolution 1559 (2004) is the cornerstone of the Council's approach to Lebanon. This resolution demanded the holding of free and credible parliamentary elections in May and June 2005, largely echoing the so-called Taif accords.[48] Resolution 1680 (2006) noted positively that sig-

---

[46] The Council has also intervened in other instances in order to protect elements of the standard. In the case of Haiti, the Council, under Chapter VII, condemned the violent overthrow of the elected government, but it did not do so in the case of Indonesia. With respect to the Congo, the Council acted under Chapter VII to protect free and fair presidential elections there, authorizing the deployment of an EU-led peace-keeping force to that end.

[47] See resolution 1701 (2006), preamb. para. 1: "*Welcoming* the efforts of the Lebanese Prime Minister and the commitment of the Government of Lebanon, in its seven-point plan, to extend its authority over its territory, through its own legitimate armed forces, such that there will be no weapons without the consent of the Government of Lebanon and no authority other than that of the Government of Lebanon".

[48] A comparison of the main points of the Taif Accord and those of Resolution 1559 shows that in principle there are no significant differences between the two documents regarding the main issues of the current internal Lebanese political and international agenda. As might be expected, the Taif Accord is more detailed, covers a wider range of domestic Lebanese matters and is vaguer with regard to issues which Syria finds problematical or unacceptable, dealing

nificant progress had been made towards implementing in full all provisions of resolution 1559 (2004), in particular through the *Lebanese national dialogue*, but noted with regret that other provisions of resolution 1559 (2004) had not yet been fully implemented, namely the disbanding and disarming of Lebanese and non-Lebanese militias, the extension of the control of the Government of Lebanon over all its territory, strict respect for the sovereignty, territorial integrity, unity and political independence of Lebanon, and free and fair presidential elections conducted according to the Lebanese constitutional rules, without foreign interference and influence. The Council noted with concern the conclusion of the Secretary-General's report[49] that there had been movements of arms into Lebanese territory for militias. Both resolution also directly addressed Syria. Resolution 1559 (2004) demanded the withdrawal of Syrian forces from Lebanon[50] and resolution 1680 (2006) demanded further *bilateral dialogue*, urging Syria to respond positively to the request made by the Government of Lebanon, in line with the agreements of the so-called Lebanese national dialogue, to delineate their common border and to establish full diplomatic relations and representation, noting that such measures would constitute a significant step towards asserting Lebanon's sovereignty, territorial integrity and political independence.[51] It also called on Syria to take measures against

---

with topics not mentioned in Resolution 1559. It should be noted that both the Taif Accord and Resolution 1559 state that the Syrian army is to leave Lebanese territory (although, according to the Taif Accord, the army was to pull out in two stages), that the Lebanese militias (i.e., Hezbollah) and non-Lebanese militias (i.e., Palestinian terrorist organizations) are to be disbanded and disarmed, and that the Lebanese army and the Lebanese government are to be sovereign in south Lebanon and security and stability are to be restored to the Israeli-Lebanese border. Both documents express support for Lebanese sovereignty and independence. It should also be noted that Syria selectively imposed the Taif Accord, completely ignoring all articles it found unacceptable to itself and its proxies, and thus turned the Accord into an important tool for maintaining its control in Lebanon. The Taif Accord was fundamentally a compromise between the various sects and rival factions that were involved in the Lebanese civil war and became, after it was approved, the cornerstone of the relations between them.

49 S/2006/24.

50 Res. 1559 (2004).

51 Res. 1680 (2006), para. 4.

movements of arms into Lebanese territory.[52] The Security Council has returned to these issues through presidential statements.[53]

After Israel had invaded Lebanon, the Security Council adopted resolution 1701 (2006) which contained measures amounting to a graduated approach to solving the crisis. In resolution 1701 (2006) taken under Chapter VII UN Charter, the Council demanded an immediate cessation of all military activities by Hezbollah and Israel and the withdrawal of the latter's military forces in parallel with the establishment of a UN peacekeeping force.[54] Mirroring the principles of resolution 1559 (2004), resolution 1701 (2006) further required that the Government of Lebanon extend full control over its territory in accordance with the provisions of resolutions 1559 (2004) and 1680 (2006), and of the relevant provisions of the *Taif Accords*.[55] Then it declared all parties respon-

---

52 Res. 1680 (2006), para. 5.

53 As recently as 30 October 2006, a presidential statement again turned to this matter (S/PRST/2006/43): "The Security Council welcomes the fourth semi-annual report to the Security Council of 19 October 2006 on the implementation of resolution 1559 (2004). The Security Council notes that important progress has been made towards the implementation of resolution 1559 (2004), in particular through the deployment of the Lebanese Armed Forces in the south of the country for the first time in three decades, but it also notes with regret that some provisions of resolution 1559 (2004) have yet to be implemented, namely the disbanding and disarming of Lebanese and non-Lebanese militias, the strict respect for the sovereignty, territorial integrity, unity, and political independence of Lebanon, and free and fair presidential elections conducted according to the Lebanese constitutional rules, without any foreign interference and influence. The Security Council commends the Lebanese Government for extending its authority throughout its territory, particularly in the South, and encourages it to continue its efforts in this regard. The Security Council reiterates its call for the full implementation of resolution 1559 (2004) and urges all concerned States and parties as mentioned in the report to cooperate fully with the Government of Lebanon, the Security Council, and the Secretary-General to achieve this goal".

54 Essentially, this may be interpreted as the Security Council foreclosing further reliance by Israel on its inherent right to self-defence, an action referred to in Art. 51 UN Charter. In contrast, resolution 1697 (2006) of 31 July 2006, passed roughly three weeks after the commencement of the Israeli invasion on 12 July 2206, had avoided taking any stance and had simply expressed deepest concern at the escalation of hostilities in Lebanon and Israel in its preamble.

55 Res. 1701 (2006), para. 3 "emphasizes the importance of the extension of the control of the Government of Lebanon over all Lebanese territory in accordance with the provisions of resolution 1559 (2004) and resolution 1680 (2006),

sible for the search for a long-term solution, humanitarian access to civilian populations, including safe passage for humanitarian convoys, or the voluntary and safe return of displaced persons. It calls on all parties to comply with this responsibility and to cooperate with the Security Council. These principles reflect the Council's emphasis on the Lebanese state institutions and their effective control over their territory as set out in resolution 1559 (2004), enriched by the focus on specific border issues with Israel and the role of UNIFIL.[56] The Secretary-General was requested to develop, in liaison with relevant international actors and the parties concerned, proposals for implementing the relevant provisions of the Taif Accords, and resolution 1559 (2004) and 1680 (2006), including disarmament, and for the delineation of the international borders of Lebanon, especially in those areas where the border is disputed or uncertain, including by dealing with the Shebaa farms area, and to present those proposals to the Security Council within thirty days.[57] For lack of any formulated outside negotiating proposal or forum, the resolution itself sets out the basic principles for a long-term solution to be negotiated in detail between the parties. Exceptionally, the Security Council defines a framework for negotiations between the parties to the dispute. This is most clearly visible in the Lebanese case where the Council had to come up with such framework *faute de*

---

and of the relevant provisions of the Taif Accords, for it to exercise its full sovereignty, so that there will be no weapons without the consent of the Government of Lebanon and no authority other than that of the Government of Lebanon".

[56] In particular: full respect for the Blue Line by both parties; security arrangements to prevent the resumption of hostilities, including the establishment between the Blue Line and the Litani river of an area free of any armed personnel, assets and weapons other than those of the Government of Lebanon and of UNIFIL as authorized in paragraph 11, deployed in this area; full implementation of the relevant provisions of the Taif Accords, and of resolution 1559 (2004) and 1680 (2006), that require the disarming of all armed groups in Lebanon, so that, pursuant to the Lebanese cabinet decision of 27 July 2006, there will be no weapons or authority in Lebanon other than those of the Lebanese State; no foreign forces in Lebanon without the consent of its Government; no sale or supply of arms and related material to Lebanon except as authorized by its Government; and the ceding to the United Nations of all remaining maps of landmined areas in Lebanon in Israel's possession.

[57] See Activities of United Nations Secretary-General in Lebanon, Israel, Occupied Palestinian Territory, 28-30 August, SG/T/2509; SG reports on the implementation of Security Council resolution 1701 (2006) (S/2006/670; S/2006/730, S/2006/780, S/2006/933).

mieux. Essentially, however, even, here the Council endorsed the outcome of prior negotiations among the internal and external actors involved in the Lebanon and the Lebanese civil war. Clearly, the Council favoured the further involvement of European and other states in Lebanon. In the Lebanese context, the informal contact group was the so-called *quartet* consisting of the EU, the UN, Russia, and the US. This contact group, however, had not been very active of late, although Germany will undertake to revive it on the basis of its presidency of both the EU and the G8 in 2007.[58] In the case of Lebanon, the UNIFIL [-]peacekeeping force was also designed as a mechanism to help determine that circle of States ready to assume responsibility for resolving the crises.

---

[58] See H. Williamson, "Berlin aims to revive Mideast 'quartet'", *FT*, 10 November 2006: "Germany will try to advance the Middle East peace process next year by reviving the joint diplomatic efforts in the region by the US, European Union, Russia and the United Nations, Angela Merkel, chancellor, said on Friday. Speaking at a security conference in Berlin, Ms Merkel said Germany would use its EU presidency from January onwards to breathe new life into the Middle East "Quartet" involving these four international interests. Officials said the chancellor's comments reflected frustration in Germany and the EU that the quartet had been largely inactive in recent months, despite the tensions and violence in the Middle East. Germany in January assumes both the six-month EU presidency and the year-long presidency of the G8 group of industrial countries and German diplomats admit that Berlin is under pressure to take a heavyweight leadership role in the Middle East and elsewhere in this period. Ms Merkel's announcement followed repeated suggestions by Frank-Walter Steinmeier, foreign minister, that the quartet structure be revived, in particular to draw Washington into broader international initiatives in the Middle East. In order to reinforce the quartet's role, its mandate could be expanded to include related regional conflicts, such as that between Israel and Lebanon, Mr. Steinmeier has argued. In addition, other countries, such as Egypt, could be drawn into the talks to make them more representative. The quartet's last big policy decision was in January 2006, when, after a meeting in London attended by Condoleezza Rice, US secretary of state, it called on Hamas to recognize Israel's right to exist, abide by past agreements and renounce violence. Some diplomats now fear that Europe and the US could be diverging, particularly if the Palestinians succeed in their attempts to form a national unity government. While the EU would like to recognize and work with such a government, Washington is much less enthusiastic.

2. Responsibility to protect

Action on Sudan adds a further element to the standard of legitimate government enunciated in part above. For this is first about the issue of a representative and therefore legitimate, government. In the case of Sudan, such representative government will require both the North and the South to be represented on it. The situation in Sudan is marked by several internal conflicts involving the central government and a number of other actors. The Security Council has been extremely concerned with Sudan's internal violence since 2003 using its Chapter VII powers.[59] The Council supported and endorsed the Naivasha agreement and the Comprehensive Peace Agreement of 9 January 2005 signed by the Government of Sudan and the Sudan People's Liberation Movement, commended the IGAD and the Kenyan government on its conclusion and urged the parties to implement the Agreement.[60] The Council supported this objective through the mandating of UNMIS, the mandate of which is extended continuously.[61] It encouraged deployment in order for UNMIS to support the timely implementation of the Comprehensive Peace Agreement. To this effect, the Council has determined that the situation in the Sudan *continues to constitute a threat to international peace and security*.[62]

After the conclusion of the civil war between the North and the South, the Darfur humanitarian disaster erupted.[63] It involves a further emerg-

---

[59] Beginning with resolution 1502 (2003) and resolution 1547 (2004), resolution 1556 (2004), 1564 (2004), 1574 (2004), 1591 (2005), 1593 (2005), 1651 (2005), 1665 (2006), 1703, 1713 (2007), 1714 (2007). The most recent resolution 1714 recalls its previous resolutions, in particular resolutions 1709 (2006) of 22 September 2006, 1706 (2006) of 31 August 2006, 1679 (2006) of 16 May 2006, 1663 (2006) of 24 March 2006, 1653 (2006) of 27 January 2006, 1627 (2005) of 23 September 2005 and 1590 (2005) of 24 March 2005, and the statements of its President, in particular that of 3 February 2006, concerning the situation in the Sudan.

[60] Res. 1714 (2006)

[61] Res. 1714 (2006), para. 1.

[62] Res. 1714 (2006).

[63] This has also spilt over into an international armed conflict of low intensity with neighbouring countries, namely Chad. See monthly report of the SG on Darfur, September 2006, S/2006/870, para. 16: "Despite the agreement of 26 July and the resumption of diplomatic relations between the Sudan and Chad on 8 August, fighting between Chadian armed opposition groups and the Chadian regular forces (FANT) continued in September. On 16 September,

ing standard, the so-called responsibility to protect.[64] In 2004 violence broke out in Darfur, a province of western Sudan. In the Sudan context, again a presidential statement initially set forth the principles and demands that the Council considers being of relevance in order to solve this crisis. These exact demands were then translated fist into resolution 1545 (2004) and then 1556 (2004) – the latter passed under Chapter VII giving them legally mandatory force. In resolution 1556 (2004), the Council identified this violence *per se* as a threat to international peace and security in the region within the meaning of Art. 39 UN Charter, and it has continued to do so.[65] There may in fact be room for debate whether purely internal human rights violations or an international dimension in the form of cross-border effects would meet the requirements of Art. 39. Any of them may do so.[66] What is important is that the internally precarious situation of Sudan attracts Council attention to it. The Council set forth the "responsibility to protect"[67] and the protection of civilians in armed conflict[68], as the standards controlling

---

Chadian armed opposition group rebels and FANT clashed in Jebel Merfain, 70 kilometers north-west of El Geneina, on the Chadian side of the border. The groups were reinforced from Western Darfur on 19 September and engaged in heavy clashes with FANT forces on the same day in Jebel Merfain. The Chadian armed opposition groups reportedly captured 60 Chadian soldiers and numerous tanks and vehicles in the attack".

[64] Originally, the 2005 World Summit Outcome recognized the responsibility to protect (para. 138 and 139). Subsequently, on 28 April 2006, the Security Council passed resolution 1674 (2006) reaffirming the provisions of para. 138 and 139 of the World Summit Outcome. The High-Level Mission on the situation of human rights in Darfur has applied the responsibility to protect to the Darfur situation. See Report of High-Level Mission on the situation of human rights in Darfur pursuant to Human Rights Council decision S-4/101, UN Doc A/HRC/4/80, 9 March 2007, para. 19-23, 38-43.

[65] See resolution 1713 (2006).

[66] In fact, resolution 1547 (2004) and resolution 1556 (2006), both under Chapter VII, mention the cross-border effects. But it is by no means clear that this is a necessary condition. The humanitarian plight in Darfur equally mentioned by the SC might otherwise be enough.

[67] Res. 1556 (2004), preamb para. 9 reads: "Recalling in this regard that the Government of Sudan bears the primary responsibility to respect human rights while maintaining law and order and protecting its population within its territory and that all parties are obliged to respect international humanitarian law".

[68] Res. 1755 (2007) recalling resolution 1674 (2006), which reaffirms, inter alia, the relevant provisions of the UN World Summit Outcome document.

the situation. The Council demanded that the Government and rebel forces and all other groups immediately cease all violence and attacks.[69] In resolution 1556 (2004) the Council furthermore demanded that the Government of Sudan fulfil its commitments to disarm the Janjaweed militias and apprehend and bring to justice their leaders, and threatened further actions, including measures provided for in Art. 41 UN Charter.[70]

III. From sanctions to judicialising contentious issues in Sudan and Lebanon

The Security Council seeks compliance with the demands it formulates with respect to precarious states. It does so by moving from sanctions to judicializing contentious issues.

In the Sudanese case, the Council escalated its sanctions from those intended to hemming in the Darfur conflict (arms embargo) to general economic and individualized sanctions. The Security Council first threatened economic sanctions and imposed an arms embargo on all non-governmental entities and individuals, including the Janjaweed, operating in the states of North Darfur, South Darfur and West Darfur on 30 July 2004 with the adoption of resolution 1556. Resolution 1591 (2005) expanded the scope of the arms embargo. The Security Council first threatened economic sanctions with the adoption of resolution 1556 (2004). Resolution 1564 (2004) concretized the threat of economic sanctions to the Sudan oil sector. Resolution 1591 (2004) specified additional measures including a travel ban and an assets freeze to be imposed on individuals[71] because they "impede the peace process, consti-

---

[69] Res. 1574 (2004).

[70] The Council reiterates its demand to end impunity to the Government of Sudan in resolution 1564 (2004).

[71] Res. 1591, para. 3(d) states that all States shall take the necessary measures to prevent entry into or transit through their territories of all persons as designated by the Committee, provided that nothing in this paragraph shall oblige a state to refuse entry into its territory to its own nationals; para. 3(e) that all States shall freeze all funds, financial assets and economic resources that are on their territories on the date of adoption of this resolution or at any time thereafter, that are owned or controlled, directly or indirectly, by the persons designated by the Committee, or that are held by entities owned or controlled, directly or indirectly, by such persons or by persons acting on their behalf or at

tute a threat to stability in Darfur and the region, commit violations of international humanitarian or human rights law or other atrocities, violate the measures implemented by member states in accordance with resolution 1556 (2004) or are responsible for the offensive military overflights". Resolution 1591 (2005) set up a Security Council Committee pursuant to rule 28 of its provisional rules of procedure supported by a panel of experts to monitor the implementation of these measures and to designate certain individuals subject to the financial and travel restrictions.[72] With resolution 1672 (2006), the Security Council decided that all states shall implement the measures specified in resolution 1591 (2005) with respect to certain named individuals.[73] Resolution 1669 (2006) threatens further individualized sanctions against persons who are in violation of the Darfur Peace Agreement.

It remains for the Security Council to internationalize those of its demands that a State is either unwilling or unable to fulfil. In particular, by transferring a case or situation to an international tribunal for this purpose, the Council neutralizes the issue and ensures that its demands are effectively taken care of. This applied in the case of Sudan where the Council eventually internationalized its demand to end impunity in Darfur originally addressed to the Sudanese government. While this demand was directed at the Sudanese Government, the Council subsequently called for the Secretary-General to send a commission of enquiry to Sudan.[74] This was an executive and legally non-binding form of

---

their direction, and decides further that all states shall ensure that no funds, financial assets or economic resources are made available by their nationals or by any persons within their territories to or for the benefit of such persons or entities.

72 Res. 1591 (2005), extended by resolution 1651 (2005) and 1665 (2006). The SG apppointed five persons on 28 September 2006, S/2006/926. The Council has urged all States, relevant United Nations bodies, the African Union and other interested parties, to cooperate fully with the Committee and the Panel of Experts, in particular by supplying any information at their disposal on the implementation of the measures imposed by resolution 1591 (2005).

73 Major General Gaffar Mohamed Elhassan (Commander of the Western Military Region for the Sudanese Armed Forces); – Sheikh Musa Hilal (Paramount Chief of the Jalul Tribe in North Darfur); – Adam Yacub Shant (Sudanese Liberation Army Commander); – Gabril Abdul Kareem Badri (National Movement for Reform and Development Field Commander).

74 Under Chapter VII, resolution 1564 (2004) requests that a commission of inquiry be established by the Secretary General (Press Release UN Doc SG/A/890).

internationalization. The Council then, in resolution 1593 (2005), in a second step, referred the situation since 2002 to the International Criminal Court pursuant under Chapter VII.[75] This was a legally binding form of judicial internationalization.[76] The Council thus referred the case to an institution that involves a much larger group of States than another ad hoc tribunal in the mold of the tribunals for the former Yugoslavia and for Rwanda would.[77]

The Council has also endeavoured to do so in the case of Lebanon with the hybrid international-national tribunal charged with the criminal prosecution of the assassins of Prime Minister Hariri for which the Lebanese government had turned to the Council for help. The Security Council considered that as a precondition for lasting peace in the country, steps had to be taken to end the impunity of the perpetrators of odious crimes such as this assassination. Resolution 1644 (2005) initiated the process of setting up a hybrid international-national tribunal for this purpose.[78] Resolution 1664 (2006) requested the Secretary-

---

75 Pursuant to Art. 13 lit. b Rome Statute and Art. 17(1) Negotiated Relationship Agreement between the International Criminal Court and the United Nations.

76 31 March 2005. On 6 June 2005, the Prosecutor of the ICC, Mr. Luis Moreno-Ocampo officially opened an investigation into crimes committed in Darfur. The situation of Darfur, Sudan, has been assigned to Pre-Trial Chamber I.

77 The Darfurian crisis illustrates that relevant Security Council action may be complemented by other institutional action, which essentially sanctions deviant behaviour by means of public exposure. The newly minted Human Rights Council (HRC) – successor to the discredited Human Rights Commission – has entered the fray. See Report of High-Level Mission on the situation of human rights in Darfur pursuant to Human Rights Council decision S-4/101, UN Doc A/HRC/4/80, 9 March 2007, para. 19-23.

78 The tribunal will be competent to try those responsible for the attack on former Prime Minister Hariri. It will have jurisdiction over the perpetrators of other attacks only under very strict conditions: the attacks must be on the list of 14 attacks annexed to the report, and they must be connected to the attack on Mr. Hariri. The prosecution and punishment of the crimes under the jurisdiction of the tribunal shall be governed by Lebanese criminal law, specifically the provisions referred to in article 2 of the draft statute. Both the international and the national judges of the tribunal will be selected through an international procedure. The objectivity and impartiality of the process will be assured through the establishment of a selection panel consisting of two international judges and a representative of the Secretary-General. Finally, the Secretary-General will appoint the judges upon the recommendation of the selection panel.

General to negotiate an agreement with the Government of Lebanon aimed at setting up a tribunal of an international character taking into account the recommendations in his report[79] and the views expressed by Council members. The results of these negotiations[80] have met with the approval of the Security Council[81] but there has as yet been no formal Lebanese acceptance of the agreement pursuant to the Lebanese constitution.[82] They constitute the attempt judicially to internationalize

---

[79] UN Doc S/2006/176.

[80] S/2006/893. The Agreement is annexed to the report, including the draft Statute of the Special Tribunal

[81] S/2006/911. It is understood that the Secretary-General will begin the process of establishing the Tribunal when he has sufficient contributions in hand to finance it and twelve months of its operation[s], plus pledges equal to the anticipated expenses of the next twenty-four months of the Tribunal's operation.

[82] See report of the SG's Legal Advisor to the SC, 24 November 2006, S/2006/893/Add.1: "By Security Council resolution 1664 (2006) you requested the Secretary-General to negotiate an agreement with the Government of Lebanon aimed at establishing a tribunal of an international character based on the highest international standards of criminal justice, taking into account the recommendations in the report of the Secretary-General of 21 March 2006 and the views that had been expressed by Council members. The negotiations were conducted on that basis and in that spirit. The report of the Secretary-General on the establishment of the tribunal provides a glimpse of the negotiations. The following additional information will be useful. First, it must be emphasized that the Lebanese negotiators were designated by a consensus decision of the Government of Lebanon, under the leadership of the President himself. Accordingly, the Lebanese delegation was fully empowered to negotiate on behalf of the national authorities. Secondly, both the principle and the substance of the negotiations benefited from the unanimous support for the establishment of the tribunal expressed by the Lebanese national dialogue at its first meeting. Thirdly, the Lebanese constitutional process for the conclusion of an agreement with the United Nations has not been completed. Major steps remain to be taken, in particular formal approval by the Government, which is the prerequisite for the signature of the treaty and its submission for parliamentary approval and, ultimately, its ratification. Only after this process has been completed will Lebanon have entered into an internationally binding commitment. Although the decision by the Government on Monday, 13 November 2006, to support the draft agreement and statute is of considerable political importance, it is not a formal step in the process of concluding the treaty. Accordingly, and pending a decision by the Government, at this stage the Republic of Lebanon has not entered into an internationally binding commitment. It will have done so only

one specific issue and act of political violence,[83] which could not have been done under the Rome Statute with its broad jurisdictional categories of crimes against humanity et al.[84]

IV. Peacekeeping

Implementation of Council demands with respect to precarious states will most often require that international peacekeepers be stationed in the country essentially internationalizing the compliance issue. Such an international peacekeeping force will have to provide that security that the national forces of the precarious state cannot. Importantly, under the Council's current practice, such peacekeeping forces are set up to ensure the implementation of specific Council principles and demands, not simply to separate warring states or other entities. The peacekeeping force will require the consent of the territorial State but receive a so-called robust mandate containing Chapter VII elements.[85] In both the Sudan and the Lebanon cases, the Security Council pursued this strat-

once the constitutional process has been completed and the treaty has been ratified".

83 When the Council unanimously decided to request the SG to negotiate an agreement with Lebanon, it was responding to a request for assistance from the Lebanese authorities. Faced with a series of heinous attacks, in particular the highly symbolic one that took the life of former Prime Minister Hariri, those authorities, with the support of an entire people, called for justice to be done. But they were convinced that, given the circumstances, the national justice system would not be able to meet that objective.

84 Early in the negotiations the possibility was raised of incorporating legal grounds that would enable the judges, in certain circumstances and with sufficient evidence, to qualify crimes as crimes against humanity. The draft document does not include this possibility. The text of the statute, the language of the report, the preparatory work and the background of the negotiations clearly demonstrate that the tribunal will not be competent to qualify the attacks as crimes against humanity. See report by the SG's Legal Adviser, S/2006/893Add.1.

85 See T. Findlay, *The Use of Force in UN Peace Operations*, 2002, J. Fink, "From Peacekeeping to Peace Enforcement. The blurring of the mandate for the use of force in maintaining international peace and security", *Maryland Journal of International Law and Trade* 19 (1995), 1; K. Cox, "Beyond Self-Defense: United Nations Peacekeeping Operations & the Use of Force", *Denver J. Int'l L & Pol'y* 27 (1998-1999), 239.

egy. This strategy included the deployment of international peacekeepers with a specific, robust mandate. The robust mandate of the UN peacekeeping force (UNIFIL) is designed to support the implementation of this gradual approach, essentially to buy the time necessary to find the negotiated solutions the basic contours of which are sketched out in resolution 1701 (2006).

V. Decentralisation: the role of the African Union in Sudan

Both the search for negotiated solutions and the deployment of peacekeepers are issues that the Council will approach on the basis of subsidiarity.[86] Sudan illustrates this very clearly. The Security Council emphasized that there can be no military solution to the conflict in Darfur, called on the parties to the conflict, including the Government of National Unity, to resume the Abuja Peace Talks under the auspices of the African Union[87] and stressed its firm commitment to the Darfur Peace Agreement,[88] urging those parties that have not signed the Darfur Peace Agreement to do so and threatening measures such as an asset freeze or travel ban against any individual or group that violates or attempts to block the implementation of the agreement.[89] The Council also endorsed a regional organization-supported peacekeeping force – the African Union's Mission in Sudan (AMIS).[90] The Security Council strongly supported the decision of the AU to increase its mission in Darfur and urged all States to support this mission logistically.[91] But the Council has gradually moved towards giving international support to

---

[86] See, in particular, resolution 1625 (2005), where the Council, meeting at the level of heads of states and governments, adopted a declaration on strengthening the effectiveness of the SC's role in conflict prevention, particularly in Africa. The resolution mentions the need to develop effective partnerships between the Council and regional organizations, in particular the AU and its subregional organisations.

[87] E.g. res. 1591 (2005), para. 2.

[88] Res. 1713 (2006).

[89] Res. 1706 (2006), para. 14. On the implementation of that agreement see the SG's monthly report on Darfur to the SC.

[90] Pursuant to the AU Peace and Security Council Communiqué of 20 October 2004, para. 6.

[91] Res. 1590 (2005).

that regional force. Resolution 1706 (2006) gave UNMIS a robust mandate to protect the implementation of the Darfur Peace Agreement. The Security Council wants UNMIS to provide transitional assistance to AMIS essentially turning this into a hybrid AU-UN peacekeeping operation.

VI. Concluding observations on the risk presented by precarious states Lebanon and Sudan

Precarious states are a risk to regional and global stability, and the Council assessed both Lebanon and Sudan to fall under this category and thus warrant international supervision a long time ago. Its actions in these cases follow the management scheme identified above: standard-setting, compliance control and room for negotiated solutions, the latter two elements carried out by regional organisations if possible.

D. Risk management and the reach of Chapter VII UN Charter

Risk management by the Security Council forces the rethinking of Chapter VII of the UN Charter and the Security Council as its central institution.[92]

I. The Security Council as legislator

Much has been said and written recently about the new (quasi-)legislative function that the Security Council has assumed in the areas of anti-terrorism[93] and weapons of mass destruction,[94] where the Council

---

92 I shall use the term institution in the narrower, material sense. For a broader understanding of institution as the "set of rules that stipulate the way in which states should cooperate and compete with each other" see J.J. Mearsheimer, "The False Promise of International Institutions", *International Security* 19 (1994/95), 8. See, generally, A. Lecours, "New Institutionalism: Issues and Questions", in: id. (ed.), *New Institutionalism*, 2005, 1.

93 In particular regarding anti-terrorism resolution 1373 (2001).

promulgates detailed general provisions that states need to comply with. However, under its risk management approach outlined here, the Council turns itself into a more elaborate legislator of international law. Substantively, the Council enunciates fundamental rules for states in the conduct of their domestic policies: The NPT, protection of the legitimate government, and responsibility to protect. The Security Council uses its powers under Chapter VII to shape the legal situation. To that effect, it exercises its power under Arts. 39 (and 40) UN Charter to determine the legal standard applicable to the situation. This specific legal power of the Council is distinct from its powers to take enforcement measures under Arts. 41 and 42 UN Charter, although such enforcement measures may repeat and thus absorb previous resolutions.[95]

The Council also lays down a general legal obligation for states to cooperate and negotiate with informal groups of other states designated by the Council. In other words, the state concerned is no longer free, as it was under general international law, to decide whether or not to enter at all into negotiations and to choose its partners. The informal group of states designated receive an authorization to negotiate on behalf of the international community. That considerably enhances the legitimacy of their action. It is not the self-selected group of certain states but rather the community of states represented by the UN that is to face the state concerned.

II. Interpreting the UN Charter

This has considerable consequences for the understanding of international peace and security within the meaning of Arts. 39-42. This central notion is much thicker now because of the interpretation given to it by the Council in its risk managing practice. It comprises concepts and notions such as non-proliferation of nuclear arms and stability of states. Anti-terrorism is also a sure candidate. A future thick understanding of the notion of international peace and security may extend to environmental degradation, disease and poverty. Protection of these objectives

---

[94] See, e.g., R. Wolfrum, "Der Kampf gegen eine Verbreitung von Massenvernichtungswaffen", in: K. Dicke (ed.), *Weltinnenrecht. Liber amicorum Jost Delbrück*, 2005, 865.

[95] The differentiation of the legal basis is indicative of the Council's ability to pursue a cadenced approach to managing threats to international peace and security.

may necessitate action in individual instances by the Security Council, and it of secondary concern only whether there are tangible cross-border effects such as refugee streams in the individual instances.

The Charter specifies that all conflicts be peacefully resolved and that also applies to the Council, its responsibility and its powers under Chapter VII.[96] The Council's practice provides for again a much thicker understanding of this fundamental principle of the Charter. The Council's new practice reflects a strong emphasis on the peaceful resolution of threats to international peace and security through negotiation. Put broadly, it favours the exhaustion of peaceful means for resolving disputes and crises that the Charter requires before resort to force may be contemplated. Such negotiations shall be conducted in a decentralized or subsidiary fashion. The informal group approach involves the states, relevant regional organizations and other players in the *particular field under consideration*. Put broadly, it favours the exhaustion of peaceful means for resolving disputes and crises that the Charter requires before resort to force may be contemplated. This approach reflects lessons learned from the handling of the Iraqi situation prior to 2003, where the lack of a working forum for negotiation rendered the sanctions regime installed and administered by the UN politically ineffective. In other words, the Security Council is ready to take from the panoply of its responsibility and its powers under Art. 24 UN Charter the power to *devise* a crisis solution and to confer it on such informal groups even if they are composed of states that are not (permanent or non-permanent) members of the Council. The power to prescribe measures with content of the Security Council's own design arguably comprises the power to prescribe compliance with the *substance* of a regime/crisis solution determined externally. This in some ways goes back to the fundamental idea underlying the collective system of the UN, as evidenced by Chapter VIII. It is certainly in line with the "logic of the overall system contemplated by the Charter", to quote the International Court of Justice in *Legality of the Use by a State of Nuclear Weapons in Armed Conflict*.[97] The effectiveness of this firmly "bottom-up" approach is evident: Whenever possible the Security Council makes use of the superior knowledge of the parties close to the crisis. The Council seeks to take

---

[96] See resolution 1540 (2004), preamb. para 3: "Recalling also that the Statement underlined the need for all Member States to resolve peacefully in accordance with the Charter any problems in that context threatening or disrupting the maintenance of regional and global stability".

[97] Para. 26.

up an enabling rather than a prescriptive position. In modern parlance, this is public power reducing transaction costs. By virtue of so positioning itself, the Council itself stays one step removed from the crisis and thereby increases the options available to it. Conceivably, this is a case of delegation broadly understood. But it is probably preferable to see this as a case of shared responsibility, where the Council remains the ultimate guarantor of international peace and security (*oversight*). This implies at least a threefold safeguard[s] scheme in this specific principal-agent constellation. First, the Security Council shapes the parameters of international peace and security through its prioritizations. Secondly, it retains the position of the ultimate arbiter on the acceptability of negotiation positions and results. Thirdly, any coercion needs to be explicitly and separately authorized by the Security Council, which works as a catalyst for cooperation between the state(s) concerned by and the states most interested in the instance.

III. The direction of collective security policy within the UN institutional system

Management of international crises by the Security Council is first of all the return of institutionalized collective security as envisaged by the Charter. A firmly bottom-up approach and the assumption of a power amounting to active management of international crises by the Security Council signify the return of effective multilateralism which is currently the Security Council's *exclusive* approach. At this time, it is probably too early to say whether the Council's emphasis on the management of crises will meet with success.[98] But it definitely has brought the Council back to centre-stage in the maintenance of international peace and security quite soon after the Iraq crisis plunged it into a deep crisis of its own.[99]

---

98 The Secretary-General's report of 12 September 2006 (S/2006/780) and its update of 2 December 2006 (S/2006/933) on the implementation of Security Council resolution 1701, in particular on the operations of the United Nations Interim Force in Lebanon (UNIFIL) and other relevant United Nations activities sound a cautiously optimistic note. See also the report of 19 October 2006 on the implementation of resolution 1559 (2004) (S/2006/832).

99 It reflects an understanding of what institutionally the Council is good at. On the need to be cognizant of the Council's institutional strengths and weak-

The work of the Security Council needs to be evaluated against the backdrop of the recent surge to reform the UN as a response to drastically changed circumstances after the end of the Cold War and after 9/11. Much of this was anticipated by the now famous Panel Report, which in turn was in large part endorsed by the General Assembly meeting at the level of heads of state and government.[100] The Panel report identified four central threats, and recommended addressing them through preventive and responsive action. In terms of prevention, the Panel emphasized the need to develop strong norms: the famous report of the High-level Panel on Threats, Challenges and Change of 2004 identified the *proliferation* of weapons of mass destruction and in particular of nuclear bombs as one of the central challenges for international peace and security in the 21st century.[101] The Panel report recommended making the Treaty on the Non-Proliferation of Nuclear Weapons, which restricts the lawful possession of nuclear weapons to the declared powers, the centrepiece of the international community's response to this challenge.[102] As regards national (state-internal) violence, the Panel report recommended the development of strong norms to protect the legitimate government, and it urged the UN (and its member states) to ensure enforcement of these norms and standards. The Security Council has implemented these policy recommendations as demonstrated above. However, the Panel report went much further in respect of UN Security Council reform. In fact, it recommended in-

---

nesses see D. Malone, "Introduction", in: id. (ed.), *The UN Security Council: From the Cold War to the 21 Century*, 2004, 1.

[100] As is well known, the former Secretary-General Kofi Annan initiated such reform on the occasion of the organisation's 60th anniversary. For that purpose, he set up an advisory body of independent experts. That body came up with an analysis of the challenges facing the UN today and a number of recommendations for reforms to tackle them. Most of these recommendations were endorsed by the Members' Heads of State and Governments meeting in New York in 2006, A/RES/60/1.

[101] UN Doc A/59/565.

[102] A/59/565, para. 110 et seq. The Panel also recommends strengthening the regime through the Additional Protocol; to provide incentives for States to forego the development of domestic uranium enrichment and reprocessing facilities; for a voluntary time-limited moratorium on the construction of any such facilities and the negotiation of a verifiable fissile material cut -off treaty that ends production of highly enriched uranium for non-weapon and weapon purposes. See also the Note of the Secretary-General on the Panel report, A/59/565, para. 12.

stitutional reform. Such reform was meant to broaden the Council's membership in an effort to make it more inclusive, and thereby strengthen both its effectiveness and its legitimacy. However, the heads of state and government demurred. To a certain extent, however, the Security Council in fact has taken up the core ideas of the Panel's recommendations. It has done so by involving States not members of the Council in its crisis management on an ad hoc basis. More broadly, the legitimacy of the Council's action hinges on inclusiveness. This is not formal inclusiveness but functional or meritorious inclusiveness. States ready to take on an increased responsibility for the management of international crises may do so on their own initiative simply by forming or joining an informal group. In other words: if the self-selected contact group/informal group effectively engages in a discourse on the crisis and comes up with a plan to solve it, it will receive support from the Security Council.[103] States making up the contact group, while not being (permanent) members of the Council are indirectly involved in the Council's decision-making. For that body's decisions relate to and are based on the grouping's prior actions. By the same token, the issue of formal membership for the Council's representativeness loses some, if not all, of its practical significance.

Essentially, this is also an issue of the quasi-constitutional law of the United Nations. For the relevant broad policies that the Security Council implements were decided at the General Assembly meeting at the level of the heads of states and government. In that respect, it is the General Assembly that formulates the interests of the international community in the field of collective security. And it is the Security Council that has the exclusive legal power to implement and enforce them. However, the issue of membership also demonstrates the limits of informal infra-treaty institutional evolution.

IV. Collective security in the age of globalisation

Iraq has taught the lesson that the model of ad hoc intervention in a crisis does not really work. As a result of its flagrant failure to secure in-

---

[103] Cf. World Summit Outcome resolving: "We recommend that the Security Council continue to adapt its working methods so as to increase the involvement of States not members of the Council in its work, as appropriate, enhance its accountability to the membership and increase the transparency of its work" A/RES/60/1, para. 154.

ternational peace in this case, the Council lost a great deal of trust that international (collective) action would secure international peace. In an attempt to rebuild that lost trust in the effectiveness of collective action, the Council has refocused its activity and retooled its working methods.[104] The Council's practice here is part and parcel of an effort to redefine the objectives of the UN as an organisation and to provide it with the requisite means. Securing the stability of an increasingly globalizing world is clearly a, if not the, central objective of the UN and all its organs. In that respect, the Council's practice signals the move from state-centred coordination towards a functional international system, in which international security is a much more ambitious concept than in a system based on self-coordinating but still largely self-contained states. As a consequence, the prohibition to intervene in internal affairs that Art. 2(7) UN Charter sets forth no longer functions as a protective shield for states. It is only being in compliance with the relevant standards that states will be able to rely on in the future.

---

104 The importance of this development is obvious if compared to the handling of the Iraq crisis. That case was marked by a direct confrontation between the Security Council and Iraq, aggravated by the broad formulation of the Council's objectives and demands. See A. Cassese, *International Law*, 2nd ed., 2005, at 348-49, discussing resolution 678 (1990) and resolution 1511 (2003), 1546 (2004), on Iraq.

Comment on the Contribution by Volker Röben

*Michael Köbele**

Thank you for giving me the floor. I am certainly honoured to be here today to speak at Professor Wolfrum's 65th birthday symposium. I am proud and, at the same time, humbled, to be part of an event marking another milestone in the life of an esteemed internationally recognized legal luminary.

I think we all agree that the latest developments in the management of crises by the United Nations Security Council deserve closer attention from academe. And we all likewise agree that we have seen a very accurate, insightful, and sharp presentation from Volker Röben. The few comments that I will make are of a marginal nature and, admittedly, draw largely from Volker Röben's convincing and thought-through contribution.

Before going into the details, I would like to make one reservation and one preliminary remark.

The reservation is that in the evaluation of the facts presented to us, legal rules are of a significant but not decisive importance. Volker Röben's presentation reaches the edges of law, but it may well be that by turning to political scientists, sociologists, historians, or even psychologists, the intellectual return gained may be far greater and that I, as a German law-educated lawyer, may not find myself in the best position to evaluate the situation the UN Security Council finds itself in at the end of the year 2006.

---

* This paper is based on a comment on the presentation by Volker Röben given at the symposium entitled "International Law Today: New Challenges and the Need for Reform?" in Heidelberg, December 2006. The structure and style of the oral presentation have been maintained.

My preliminary remark is that, unlike what most of us, including myself, were thinking when Volker Röben started drafting his paper on the management of crises by the UN Security Council, the topic has lost some of its urgency in the meantime. The report of the non-partisan Iraq Study Group chaired by James Baker and Lee Hamilton gave a first indication of a shift in public opinion in the United States. Further, with the great loss of votes in the recent US mid-term elections by those who openly advocated a strong unilateral approach in the external relations of the United States, any purely hegemonic, unilateral approach to the management of international crises has become, to a certain degree, less likely, at least without the occurrence of new events such as major terrorist attacks. Thus, regardless of how one views the management of crises by the UN Security Council, mere power-based reliance on a "coalition of the willing" loosely tied together by an ad hoc type of common interest seems to be currently off the table as a discredited approach, even by those who belittle the capabilities of the United Nations and one of its most prominent organs, the Security Council, at least for some years to come.

Having stated my caveat and preliminary comment, I come to my first question. Which deficiencies of the UN Security Council can be addressed in its practice?

The deficiencies are well-known and frequently reiterated.

In his report entitled *In Larger Freedom – Towards Development, Security and Human Rights for All of 2005*, the then incumbent Secretary-General of the United Nations, Kofi Annan, put it, and I quote: "[a] change in the [Security] Council's composition is needed to make it more broadly representative of the international community as a whole, as well as of the geopolitical realities of today, and thereby more legitimate in the eyes of the world" and that "its working methods are made more efficient". The report, in accordance with organizational theory, distinguishes input and output legitimacy. Output legitimacy refers to the performance or the achievement of the substantive purposes of an organ, i.e., efficiency in practice, whereas input legitimacy refers to the processes by which decisions are made. The frequent use of contact groups in the management of international crises as described by Volker Röben brings in new experience, expertise, and stakeholders with a true interest in solving the conflict and, thereby, enhances input legitimacy. The same holds true for expert commissions as depicted by Volker Röben. And the use of the Non-Proliferation Treaty, the International Criminal Court, and regional organizations as a point of reference in, as Volker Röben calls it, the "calibrated use" of the UN Security Council's powers under Chapter VII does have a taming and rationalizing effect even though the regimes referred to by the UN Security Council do not present the ultimate and optimal regulatory solution to a given problem, and are themselves subject to criticism, including criticism relating to fairness and legitimacy.

Through such refinement of its law and practice under Chapter VII, the UN Security Council reduces the risk of giving a carte blanche which would allow States to have recourse to military force without adequate authorization from it. This shows that the UN Security Council's new approach not only aims at the better and more effective management of international crises but also addresses the UN Security Council's inability to prevent a Security Council member with a veto power from invading another country under the pretext of implementing previous Security Council resolution(s). The most striking example, of course, is the invasion of Iraq in 2003 led by the US. But in the future, other veto powers may follow the US-American example and pursue a similar strategy when facing existing or alleged security problems.

It is to this process of refinement of the UN Security Council's law and practice that I believe we, as lawyers, can certainly contribute using the methods and theories our profession has to offer. Altogether, this new approach taken by the UN Security Council adds not only to its legitimacy, due to broader participation and heightened inclusiveness, but also to the legitimacy of the groups and commissions it is authorizing. This is a classical win-win situation and this is the good news.

What, then, is the bad news? Theory and experience would suggest that with the rise of input legitimacy, output legitimacy/efficiency would likewise increase. Yet, if one looks at the examples presented, there are serious doubts in practically all the countries cited whether the situation has actually improved. To illustrate the discrepancy, I could read some excerpts from the UN Security Council resolutions referred to by Volker Röben and compare them to the reality now. I abstain from doing so because I see so many prominent experts in the room and see no need to repeat what these resolutions, the contents of which are well-known to you, state. One needs to wear rose-coloured spectacles to view the crisis management of this year as an ultimate success. And even in Lebanon, where the guns are silent now between Hezbollah and the Israeli Army, the change of strategy from confrontation to conflict avoidance, as opposed to conflict resolution, was within the internal logic of conflict, as Hezbollah had successfully established itself as a political and military power in the Middle East. And the UN Security Council's claim to disarm Hezbollah does not show any progress at the moment, and, in fact, it is Hezbollah which is leading the protests demanding that the Security Council-backed government step down. This is the bad news.

Thus, no matter how promising the new approach is, the increase in input legitimacy will most likely not lead to any significant progress in the near future. In fact, in almost all the case studies Volker Röben presented to us, the international community may ultimately fail and be unable to restore lasting peace, in particular with respect to institutionally weak States, such as Sudan. In less hopeless cases, the lack of trust among countries and the complexity of the interests involved may simply not allow overcoming prisoner's dilemmas for the parties to the negotiations. At the same time, and making things even more complicated, it is likely that there will always be States which tend to take the path of unilateralism and, worse, there will likewise always be States which prefer to remain passive and reluctant when called upon to participate in collective action when facing a threat to international peace.

Be that as it may, this does not distract from the general proposition that, as such, the approach taken by the UN Security Council is promising and valuable. At the very least, it leaves the door open to further negotiations which may occur or not occur in the future and which reduces the incentives to turn to military solutions outside the UN framework. It is a promising bottom-up approach which tries to ensure that the contact groups in all circumstances are more representative than the UN Security Council, and actually include all the necessary stakeholders, and not just those with the necessary economic or military power grip. In addition, transparency may allow for an open and robust discussion to ensure that the contact groups stay within the framework imposed by the UN Security Council and not vice versa. If this approach prevails for a long time, it would also be worthwhile to look at its impact on other UN organs, including the General Assembly and the Secretary-General.

My last point relates to the possibility of reform of the UN Security Council which is still on the agenda, even though the prospects for a major reform in the near future may be slim. Again, much has been said about this. I wonder, though, whether the emergence of contact groups to some degree relieves the pressure for reform because the relevant candidates are already members of the contact groups. With respect to Germany, Chancellor Merkel, to the surprise of many, officially announced and confirmed Germany's long-term goal of achieving a permanent seat in the UN Security Council. This statement seems to suggest the opposite. Also, in the report mentioned above, criticism of the

UN Security Council also clearly distinguishes between the composition of the Security Council and its working style and procedures. This distinction suggests that changing the latter may not necessarily reduce the need for reform of the former. In addition, one could make the point that by joining various contact groups, Japan and Germany have taken over a greater share of responsibility than mere financial responsibility compared to the past and that, therefore, their admission as permanent members should be merely a matter of time. As a consequence, other middle powers which remain relatively passive may have a difficult time justifying their continuing opposition to such admission of Japan and Germany to the UN Security Council as permanent members. Accordingly, changes in the working procedures of the UN Security Council do not reduce the need for reform with respect to the Security Council's composition, although in practice it is predictable that opponents of any change in the status quo in the United Nations may argue exactly on this basis in years to come.

Thank you for your attention, and I thank Professor Wolfrum for giving me the opportunity to learn from and, if I may be allowed to be presumptuous, with him and for helping to open doors for me outside the Max Planck Institute for Comparative Public Law and International Law.

Promoting the Unity of International Law: Standard-Setting by International Tribunals

Nele Matz-Lück

I. Overlapping Jurisdictions and Fragmentation of International Law

The consequences resulting from the growing number of international courts, tribunals and other permanent or at least systematic dispute settlement mechanisms for public international law have been discussed for the last 20 years. In the 1990s some judges at the International Court of Justice (ICJ) in The Hague rang the alarm bell concerning a "proliferation" of tribunals. They emphasised the potential negative effects a growing number of specialised courts and tribunals might have on the unity of public international law. The main reason for the ICJ judges' expression of concern at that time was the establishment of the International Tribunal for the Law of the Sea (ITLOS) with its broad mandate concerning issues covered by the 1982 Convention on the Law of the Sea (UNCLOS).[1] Its jurisdiction to settle disputes includes subjects traditionally within the jurisdiction of the ICJ,[2] e.g. maritime boundaries.[3] In 1998 New York University (NYU) organised a well-known symposium on "The Proliferation of International Tribunals: Piecing together the Puzzle" to which more than ten experts contributed, and which covered general aspects as well as specific perspectives on human rights tribunals, the ITLOS, the World Trade Organization (WTO) or the Economic Court of the Commonwealth of Independent States.[4]

Since the early 1990s a considerable number of new courts, tribunals and permanent dispute settlement mechanisms have been established.[5]

---

1 *ILM* 21 (1982), 1261 et seq.

2 On the relationship between the ICJ and ITLOS see T. Treves, "Conflicts between the International Tribunal for the Law of the Sea and the International Court of Justice", *N.Y.U. J. Int'l L. & Pol.* 31 (1999), 809 et seq.

3 Throughout its existence the ICJ has frequently settled international disputes between States concerning maritime boundaries of adjacent or opposite territories in the world's seas. As an example of cases decided within the last five years see the case concerning the *Land and Maritime Boundary between Cameroon and Nigeria (Cameroon v. Nigeria: Equatorial Guinea Intervening)* which was decided in 2002, ICJ Reports 2002, 303 et seq. The case concerning *Maritime Delimitation in the Black Sea (Romania v. Ukraine)* which began in the ICJ 2004 is still pending. After the public hearings were concluded in March 2007 the court started its deliberations in the case concerning *Maritime Delimitation between Nicaragua and Honduras in the Caribbean Sea (Nicaragua v. Honduras)*. In the *Case Concerning the Territorial and Maritime Dispute (Nicaragua v. Colombia)* which has been pending since 2001 the public oral hearing will take place in June 2007. Although, no Member State to the Convention on the Law of the Sea has yet taken a case concerning the extent and fixing of maritime boundaries to the ITLOS, the court adopted a resolution in accordance with Art. 15 para. 1 of the Tribunal's Statute in its 2007 spring session by which it established a standing special chamber to deal with maritime delimitation disputes, ITLOS/Press 108, 16 March 2007, accessible via <http://www.itlos.org/start2_en.html> (last visited 20 April 2007).

4 The complete collection of papers presented at this workshop is published in *N.Y.U. J. Int'l L. & Pol.* 31 (1999), 679 et seq.

5 For an approach to an explanation of why the 1990s were the decade with the largest quantitative increase in international judicial bodies, see C. Romano,

The World Trade Organization's Dispute Settlement Body (DSB) which was established in 1995 by the Dispute Settlement Understanding (DSU)[6] as part of the WTO agreements is one example of a specialised institution with a clear mandate to settle trade disputes between the parties. Another case of a specific judicial mechanism is the evolution of the institutional dimension of international criminal law. After the establishment of the International Criminal Tribunal for the Former Yugoslavia (ICTY) in 1993[7] and the International Criminal Tribunal for Rwanda (ICTR) in 1994[8] the establishment of the International Criminal Court (ICC) by the Rome Statute of the International Criminal Court (1998)[9] marked a milestone for the specification of international criminal law. Once the ICC starts delivering judgments on the cases that are currently being prepared by the Office of the Prosecutor, its role in further developing international criminal law will be substantial.

Despite the fact that specialised tribunals operate within the realm of distinct mandates their jurisdictions may overlap. With the exception of the ICJ as the only general international "world court" which is restricted neither by material nor by regional restraints and which is said to "pride[ ] itself on the global character of its clientele",[10] other courts and tribunals confine their jurisdiction to specific branches of law and limit the body of applicable law.[11] However, despite such specialisation and limitation of jurisdiction the facts of cases may justify possible alternative competent fora, e.g. by being concerned with trade and fishing

---

"The Proliferation of International Judicial Bodies: The Pieces of the Puzzle", *N.Y.U. J. Int'l L. & Pol.* 31 (1999), 709, 728 et seq.

6 UNTS Vol. 1869, 401.

7 S/RES/827 of 23 May 1993.

8 S/RES/955 of 8 November 1994.

9 UNTS Vol. 2187 No. 3. The statute entered into force on 1 July 2002.

10 R. Higgins, "The ICJ, the ECJ, and the Integrity of International Law", *ICLQ* 52 (2003), 1, 3.

11 The issue that a court may find it difficult to chose the applicable law because of the opportunity to assess cases from different angles, e.g. from the point of view of environmental law or alternatively from a human rights perspective, is not relevant to tribunals that were established to enforce a certain treaty, although it is to the ICJ. On the issue of "locating the corpus of law at the heart of a difficult case" with reference to the ICJ's Advisory Opinion in the Nuclear Weapons Case (*Legality on the Threat or Use of Nuclear Weapons, Advisory Opinion* [1996] ICJ Reports 1996, 226 et seq.), see R. Higgins, "A Babel of Judicial Voices? Ruminations from the Bench", *ICLQ* 55 (2006), 791, 792.

as in the European Community (EC) – Chile Swordfish Case[12] or the lawful use of the sea as well as relations between European Union (EU) Member States, as in the Mox-Plant Case.[13]

One consequence of parallel or overlapping jurisdictions is that it may be largely coincidence which institution deals with a dispute and, as a result, which legal perspective is relevant for settling the case. Depending upon the dispute in question, parties may be able to choose whether a case that has both environmental and human rights implications is decided with a leaning towards the one or the other set of legal rules by opting for a specific forum. Legal writing uses the term "forum shopping" – with a negative connotation – to describe the choice of judicial body which is often guided by expectations about the most beneficial outcome. Another effect of overlapping jurisdictions may be that two or more courts deliver different and potentially contradictory rulings, if parties take the same case to different dispute settlement authorities at the same time. Unlike in national legal orders[14] there is no general rule on *lis pendens* in international law which has the effect of barring the referring of the same case to more than one tribunal.[15]

From time to time the establishment of a world environment court[16] or a single international administrative court in addition to the existing

---

[12] Proceedings in the WTO as well as at the ITLOS chamber have been adjourned but not terminated. On the background of the case see P.-T. Stoll/S. Vöneky, "The Swordfish Case: Law of the Sea v. Trade, *ZaöRV* 62 (2002), 21 et seq.; M. Orellana, "The Swordfish Dispute between the EU and Chile at the ITLOS and the WTO", *Nord. J. Int'l L.* 71 (2002), 55 et seq.

[13] See V. Röben, "The Order of the UNCLOS Annex VII Arbitral Tribunal to Suspend Proceedings in the Case of the Mox Plant at Sellafield: How Much Jurisdictional Subsidiarity?", *Nord. J Int'l L.* 73 (2004), 223 et seq.

[14] See e.g. § 261 III of the German Code of Civil Procedure as amended on 5 December 2005, *Federal Law Gazette* I (2005), 3203 et seq.; corrigendum *Federal Law Gazette* I (2006), 431 et seq.

[15] On *lis pendens* in international law see also K. Oellers-Frahm, "Multiplication of International Courts and Tribunals and Conflicting Jurisdiction – Problems and Possible Solutions", *Max Planck UNYB* 5 (2003), 67, 77 et seq.

[16] The 1990s with the "Rio Earth Summit" in 1992 can be regarded as the decade of international environmental law. In this context some authors raised the issue of an International Environmental Court, see e.g. A. Rest, "Zur Notwendigkeit eines internationalen Umweltgerichtshofs", in: G. Hafner (ed.), *Liber Amicorum: Professor Ignaz Seidl-Hohenveldern in honour of his 80th birthday*, 1998, 575 et seq. More critical voices proposed making use of the Permanent Court of Arbitration, see e.g. S.D. Murphy, "Does the World Need

courts and tribunals is subject to (academic) discussion. In practice, however, the setting up of those tribunals is rather unlikely due to the general reluctance of States to create further institutions which they will need to finance in order for them to become operational.

In the context of unity of international law the establishment of new courts and tribunals is not the only area of concern. Rather more generally, the development of different and distinct branches of public international law and the effects of such diversification on the body of public international law have in recent years been subject to increasing academic research. The specialisation of international law may be seen as an underlying reason for the creation of new courts, which may then in turn develop these branches further.[17] Hence, the issue of jurisdiction of different tribunals with their mandates to adjudicate a case from the viewpoint of a specific branch of public international law or legal regime, e.g. the law of the sea, trade law, environmental law or human rights law, is only one element of the current discussion on a substantive broadening and deepening of public international law.

In legal writing some contributions to the discussion deal with only the symptoms of a substantive diversification, e.g. with only the creation of different courts,[18] whereas other studies restrict themselves to discussing only the underlying specialisation of the material law without considering the institutional and jurisdictional effects of such development.[19] As is shown in his written work *Rüdiger Wolfrum* has been interested in all aspects of these questions, covering both the substantive

---

a New International Environmental Court?", *Geo. Wash. J. Int'l L. & Econ.* 32 (2000), 333 et seq.

17 See *infra* III 1.

18 The approach of the symposium on the proliferation of courts, see note 4, as indicated by its title, focused on this aspect.

19 This approach was adopted by the International Law Commission (ILC), *Fragmentation of International Law: Difficulties Arising from the Diversification and Expansion of International Law*, Report of the Study Group of the ILC, Finalised by Martti Koskenniemi, Doc. A/CN.4/L.682 of 13 April 2006 (hereinafter ILC Report), para. 13. Likewise, the symposium on the 25th anniversary of the Michigan Journal of International Law entitled "Diversity or Cacophony? New Sources of Norms in International Law" focused more on the substantive fragmentation of international law, although Bruno Simma in his introduction mentions both the proliferation of courts and substantive fragmentation of norms as elements of the general issue, see B. Simma, "Fragmentation in a Positive Light", *Mich. J. Int'l L.* 25 (2003/2004), 845, 855 et seq.

and jurisdictional implications. He dealt with these questions at a time when terminology still referred to conflicts in public international law, colliding regimes and problems resulting from overlapping jurisdictional competences,[20] i.e. before these issues had been commonly labelled "fragmentation of international law".

This paper attempts to characterise the international legal system's nature with reference to fragmentation and unity of law and to define the role of international tribunals in this context. It is not the aim of this article to rehearse the different arguments in favour and against an increase in the number of international tribunals. Rather, when assessing the role of international tribunals and their potential influence on the unity of public international law, the article focuses on the arguments relevant to the current debate on the substantive fragmentation of the law. It will end with some conclusions sparked by the report of the Study Group of the International Law Commission (ILC) on fragmentation of international law which was submitted to the United Nations General Assembly in the summer of 2006.[21] In this context the question whether a kind of "general international law" is evolving which may be promoted by decisions of different international tribunals is subjected to further elaboration.[22]

II. The Nature of the International Legal System: Fragmentation vs. Unity

1. The Existence of an International Legal System

When dealing with the fragmented nature of a legal system one must necessarily presuppose that the relevant rules and institutions establish

[20] R. Wolfrum, "Konkurrierende Zuständigkeiten internationaler Streitentscheidungsinstanzen: Notwendigkeit für Lösungsmöglichkeiten und deren Grenzen", in N. Ando et al. (eds), *Liber Amicorum Judge Shigeru Oda*, 2002, 651 et seq.; R. Wolfrum/N. Matz, *Conflicts in International Environmental Law*, 2003; R. Wolfrum/N. Matz, "The Interplay of the United Nations Convention on the Law of the Sea and the United Nations Convention on Biological Diversity", *Max Planck UNYB* 4 (2000), 445 et seq.

[21] The short report submitted to the General Assembly on 18 July 2006, Doc. A/CN.4/L.702, bears the same title as the extended one referred to in note 19.

[22] See *infra* IV.

systematic structures that warrant the label "legal system". While the existence of legal systems established by and containing the body of applicable law is not in doubt as far as municipal legal orders or the supranational legal order established by the primary and secondary law of the European Community are concerned, this is less obviously so in the field of public international law. The ILC's report on fragmentation however, has been very explicit in affirming the existence of an international legal system:

> "International law is a legal system. Its rules and principles (i.e. its norms) act in relation to and should be interpreted against the background of other rules and principles. As a legal system, international law is not a random collection of such norms."[23]

This view is not yet shared by all legal scholars.[24] Yet, the international set of rules and competencies has a systematic content in the sense that its rules are not independent of one another; neither at the time of their creation nor during their existence and implementation. As in domestic legal systems no new norm is created in the void at the international level. Instead, international legal norms are born into the existing conglomerate of international law and interact in many ways with the other components of this system.[25] Furthermore, international law is distinguishable from other legal orders by reliance upon a different basis of legitimacy, different mechanisms for creating, applying and implementing its rules.[26]

Despite the fact that the international legal order is more than a random assembly of primary and secondary rules, it must be admitted that it has certain characteristics that remind us of a more or less loose-knit net of

---

[23] Conclusions of the ILC Study Group, see note 21, para. 14 (1).

[24] See e.g. G. Hafner, "Pros and Cons Ensuing From Fragmentation of International Law", *Mich. J. Int'l L.* 25 (2003/2004), 849, 850 finds that there is "no homogeneous system of international law" but that international law consists of "erratic blocks and elements; different partial systems" and various sub- and sub-subsystems that all interact with one another. On the discussion see also B. Kingsbury, "The International Legal Order", *IILJ Working Paper* 2003/1, History and Theory of International Law Series, electronic resource available at <www.iilj.org> (last visited 20 April 2007), 11 et seq.

[25] Or as Higgins, see note 10, 6 puts it, "[n]o set of legal rules exists in a systemic vacuum".

[26] On criteria for legal orders see G. Abi-Saab, "Fragmentation or Unification: Some Concluding Remarks", *N.Y.U. J. Int'l L. & Pol.* 31 (1999), 919, 920 et seq.

competences, legal rules and policies. The system's deficiencies in structure and density become apparent if we compare the international legal system with "closed" legal systems with a single legislator, a limited number of other actors competent to enact legal rules and a tight net of legal regulations. In the end, however, not much is gained from deciding whether international law should be perceived as a legal system, albeit lacking systematic coherence and comparability to other (domestic) legal systems or whether it is said to lack the quality of a legal system by reason of friction, contradictions and conflicts. It is important to note that it is not in question that rules and regulations of international law are not isolated from one another and that they interact and potentially contradict one another; neither is it in question that rules are not coherent.

Even if we assume that existing mechanisms to co-ordinate treaties and generally to streamline public international law are not sufficient,[27] and that there is no "judicial system" in the sense of a correlated "constellation" of courts,[28] this does not alter the conclusion that substantive international legal norms are not and cannot be without relevance for one another. Accordingly, although structural deficits in comparison to national orders and to the EC supranational legal system are clearly discernable, the international legal system can be characterised as an "operating system" which comprises treaties, custom, general principles of law and the secondary rules created by international organisations and in which these rules function.[29]

2. Unity as Fiction

The international legal system is not only horizontal in the sense that it lacks a hierarchy of competences but also fragmented by its nature or, as the ILC experts pointed out in their report on fragmentation: "normative conflict is endemic to international law".[30] Its fragmented nature results *inter alia* from the general lack within the system of hierarchies of norms and the growing degree of specialisation by a considerable

---

[27] See Wolfrum/Matz, see note 20, 210 et seq.

[28] Abi-Saab, see note 26, 921.

[29] J. Pauwelyn, "Fragmentation of International Law", in: R. Wolfrum (ed.), *Max Planck Encyclopedia of Public International Law*, 2007, in preparation.

[30] ILC Report, see note 19, para. 486.

number of international institutions and organisations resulting in a further differentiation between rules and standards in both substance and procedure. Another element which leads to a proliferation of norms and specific dispute settlement procedures is the growing significance of the individual as an actor in public international law.[31] In this context "fragmentation of international law" is a term that allows discussion of all the different aspects of lack of coherence or integrity in public international law and has been recognised as a valuable broadening of legal terminology in public international law.[32]

International law does not and cannot experience a degree of unity or coherence of law comparable to that in national legal orders. The reasons for such lack are obvious: a horizontal structure with only rudimentary hierarchical elements and the lack of viable mechanisms that structure or harmonise public international law stemming from different sources or those rules emanating from the same source. The fact that the largest group of rules, those stemming from treaty law, are not of a universal character but applicable only to the relevant parties leads to a legal system that has no common *corpus* of law. Due to these deficiencies references here to "unity" of the international legal system mean unity within the limits achievable in a fragmented legal system. This article focuses on the efforts to promote a high degree of coherence as a counterbalance to some negative effects of fragmentation. Unity in the strict sense, i.e. a system without contradictions, will never be fully achieved in the fragmented international legal system. To this extent the unity of international law is fiction rather than a realistic objective.

In the context of the coherence of the international system one must ask not only whether unity is achievable but also whether it is desirable. However, the idea of unity in the sense of an active process, i.e. striving for at least some overarching legal standards that build a common, uniform denominator, seems beneficial in order to prevent and cope with some of the acknowledged difficulties of fragmentation. The drifting apart not only of substantial rules but also of methodologies and techniques for law-making, the application of law, implementation, and compliance weaken international law as the normative order governing

---

31 See Higgins, see note 10, 12; W. Burke-White, "International Legal Pluralism", *Mich. J. Int'l L.* 25 (2003/2004), 963, 969.

32 The inclusion of the term "Fragmentation of International Law" in the catalogue of entries for the new edition of the *Max Planck Encyclopedia of Public International Law* affirms its acceptance by scholarship.

the conduct of States, organisations and individuals. While this paper will emphasise certain positive aspects of fragmentation – the ILC Study Group understands fragmentation as a potential expression of a vital and viable development of law[33] – the effectiveness of the legal system and the safeguarding of a minimum standard of predictability and stability merit efforts to promote an idea of coherence in substance and methodology. Hence, this article calls for the acceptance of factual restrictions without losing sight of improvement and for the acknowledgement of positive aspects of fragmentation without sacrificing the idea of some overarching unity and integrity of the international legal system.

III. The Role of International Courts and Tribunals

When the ILC prepared and finalised its report on the fragmentation of public international law, conflicting competences of different tribunals were omitted from the scope of the study. The reason for this omission was that, according to the view of the experts, tribunals could and should handle conflicts of jurisdiction themselves,[34] whereas the fragmentation of the substantial law was a different matter. This restriction of their terms of reference imposed by the experts themselves may have had political motives for the prevention of institutional interferences. The ILC Study Group may be right that conflicts of jurisdiction in the strict sense, i.e. that the questions for tribunals to decide, if a case can be brought before different dispute settlement mechanisms (e.g. the Mox Plant Case, the EC – Chile Swordfish Case), should be addressed by them alone. However, conflicts of jurisprudence, i.e. diverging decisions on the substantive law, go to the core of the fragmentation debate. Hence, the separation of these aspects into substantive on the one hand and institutional on the other seems to be to some extent artificial. From the perspective of the unity of public international law it is essential to consider both elements.

---

33 This understanding is indicated by the change of the study's title at the request of the study group from "Risks Ensuing from the Fragmentation of International Law" to the slightly more optimistic "Fragmentation of International Law: Difficulties Arising from the Diversification and Expansion of International Law" in 2002, see ILC Report, see note 19, para. 14.

34 ILC Report, see note 19, para. 13.

All existing international courts and tribunals are part of the same legal system.[35] Two consequences result from the establishment of formalised dispute settlement mechanisms within the framework of the international legal system. First, existing public international law, whether in the form of customary law, certain applicable treaty law, the statutes of the relevant tribunals or relevant secondary rules by institutions, governs decisions by international tribunals. Second, the decisions themselves, even if legally binding only *inter partes*, e.g. in accordance with Art. 59 of the Statute for the ICJ or Art. 296 para. 2 UNCLOS, contribute to the body of public international law, interact with existing rules and decisions and may also have an influence on future decisions.

The factual interrelation between international courts and tribunals shows that the ICTY Appeals Chamber in one of the decisions on the *Tadić* Case was mistaken when it held that, in principle, "every tribunal is a self-contained system".[36] From a formal point of view the ICTY is right in that there is no court system that has tribunals at different levels with a single "world court" at the top.[37] Neither are decisions of international tribunals binding on other courts. International courts are generally not even bound by their own previous decisions, although they seem to refer to their own precedent and derogate from it only in exceptional circumstances.[38] Yet, the contribution to the legal system made by decisions of international courts and tribunals cannot be reduced to the relevant outcome for one of the parties or even to the legal findings in the case.

Since the decision-making of international tribunals is governed by a variety of rules within the framework of the international legal system, their decisions also contribute to reinforcing certain legal standards. While some substantive legal standards may be particularly relevant to only one or two specific branches of international law, e.g. the question whether there is a normative precautionary principle in international

---

35 T. Buergenthal, "Proliferation of International Courts and Tribunals: Is it good or bad?", *LJIL* 14 (2001), 267, 274.

36 *Prosecutor v. Tadić*, Case No. IT-94-1-AR72, Decision on the Defence Motion for Interlocutory Appeal on Jurisdiction of 2 October 1995, *ILM* 35 (1996), 32 et seq., para. 11.

37 On the decentralisation and independence of international courts see Oellers-Frahm, see note 15, 75 et seq.

38 Ibid, 76.

environmental law,[39] standards concerning procedure and methodology, e.g. the interpretation of public international law, gain relevance for the settlement of any international dispute and hence for the development of public international law in a more general manner.[40]

1. A Proliferation of Courts and Tribunals: Cause or Consequence of Fragmentation?

The international legal order that we experience today is the result of many individual decisions that international actors perceived as viable and necessary approaches to solving the particular difficulties arising from globalised interrelations. The argument that it was no wonder that international law was homogenous neither in substance nor procedure because of a multitude of international courts and tribunals instead of the centralised, hierarchical law-enforcement system known in domestic legal systems can be turned upside down: it is no wonder that international law that is by its process of creation homogenous neither in substance nor procedure results in the conception of a multitude of different international courts and tribunals that apply the existing law according to their jurisdictions and mandates.

Like the fragmentation of legal rules the fragmentation of the accompanying jurisdictional mechanisms can be separated along functionally defined areas on the one hand, e.g. courts and other dispute settlement mechanisms concerning human rights, the law of the sea or trade law, and along regional lines on the other, e.g. the European Court of Human Rights (ECtHR) and the Inter-American Court of Human Rights. Although the competences of regional courts dealing with the same subject matter are unlikely to conflict with regard to individual cases due to rules on regional restrictions concerning jurisdiction, they may develop in different directions, creating specific regional international

---

39 In fact this question is also relevant to trade disputes in the context of the WTO's SPS Agreement, see e.g. the report of the Appellate Body in *EC Measures Concerning Meat and Meat Products (Hormones)*, WT/DS26/AB/R and WT/DS48/AB/R of 16 January 1998 and the Panel report in *European Communities – Measures Affecting the Approval and Marketing of Biotech Products*, WT/DS291/R, WT/DS292/R, and WT/DS293/R of 29 September 2006. See also the ILC Report, see note 19, para. 55; M. Koskenniemi/P. Leino, "Fragmentation of International Law? Postmodern Anxieties", *LJIL* 15 (2002), 553, 572.

40 See *infra* III 2.

law. It is questionable whether regional international law is a threat to the unity of international law. Regional international law may be better adapted to regional peculiarities or values and, hence, only reflect the fact that there is neither a single world government or legislator nor a uniform world people. If certain rules are more strictly applied in some regions, e.g. a high standard of protection of human rights, this may even serve as a role model and strengthen effective standards on a wider level. Such effects are *inter alia* referred to when fragmentation is described as a sign of a vital and viable system.

In principle, the existence of and relationship between different courts and tribunals reflect rather than cause the existing fragmentation of public international law, although a potential catalytic effect cannot be denied. Yet, international law would not necessarily be more coherent if we had fewer courts and tribunals. International law might even be less effective, since fewer courts and tribunals would certainly not have the consequence that the existing courts would decide all potential cases in a co-ordinated manner. Instead, many cases would not be brought before dispute settlement bodies at all. This could have the effect that the underlying objective in international relations, that States should solve all disputes in a formalised and peaceful manner, would suffer. In the same way, Judge Higgins, unlike her ICJ colleagues who warned against a proliferation of courts, stressed the desirability of the trend to resolve disputes in a peaceful manner that was reflected in the widening and diversification of the judicial map in the last 20 years.[41] Viewed from this perspective the proliferation of courts is "a powerful element" in reducing in number those fields of international relations that lack judicial control.[42]

Legal pluralism is the reason and at the same time a justification for a multitude of different dispute settlement mechanisms. In this context, it appears particularly important to perceive the rule of law in international law with its procedural and material implications as a unifying objective that is better achieved by a vital international legal system allowing for development and change than by strict "frozen" hierarchies. The ILC's argument that deviations in treaty law should not be seen as

[41] At the same time, however, she does not deny that a proliferation of courts may lead to courts giving contradictory judgments with negative implications, Higgins, see note 10, 18.

[42] P.-M. Dupuy, "The Danger of Fragmentation or Unification of the International Legal System and the International Court of Justice", *N.Y.U. J. Int'l L. & Pol.* 31 (1999), 791, 796.

"legal-technical 'mistakes'" but rather as reflecting the "differing pursuits and preferences that actors in a pluralistic (global) society have",[43] can be transferred in an even more viable manner to the context of the diversification of dispute settlement procedures. The establishment of courts or dispute settlement mechanisms that can rule with legally binding effect is not easy to negotiate. From the perspective of sovereignty one must assume that States will be reluctant and cautious in creating institutions with jurisdiction over them. Despite subjective political reasons why States may support the development of further courts, "mistakes" in the sense of a lack of objective reasons for the establishment of a specialised court are unlikely.

As the ILC Study Group indicates throughout its report, competition between rules and between the institutions that interpret and apply them can benefit a dynamic development of international law. The widening and deepening of public international law that is reflected both by the creation of legal rules and by the establishment of courts and tribunals draws the different branches closer together[44] as the net of rules tightens and, hopefully, becomes more reliable. This necessarily leads to the application of the same international rules and standards by different tribunals and has risks but also opportunities to achieve coherence of the international legal system. It is for the courts to be aware of their role in this context and to act accordingly with a view to enhancing the degree of integrity of the international legal order of which they form a vital part.

2. Potential for Standard-Setting by International Tribunals

a) The stare decisis Rule and de facto Precedent

Clearly a technically viable approach to providing for enhanced coherence in the world of international courts and tribunals or other dispute settlement bodies would be a *stare decisis* rule, i.e. binding precedent. In addition to the precedent observed by a court in regard to its own prior rulings, such a rule could oblige different courts either vertically within the same branch of international law or even horizontally between distinct branches to follow earlier decisions. Binding precedent within the same or between different courts would set standards in accordance

[43] ILC Report, see note 19, para. 16; Koskenniemi/Leino, see note 39, 561.

[44] Pauwelyn, see note 29.

with procedural and material norms. Eventually, like a hierarchy of courts, this would promote stability, reliability and, ultimately, a high degree of unity as courts could, in principle, not deviate from those standards already set. However, if binding precedent were to extend over different courts and different branches of international law, such a process would fly in the face of the reasons why different tribunals were established and suppress the positive aspects of fragmentation, i.e. the vitality of the legal system as a result of diversification and specialisation. Likewise, even if an international tribunal were bound by its own previous rulings this would deny the particular dynamic element in international law.

Furthermore, in the absence of a hierarchical order of courts it would be difficult to establish which decisions by what tribunals constituted binding precedent for the others. Although a *stare decisis* rule would not have direct effect on States it would also raise questions as to the position of third States and the general rules that States are bound neither by treaties nor by decisions concerning disputes to which they are not party. In the worst cases the adoption of a *stare decisis* approach to achieving greater coherence might have the opposite effect. It is not unlikely that States would refrain from dispute settlement if they sought to avoid the (indirect) application of rulings of courts whose jurisdiction they had not accepted. If a decision by a court for a special treaty regime, e.g. the ITLOS for the law of the sea, were to have legally binding effect on the ICJ when dealing with maritime delimitation cases, States deliberately not ratifying the Convention on the Law of the Sea might still be subjected to its regime via the ICJ. If such a result is the effect of a *stare decisis* rule, this is legally more problematic than where courts interpret material norms with respect to each others' decisions because they are convinced of the customary nature and applicability of the underlying legal standards. In the latter case a court's ruling reflects the development of international law, but only and to the extent that it agrees with the prior findings of the other tribunal. The restriction of the application of a *stare decisis* rule to the interpretation of customary international law or general principles of international law could solve some difficulties but would not defeat others.

In the absence of a formal *stare decisis* rule in international law, standard-setting as a consequence of decisions made by international courts and tribunals will take the form of enforcement or reinforcement of norms by "informal" repetition. If certain general rules have already been relied upon by different courts and in different decisions this will have a reinforcing effect and considerably strengthen the particular legal rule, and in such a way that we can speak of *de facto* precedent. In contrast to a legal *stare decisis* rule, however, such a process is not predictable. There is no methodology to define or predict what rules will be subject to such a reinforcing setting of precedence.

While courts cite previous case law of other tribunals in their decisions, they do not refer to the coherence of international law as a legal reason for following *de facto* precedent. Hence, we can only presume that repetition is also based upon a wish to avoid contradictions.[45] An analysis of decisions by international tribunals shows increasing reliance upon prior reasoning.[46] In particular the recognised more general international law must not be and is in fact not reinvented or reinterpreted with every new decision. The diversification of law and the resulting specialisation of tribunals was clearly not intended to leave behind the foundations of international law completely but to provide for competence in specialised matters such as trade, financial and investment issues, law of the sea etc. As a result, different branches of international law still share a common basis of rules that may be termed "general international law", although there is still no common understanding of this term.[47] The definition of a category of "general international law" is not a suitable means, however, of overcoming difficulties concerning the predictability of rules subject to *de facto* precedent because the label does not give any indications as to its potential content.

b) Categories of Standards: Procedure, Methodology and Material Law

The setting, or rather the reinforcement, of existing standards by international courts and tribunals is particularly relevant in the case of rules filling gaps left by those treaties or rules of procedure which are applied in dispute settlement proceedings. If all courts and tribunals only applied the specific treaty or treaties relevant to the specialised regime

---

[45] Simma, see note 19, 846, emphasises the caution exercised by courts not to contradict one another and goes as far as to say that "if there are international institutions that are constantly and painstakingly aware of the necessity to preserve the coherence of international law, it is the international courts and tribunals." Likewise, Higgins, see note 11, 797 stresses the importance of the "tremendous efforts that courts and tribunals make, both to be consistent inter se and to follow the International Court of Justice."

[46] See J. Charney, "Is International Law Threatened by Multiple International Tribunals?", *RdC* 271 (1998), 101, 129.

[47] ILC Report, see note 19, para. 493.

they were established by and for, the risk of conflicts of law would decrease but dispute settlement would not be practicable.

Treaties tend to regulate only the specific issue they were drafted to address instead of repeating the whole canon of applicable international law. This is particularly so, as it is difficult to maintain the complete "applicable law" in a treaty instrument, since applicability of norms depends to the greatest extent upon and changes with each party in relation to any other party. Although certain fundamental standards are likely to be agreed upon by all States and claim applicability as supplementary customary law, it is usually not until the settling of a given dispute that such questions arise in relation to a special treaty regime. Any settling of disputes requires certain rules of procedure, methodology and material law in addition to the specific treaty law applicable. One can draw the conclusion from the reliance on overarching international law by different tribunals that there is some "general international law" or a "fall-back" of rules, i.e. a universal practice of international organisations, courts and tribunals.

aa) Procedural Standards

While special procedures, e.g. the prompt release procedure for vessels in accordance with Art. 292 UNCLOS, are a sign of a vital system of peaceful settlement of different disputes, all judicial proceedings have some general rules in common. The acceptance of underlying common procedural standards is a process independent of the courts' potential influence on diversification or unity of the substantive law.

There are certain standards widely accepted in international law that are crucial in governing decisions by international tribunals. Even if international tribunals operate independently of one another, there is a unifying element that would promote stability of the system if procedural standards were reliable and applied in a uniform manner. Tribunals borrow procedural practices from one another. Although one cannot speak of "international rules of procedure",[48] courts and tribunals have developed some procedural standards, e.g. those concerning the burden and standard of proof, in reliance upon one another in order to fill gaps left by the written rules of procedure. International judicial procedure can be described as a completely autonomous and independent institution

[48] A. Watts, "Enhancing the Effectiveness of Procedures of International Dispute Settlement", *Max Planck UNYB* 5 (2001), 21.

that is distinct to national rules of procedure.[49] Common standards that guide the procedure of different dispute settlement mechanisms are *inter alia* estoppel, transparency, fundamental fairness and due process.[50] The recognition of formal standards enhances formal unity of the international legal system by gradually developing a reliable procedural system. At the same time this development does not hamper the opportunity to establish specific procedural frameworks that are adapted to the needs and conceptions of new courts or tribunals.

bb) Methodology

A second category of standards that has great potential for enhancing the level of unity of international law is related to methodologies for defining the applicable law. This includes all legal elements concerning sources of international law, particularly criteria for defining customary international law and for the interpretation of public international law. Such standards are positioned between purely procedural and substantive ones.

The WTO Dispute Settlement Understanding in its Article 3.2 explicitly provides that the different agreements covered by the WTO must be interpreted "in accordance with customary rules of interpretation of public international law". No other international agreement includes such a clause. Nevertheless, the standard of interpretation is not questioned but is common to all dispute settlement proceedings. The explicit reference to the applicability of rules on interpretation by the drafters of the WTO agreements demonstrates that the specialised trade regime had already alienated itself from the *corpus* of international law during the time of the former GATT.[51]

---

[49] S. Rosenne, *The Law and Practice of the International Court (1920-2005)*, 4th edition, Vol. III, 2006, 1022.

[50] S. Oeter, "Vielfalt der Gerichte – Einheit des Prozessrechts?", in: R. Hofmann/A. Reinisch/Th. Pfeiffer/S. Oeter/A. Stadler (eds), *Die Rechtskontrolle von Organen der Staatengemeinschaft, Vielfalt der Gerichte – Einheit des Prozessrechts?*, 2006, 149, 162.

[51] J. Pauwelyn, *Introductory Report on the World Trade Organization*, paper presented at the conference entitled *L'influence des sources sur l'unité et la fragmentation du droit international*, 2005, available at <http://eprints.law.duke.edu/archive/00001314/01/unityandfragmentationininternationallaw.pdf> (last visited 20 April 2007), 9.

The rules on interpretation of international law would also be included in a "fall-back" category or in "general international law". They belong to the most important conflict-avoidance mechanisms,[52] particularly if a systematic and harmonizing interpretation that takes account of "any relevant rules of international law applicable in the relations between the parties"[53] is chosen. Such an approach allows for the recognition of the rules assembled in the broader system of international law, i.e. custom, general principles and other treaties.

cc) Substantive Legal Rules

For his lecture in The Hague in 1998 *Jonathan Charney* undertook a survey of a number of substantive legal rules, e.g. the exhaustion of local remedies, the nationality of natural persons, and maritime delimitation, with a view to analysing whether these rules were applied and interpreted differently by different tribunals and, if so, were damaged as a result.[54] In short, *Charney* comes to the conclusion that multiple tribunals do not pose a threat to international law as a system but share a coherent understanding of law in several core areas of international law.[55] Likewise, rules on reparation, the termination of treaties and the use of force are issues that have been referred to in a relatively consistent manner by tribunals as general, material standards.[56]

As already discussed above under the heading of *stare decisis*, coherence of substantive standards is achieved by repetition and reliance upon the previous case law of other courts. Such a process is the consequence of the conclusion that the applicable norms are part of the greater legal system and must be interpreted against this background despite their special character. Those standards governing the law of treaties, by reference either to the Vienna Convention on the Law of Treaties[57] or to the underlying customary law, are prone to be referred to in all relevant dispute settlement decisions adjudicating on the applicability of treaty law. In this respect customary international law may unify the interna-

---

52 See Wolfrum/Matz, see note 20, 133 et seq.

53 Art. 31 para. 3 lit. c) Vienna Convention on the Law of Treaties (1969), *ILM* 8, 679 et seq.

54 See Charney, see note 46, 101 et seq.

55 Ibid, 347.

56 Pauwelyn, see note 29.

57 See note 53.

tional legal system because *de facto* reliance on precedence may be particularly common.

The existence and analysis of rules of custom serve as an example of uniform reliance upon material standards. The criteria that need to be taken into consideration when analysing the validity of a rule as part of customary law are not questioned by courts and tribunals. When courts deliberate on what is valid and applicable customary law, they apply common material standards taken from Art. 38 lit. b) of the Statute of the ICJ, i.e. State practice and *opinio juris*. In the absence of previous case law on a specific question, it cannot be said with certainty that two courts would necessarily have to come to the same conclusion when assessing State practice in connection with an emerging rule of customary law. Yet, at least they would both consider the same elements, increasing the likelihood of equivalent normative outcomes.

If international courts are required to establish whether a customary rule of international law exists and governs the relations between the applicant and the respondent, they regularly turn to previous decisions by other international courts and tribunals, particularly the fairly extensive case law of the ICJ, to support their argument. Customary international law is not static but the result of a process of evolution of State practice and legal opinion. As a consequence it is not unlikely for a court to decide that a rule of customary international law has emerged that had not yet been accepted when previous decisions were reached by other tribunals. If, however, case law from international tribunals exists that argues in favour of a customary rule of substantive international law, an international tribunal will take such decisions into consideration. The European Court of Justice (ECJ), for example, in its decision in *Anklagemyndigheden v Peter Michael Poulsen and Diva Navigation Corp*[58] cited several ICJ cases to substantiate its view that certain articles in the Geneva Conventions and the Convention on the Law of the Sea[59] codified general rules recognised as customary law.[60] By relying upon and repeating material standards as part of customary international law different courts contribute to their setting and strengthening. In particular reliance upon rulings of the ICJ may serve

---

[58] Case C 286/90, *ECR* (1992), I-6019.

[59] At that time the Convention had not yet entered into force.

[60] Case C 286/90, see note 58, para. 10; for a discussion on this and further examples of from the relationship between the ECJ and the ICJ see also Higgins, see note 10, 7 et seq.

as a convenient short-cut for other international tribunals to come to a legal conclusion in their relevant cases, at least as far as customary international law is concerned. Otherwise they would themselves have to undertake the often difficult analysis of practice and *opinio juris* in the face of the high probability that they would come to the same conclusion as the ICJ in the end.

Furthermore, many decisions of international tribunals show that leading general principles of international law, such as those of good faith, equity or proportionality, are material standards that govern decisions, even if they are not explicitly referred to. To support its argument the European Court of First Instance in *Opel Austria GmbH v Council of the European Union*[61] held that the principle of good faith was "a rule of customary international law, whose existence is recognised by the International Court of Justice". The acceptance of such a rule by the ICJ led the Court of First Instance to the conclusion that the principle of good faith was binding on the Community.[62]

Viewed from this perspective the question of who decides e.g. upon a maritime delimitations case may in fact be reduced to a matter of institutional competence best dealt with by the statutes of the relevant court. If the applicable substantive standards were the same, States parties and non-States parties to the Convention on the Law of the Sea could rely upon different institutions, the ITLOS on the one hand and the ICJ or an arbitral tribunal on the other, to achieve comparable results. On this basis the legal difficulties resulting from the obligatory application of a *stare decisis* rule would not arise, although the effect would be similar.

IV. Conclusions: General International Law" as a "Fall-Back" Common to All Courts and Tribunals?

The "fall-back" on certain rules of international law without the need for any explicit incorporation in the treaty relevant to the settling of a dispute has been described by *Pauwelyn* as the most important tool for maintaining a minimum of coherence and interaction between different branches of specialised international law.[63] While such a "fall-back" in-

---

61 Case T-115/94, *ECR* (1997), II-39

62 Ibid.

63 Pauwelyn, see note 29.

deed has great potential, its characterisation as a legal tool is questionable.

When one looks more closely at judgments of international courts and tribunals, it becomes apparent that certain legal rules or, particularly, legal definitions, e.g. the definition of a State according to public international law, are accepted without any reference to sources or applicability and without any further explanation. Although hardly any of the specialised agreements applicable to different branches of international law contain provisions on the basic definitions, e.g. concerning the question of what constitutes a State or an international organisation or the definition of an international treaty, there seems to be an underlying canon of rules and definitions that they share.[64] Even if parties to a dispute disagree on legal questions concerning the rights and obligations of States, e.g. on the applicability of treaties in a situation of State succession, the legal definition of what constitutes a State seems to be such general common knowledge that it does not need further discussion.

Reference to a temporal element in the sense that such "general international law" consists of rules that existed in the era before specialisation and diversification is not sufficient to define the content of this category. Even if we use the term "general international law" in hindsight to describe the body of rules that existed before States established different branches of international law with their own rules and dispute settlement mechanisms,[65] this as such does not allow for any assumptions about the persistent recognition of these rules. In some cases specialisation served the purpose of overriding certain general rules by adaptation to the specific needs of modern international relations. At this point, however, reference could also be made to the counterpart of fragmentation: the constitutionalisation of international law. While legal regimes become more specialised, at the same time the underlying fundamental rules are reinforced in order to establish a catalogue of shared legal values.[66] In essence, it depends upon each regime and set of rules whether it deviates from the general foundations or whether it builds upon them.

---

[64] This is despite the functional differentiation that they "share a common body of law which tends to preserve a unified international legal system", Burke-White, see note 31, 970.

[65] See the ILC Report, see note 19, para. 8.

[66] See also J. Delbrück, "Structural Changes in the International System and Its Legal Order: International Law in the Era of Globalization", *SZIER* 11, 1, 35.

The establishment of a further category of international law outside the terminology of the sources of public international law, the category of "general international law", is also at least misleading. In any case the characterisation of rules or legal definitions as belonging to "general international law" does not enlarge the canon of sources accepted in public international law as exemplified by Art. 38 of the Statute of the ICJ. If rules are of such a general character that they are, as a matter of fact, accepted by all parties to dispute settlement as well as by the courts and tribunals, one must assume that they are customary law. However, it is then difficult to distinguish between customary international law and "general international law". While it must be supposed that "general international law" refers to commonly accepted definitions and rules of customary international law, not all customary international law must also be considered to belong to the category of "general international law". Even if one regards only the most fundamental rules and definitions as being part of "general international law", there are no criteria for identifying them.

What will in future be part of "general international law" is not predictable since there are no decisive factors concerning what rules will be generally accepted and further promoted by tribunals. Hence, only by a review of the current situation at a given time can we conclude what rules deserve that label. Even such a result is then subject to further development and change. For the same reason a "fall-back" cannot be a tool, but must merely be accepted as a positive factual development without having a steering element. Consequently, standard-setting by international courts and tribunals that leads to the greater unity of international law remains a *de facto* phenomenon. The current suggestions on how to formalise relationships between tribunals – even without creating hierarchies or a *stare decisis* rule – should be explored further in order to reduce the element of coincidence in the development.

However, if we conclude that courts and tribunals, while part of a highly fragmented legal system, show a tendency to promote certain rules of international law, it may be justified to consider these common standards to be part of "general international law". Such a process would label them, regardless of their source, with a term that allowed for discussion of the phenomenon. As the ILC concluded, the content and legal nature of a category of "general international law" will and should be subject to further research.

Where Unity Is at Risk: When International Tribunals Proliferate

Holger Hestermeyer[*]

There is a growing consensus among international law scholars that the structure of international law has changed. The "Westphalian System", always more of a paradigm than an actual description of reality, has been swept away.[1] With drastically reduced transportation costs, instant global communication and the advent of technologies affecting and at times threatening all humanity, interdependence between countries has grown. No country can tackle such difficult issues as the threat to the ozone layer or climate change,[2] international transportation,[3] international communication,[4] terrorism[5] and scores of other topics[6] alone.

---

[*] I would like to thank Prof. Dr. Riedel and Dr. Trevisanut for helpful comments – which, of course, does not imply that they incur responsibility for any of my mistakes or agree with any of my views.

[1] S. Rosenne, "The Perplexities of Modern International Law. General Course on Public International Law", *RdC* 291 (2001), 9, 23.

[2] Montreal Protocol on Substances that Deplete the Ozone Layer; Kyoto Protocol to the United Nations Framework Convention on Climate Change; R.

Friedmann has described the change as one from an "international law of coexistence" to an "international law of co-operation". In the former "rules aim at the peaceful coexistence of all states regardless of their social and economic structure. The principal object of these rules of coexistence is the regulation of the conditions of mutual diplomatic intercourse and, in particular, of the rules of mutual respect for national sovereignty."[7] The latter is characterized by the fact that "modern needs and developments have added many new areas expressing the need for positive cooperation which has to be implemented by international treaties and in many cases permanent international organizations."[8] The multiplication of legal instruments regulating separate issue areas has accelerated to a speed that is nothing short of astonishing, inducing one scholar to speak of international society's "insatiable hunger for legal norms".[9] The increasing specialization of members of the international legal community in a limited number of these issue areas and the ongoing development of norms for single issue areas have given rise to the fear of "fragmentation" of international law – spurring a lively debate

---

Wolfrum, "Purposes and Principles of International Environmental Law", *GYIL* 33 (1990), 308.

3 For examples concerning air, sea and land transportation see e.g. International Air Services Transit Agreement; Convention on the International Regulations for Preventing Collisions at Sea; Directive 2004/50/EC of the European Parliament and of the Council of 29 April 2004 amending Council Directive 96/48/EC on the Interoperability of the Trans-European High-Speed Rail System and Directive 2001/16/EC of the European Parliament and of the Council on the Interoperability of the Trans-European Conventional Rail System.

4 A. Noll, "International Telecommunication Union", in: R. Bernhardt (ed.), *Encyclopedia of Public International Law II*, 2, 1995, 1379 (1995).

5 International Convention for the Suppression of the Financing of Terrorism and actions by the Security Council.

6 P. Malanczuk, "Globalization and the Future Role of Sovereign States", in: F. Weiss/E. Denters/P de Waart, *International Economic Law with a Human Face*, 1998, 45.

7 W. Friedmann, *The Changing Structure of International Law*, 1964, 60.

8 Ibid. 61 et seq.

9 C. Tomuschat, "International Law: Ensuring the Survival of Mankind on the Eve of a New Century. General Course on Public International Law", *RdC* 281 (1999), 9, 306.

among scholars[10] and culminating in the International Law Commission (ILC) setting up a study group on the issue.[11]

But the law of cooperation has undergone further change. Friedmann could still speak of a "modest" contribution by international courts and tribunals in the evolution of international law.[12] However, since his analysis a significant number of international courts and tribunals have been set up. Indeed, the proliferation of tribunals has reached an extent where any list of them has to include the disclaimer that it is "most likely incomplete". This very disclaimer is taken from NYU's project on International Courts and Tribunals that, in 2004, listed 43 permanent, independent international tribunals delivering binding decisions, of which 16 are currently functioning, and 82 quasi-judicial implementation control and dispute settlement bodies that include such diverse

---

10 B. Conforti, "Unité et Fragmentation du Droit International: «Glissez, Mortels, N'Appuyez Pas!»", *RGDIP* 2007, 1; B. Simma, "Fragmentation in a Positive Light", *Mich. J. Int'l L.* 25 (2004), 845 ; G. Hafner, "Pros and Cons Ensuing from Fragmentation of International Law", *Mich. J. Int'l L.* 25 (2004), 849; U. Petersmann, "Justice as Conflict Resolution: Proliferation, Fragmentation and Decentralization of Dispute Settlement in International Trade", *U. Pa. J. Int'l Econ. L.* 27 (2006), 273; J. Pauwelyn, "Bridging Fragmentation and Unity: International Law as a Universe of Inter-Connected Islands", *Mich. J. Int'l L.* 25 (2004), 903; P. Sreenivasa Rao, "Multiple International Judicial Forums: A Reflection of the Growing Strength of International Law or Its Fragmentation?", *Mich. J. Int'l L.* 25 (2004), 929; A. Fischer-Lescano/G. Teubner, "Regime-Collisions: The Vain Search for Legal Unity in the Fragmentation of Global Law", *Mich. J. Int'l L.* 25 (2004), 999; A. Fischer-Lescano/G. Teubner, *Regime-Kollisionen. Zur Fragmentierung des globalen Rechts*, 2006; K. Wellens, "Fragmentation of International Law and Establishing an Accountability Regime for International Organizations: The Role of the Judiciary in Closing the Gap", *Mich. J. Int'l L.* 25 (2004), 1159; P.-M. Dupuy, "The Danger of Fragmentation or Unification of the International Legal System and the International Court of Justice", *NYU J. Int'l L. & Pol.* 31 (1999), 791; J. H. Jackson, "Fragmentation or Unification among International Institutions: The World Trade Organization", *NYU J. Int'l L. & Pol.* 31 (1999), 823; M. Pinto, "Fragmentation or Unification among International Institutions: Human Rights Tribunals", *NYU J. Int'l L. & Pol.* 31 (1999), 833; G. Abi-Saab, "Fragmentation or Unification: Some Concluding Remarks", *NYU J. Int'l L. & Pol.* 31 (1999), 919.

11 *Fragmentation of International Law: Difficulties Arising from the Diversification and Expansion of International Law.* Report of the Study Group of the International Law Commission. Finalized by Martti Koskenniemi, UN Doc A/CN.4/L.682 (13 April 2006).

12 W. Friedmann, *The Changing Structure of International Law*, 1964, 141.

bodies as the Committee on Economic, Social and Cultural Rights, the World Bank Administrative Tribunal, the Permanent Court of Arbitration and the Eritrea-Ethiopia Claims Commission.[13] Much like the topic of "fragmentation" that of "proliferation of international tribunals" has become a staple for international law scholars.[14]

The debate about the two topics has mainly focused on the threat to the coherence of the international legal order – and thereby to the international legal order itself. Some scholars see a clear danger to the unity of international law. Thus, the former President of the International Court of Justice Gilbert Guillaume stated that "I remain convinced that the proliferation of international judicial bodies could jeopardize the unity of international law."[15] Others are of a more positive view, regarding the threat to unity as minimal – taking into account that e.g. treaty law is not an entirely homogenous system anyway – and considering both proliferation of tribunals and fragmentation as proof of international law's prevailing relevance and continuing growth.[16] The person honoured by this volume has lent his voice to the latter view, emphasizing

---

[13] The Project on International Courts and Tribunals, *The International Judiciary in Context, Version 3.0*, 2004.

[14] R. Wolfrum, "Konkurrierende Zuständigkeiten internationaler Streitentscheidungsinstanzen: Notwendigkeit für Lösungsmöglichkeiten und deren Grenzen", in: N. Ando et al. (eds.), *Liber Amicorum Judge Shigeru Oda. Volume 1*, 2002, 651; Y. Shany, *The Competing Jurisdictions of International Courts and Tribunals*, 2003; G. Guillaume, "Advantages and Risks of Proliferation: A Blueprint for Action", *J. Int'l Crim. Just.* 2 (2004), 300; C. P. R. Romano, "The Proliferation of International Judicial Bodies: The Pieces of the Puzzle", *NYU J. Int'l L. & Pol.* 31 (1999), 709; B. Kingsbury, "Foreword: Is the Proliferation of International Courts and Tribunals a Systemic Problem?", *NYU J. Int'l L. & Pol.* 31 (1999), 679; R. P. Alford, "The Proliferation of International Courts and Tribunals: International Adjudication in Ascendance", *Am. Soc'y Int'l L. Proc.* 94 (2000), 160; S. Spelliscy, "The Proliferation of International Tribunals: A Chink in the Armor", *Colum. J. Transnat'l L.* 40 (2001), 143.

[15] G. Guillaume, *Speech by His Excellency Judge Gilbert Guillaume, President of the International Court of Justice, to the Sixth Committee of the General Assembly of the United Nations* (31 October 2001), available at http://library.lawschool.cornell.edu/cijwww/icjwww/ipresscom/SPEECHES/iSpeechPresident_Guillaume_6thCommittee_2001.htm.

[16] B. Simma, "Fragmentation in a Positive Light", *Mich. J. Int'l L.* 25 (2004), 845, 846.

the astonishing consistency of the jurisprudence of different international tribunals.[17]

This contribution alleges that the threats involved in the proliferation of international tribunals have so far not been sufficiently analysed. Generally, scholars have described the risk involved in the proliferation of international tribunals as that of a "cacophony of views,"[18] the risk that several tribunals will interpret the same rule of international law differently. However, this risk presupposes the application of the same rule by different tribunals. A closer analysis of the dangers involved in the proliferation of tribunals reveals that there is a second aspect that has so far been neglected: the development of a "factual hierarchy of regimes". Which of these two threats, differing interpretations or factual hierarchy, arises depends on the law the tribunals are empowered to apply. Provisions on applicable law vary considerably. The contribution will first describe these provisions and categorize them (1). It will then discuss in brief the traditional risk associated with the proliferation of international tribunals – that of different interpretations of the same rule (2). In a third step it will introduce the notion of "factual hierarchy of regimes" and, finally, in a fourth step it will propose solutions to the perceived problem.

The contribution will not address the spectre of forum shopping, another fear commonly associated with the proliferation of international tribunals. The risk of forum shopping is substantially reduced by the fact that states generally have to consent to the jurisdiction of an international tribunal. Real risks of forum shopping therefore arise only in the limited instances in which states have agreed to compulsory jurisdiction of several tribunals without the need for a special agreement.

1. Applicable Law of Tribunals

Not all international tribunals are empowered to apply the whole gamut of public international law. Just as states can set up tribunals for

---

17 R. Wolfrum, "Konkurrierende Zuständigkeiten internationaler Streitentscheidungsinstanzen: Notwendigkeit für Lösungsmöglichkeiten und deren Grenzen", in: N. Ando et al. (eds.), *Liber Amicorum Judge Shigeru Oda. Volume 1*, 2002, 651, 659.

18 J. I. Charney, "Is International Law Threatened by Multiple International Tribunals?", *RdC* 271 (1998), 115 et seq.

numerous purposes, they are also at liberty to determine the law those tribunals are to apply – always provided that they do not contract out of *jus cogens*. This way states can create principles, norms, rules and decision-making procedures governing state behaviour in a specific issue-area of international relations (a "regime")[19] and have those rules enforced by a tribunal without having to fear that other rules interfere with the judicial decisions delivered within the regime.

The question of applicable law has to be distinguished from that of jurisdiction. The latter question is posed at an earlier stage. It determines whether a tribunal can accept a case. Only after a tribunal has done so does it have to determine which law to apply in order to decide the case.

Three types of rules on applicable law are common for international tribunals: rules allowing the application of all of international law (a), rules allowing the application of all of international law, but establishing a hierarchy that prefers the rules of the regime for which the tribunal has been created (b), and finally rules allowing the application of only some parts of international law, contracting out of the remaining rules (c).

a) Rules Allowing the Application of All of International Law

Several tribunals can apply all of international law. The most important of these certainly is the International Court of Justice (ICJ), whose provision on the applicable law (Art. 38 of the ICJ Statute) has become the *locus classicus* for an enumeration of the sources of public international law. But other tribunals, too, even bilateral arbitration tribunals, are often empowered to apply all of international law. Thus, in the Rainbow Warrior Arbitration the decision was to be made on the basis of the Agreement between New Zealand and France, the Agreement to Arbitrate "and the applicable rules and principles of international law".[20]

---

[19] For this definition of regimes going back to Krasner see A. Hasenclever/ P. Mayer/V. Rittberger, *Theories of International Regimes*, 1997, 1.

[20] Art. 2, Agreement to Arbitrate, Special Agreement of February 14, 1989, in: K. Oellers-Frahm/A. Zimmermann, *Dispute Settlement in Public International Law. Texts and Materials*, 2179 (2nd ed. 2001). On the arbitration see also *United Nations Secretary-General: Ruling on the Rainbow Warrior Affair Between France and New Zealand*, 26 I.L.M. 1346 (1987); *The Rainbow Warrior*

b) Rules Setting up a Regime-Specific Hierarchy

A second group of tribunals also may apply all of international law, however, only to the extent that it is not in conflict with the regime they are meant to enforce. Clearly, Art. 293 of the United Nations Convention on the Law of the Sea (UNCLOS)[21] falls into this category. It establishes a hierarchy for the law applicable in dispute settlement under Part XV UNCLOS: "A court or tribunal having jurisdiction under this section shall apply this Convention and other rules of international law not incompatible with this Convention." Another, less obvious, example of this group is MERCOSUR dispute settlement. At first sight it seems to belong to the first category: the Protocolo de Olivos[22] in its Art. 34 on applicable law lists the sources of MERCOSUR law and adds "as well as the principles and provision of international law that are applicable to the matter."[23] It does not establish an explicit hierarchy between the applicable norms. But the provision demonstrates that a literal reading of a provision on applicable law can lead to an incorrect classification. According to the case law of the Tribunal Permanente de Revisión of MERCOSUR, international law is applicable, but "its application always has to be solely of subsidiary nature (or at most complementary)."[24]

Arbitration Concerning the Treatment of the French Agents Mafart and Prieur, 40 I.C.L.Q. 446 (1991).

[21] 1833 UNTS 3.

[22] Protocolo de Olivos para la Solución de Controversias en el MERCOSUR, available at http://www.mercosur.int/msweb/portal%20intermediario/Normas/Tratado%20e%20Protocolos/Protocolo%20Olivos_ES.pdf.

[23] Art. 34 (Derecho aplicable) reads in part:

1. Los Tribunales Arbitrales Ad Hoc y el Tribunal Permanente de Revisión decidirán la controversia en base al Tratado de Asunción, al Protocolo de Ouro Preto, a los protocolos y acuerdos celebrados en el marco del Tratado de Asunción, a las Decisiones del Consejo del Mercado Común, a las Resoluciones del Grupo Mercado Común y a las Directivas de la Comisión de Comercio del MERCOSUR así como a los principios y disposiciones de Derecho Internacional aplicables a la materia.

[24] The relevant part reads: "Al hacer esta aseveración el TPR es conciente de que no obstante de que los principios y disposiciones del derecho internacional están incluidos en el Protocolo de Olivos como uno de los referentes jurídicos a ser aplicados (Art. 34), su aplicación siempre debe ser solo en forma subsidiaria (o en el mejor de los casos complementaria) y solo cuando fueren aplicables al caso." Laudo N°1/2005 Laudo del Tribunal Permanente de Revisión Constitui-

c) Rules Limiting the Applicable Law

Finally, a third group of tribunals is governed by provisions on applicable law that do not mention international law in general. I would submit that, apart from several human rights tribunals, WTO dispute settlement falls into this category.[25] While the Dispute Settlement Understanding (DSU)[26] does not contain a provision explicitly entitled "applicable law", Art. 7.1 DSU setting out the standard terms of reference for WTO Panels fulfils this function. It determines those standard terms of reference as:

> "To examine, in the light of the relevant provisions in (name of the covered agreement(s) cited by the parties to the dispute), the matter referred to the DSB by (name of party) in document... and to make such findings as will assist the DSB in making the recommendations or in giving the rulings provided for in that/those agreement(s)."

The provision limits the applicable law to the covered agreements.[27] Some influential scholars reject this conclusion and argue that general international law remains applicable, as it would need to be contracted out of by the norm on applicable law.[28] However, this is precisely what Art. 7.1 DSU did. Of course this does not imply, in the famous words

do para Entender en el Recurso de Revisión Presentado por la República Oriental del Uruguay contra el Laudo Arbitral del Tribunal Arbitral Ad Hoc de fecha 25 de Octubre de 2005 en la Controversia "Prohibición de Importación de Neumáticos Remoldeados Procedentes del Uruguay", para. 9.

[25] For an in-depth argument see H. Hestermeyer, *Human Rights and the WTO. The Case of Patents and Access to Medicines*, 2007, 215 et seq.

[26] Available at http://www.wto.org/English/docs_e/legal_e/28-dsu.pdf.

[27] M. Böckenförde, "Zwischen Sein und Wollen – Über den Einfluss umweltvölkerrechtlicher Verträge im Rahmen eines WTO-Streitbeilegungsverfahrens", *ZaöRV* 63 (2003), 971, 979; J. P. Trachtman, "The Domain of WTO Dispute Resolution", *Harv. Int'l L. J.* 40 (1999), 333, 342; G. Marceau, "A Call for Coherence in International Law. Praises for the Prohibition Against "Clinical Isolation" in WTO Dispute Settlement", *J.W.T.* 33 (1999), 87, 110; J. Cameron/ K. R. Gray, "Principles of International Law in the WTO Dispute Settlement Body", *I.C.L.Q.* 50 (2001), 248, 263.

[28] J. Pauwelyn, "The Role of Public International Law in the WTO: How Far Can We Go?", *AJIL* 95 (2001), 535, 561 et seq.; L. Bartels, "Applicable Law in WTO Dispute Settlement Proceedings", *J.W.T.* 35 (2001), 499, 505; citing in support *Korea – Measures Affecting Government Procurement*, WT/DS163/R, para. 7.101 FN 755 (2000).

of the Appellate Body of the WTO, that WTO Panels and, more generally, tribunals falling into this group can decide in "clinical isolation" from all international law.[29] According to Art. 3.2 DSU customary rules of interpretation of public international law apply, and therefore relevant rules of international law can be referred to in the interpretation of the covered agreements in accordance with e.g. Art. 31 (3) (c) of the Vienna Convention on the Law of Treaties. This approach is confirmed by the practice of the Appellate Body.[30] However, non-WTO law cannot be *applied*, i.e. relied on in connection with general international law rules on conflict of norms as a defence to a charge of violating WTO law, it can only be referred to in the interpretation of WTO law.

2. Different Interpretation of Identical Rules

Where tribunals apply the same law, there is a risk that they will interpret the same provision differently. The most commonly cited example is certainly the "effective control test" elaborated by the ICJ in the *Nicaragua* case. The Court had to decide whether the acts committed by the *contras* could be attributed to the United States for the purposes of state responsibility. It considered that "even the general control by the respondent State over a force with a high degree of dependency on it, would not in [itself] mean, without further evidence, that the United States directed or enforced the perpetration of the acts contrary to human rights and humanitarian law alleged by the applicant State. Such acts could well be committed by members of the *contras* without the control of the United States. For this conduct to give rise to legal responsibility of the United States, it would in principle have to be proved that that State had effective control of the military or paramili-

---

[29] *United States – Standards for Reformulated and Conventional Gasoline*, WT/DS2/AB/R, 17 (1996).

[30] *European Communities – Customs Classification of Certain Computer Equipment*, WT/DS62/AB/R, WT/DS67/AB/R, WT/DS/68/AB/R, paras. 89 et seq.; *United States – Import Prohibition of Certain Shrimp and Shrimp Products*, WT/DS58/AB/R, paras. 130 et seq. (1998). See also M. Koskenniemi, *Fragmentation of International Law: Difficulties Arising from the Diversification and Expansion of International Law. Report of the Study Group of the International Law Commission*, UN Doc. A/CN.4/L.682, para. 444 (13 April 2006).

tary operations in the course of which the alleged violations were committed."[31]

The ICTY explicitly rejected that test when it had to determine whether a *prima facie* internal armed conflict was indeed international, as the armed forces on one side had to be regarded as acting on behalf of a foreign power. To supplement the rules of international humanitarian law on that question the ICTY analysed the notion of control in the law of state responsibility.[32] Rather than just applying the test elaborated by the ICJ in *Nicaragua*, the ICTY explicitly criticized the approach of the ICJ as at odds both with the logic of the system of the law on state responsibility[33] and with international judicial and state practice.[34] According to the ICTY the *Nicaragua* test applies only to individuals or unorganized groups of individuals acting on behalf of states. With regard to military or paramilitary groups it must be proved "that the State wields overall control over the group, not only by equipping and financing the group, but also by coordinating or helping in the general planning of its military activity. ... However, it is not necessary that, in addition, the State should also issue, either to the head or to members of the group, instructions for the commission of specific acts contrary to international law."[35]

One of the most striking aspects of the ICTY's ruling is the fact that it explicitly challenged the finding in the *Nicaragua* case without any apparent need to do so, as the ICTY did not have to rule on state responsibility but rather on the question whether there was an international armed conflict. As Judge Shahabuddeen stated in his separate opinion: "the Appeals Chamber ... reviewed the general question of the responsibility of a state for the delictual acts of another. It appears to me, however, that that question does not arise in this case. The question, a dis-

---

[31] *Military and Paramilitary Activities in and against Nicaragua (Nicaragua v United States of America)*, Merits, Judgment, ICJ Reports 1986, p. 14, para. 115.

[32] ICTY, Appeals Chamber, *The Prosecutor v. Duško Tadic*, Case No.: IT-94-1-A, judgment of 15 July 1999, paras. 98, 104-105.

[33] ICTY, Appeals Chamber, *The Prosecutor v. Duško Tadic*, Case No.: IT-94-1-A, judgment of 15 July 1999, para. 116.

[34] ICTY, Appeals Chamber, *The Prosecutor v. Duško Tadic*, Case No.: IT-94-1-A, judgment of 15 July 1999, para. 124.

[35] ICTY, Appeals Chamber, *The Prosecutor v. Duško Tadic*, Case No.: IT-94-1-A, judgment of 15 July 1999, para. 131.

tinguishable one, is" whether a state was through an entity using force against another state, rather than whether it was responsible for breaches of international humanitarian law committed by that entity.[36]

The ICJ replied to the challenge by the ICTY in the *Case Concerning the Application of the Convention on the Prevention and Punishment of the Crime of Genocide*. It wisely distinguished the issue of attribution under the law of state responsibility from establishing whether an armed conflict is international, and stated that while the ICTY's test may be appropriate for the latter issue, the ICTY had no reason to rule on matters of state responsibility: "The Court has given careful consideration to the Appeals Chamber's reasoning ..., but finds itself unable to subscribe to the Chamber's view. First, the Court observes that the ICTY was not called upon in the *Tadić* case, nor is it in general called upon, to rule on questions of State responsibility, since its jurisdiction is criminal and extends over persons only. ... Insofar as the "overall control" test is employed to determine whether or not an armed conflict is international, which was the sole question which the Appeals Chamber was called upon to decide, it may well be that the test is applicable and suitable; the Court does not, however, think it appropriate to take a position on the point in the present case, as there is no need to resolve it for purposes of the present Judgment. On the other hand, the ICTY presented the "overall control" test as equally applicable under the law of State responsibility. ... In this context, the argument in favour of that test is unpersuasive. ... It should ... be observed that logic does not require the same test to be adopted in resolving the two issues, which are very different in nature ...."[37]

While the cases show that the risk of different interpretations of identical rules is real, they also demonstrate that in many cases courts can avoid inconsistencies with the decisions of other tribunals by clearly setting out the issue they have to rule on and distinguishing it from the issues the other tribunals had to decide. The fact that the same examples are cited over and over again also demonstrates that there are too few instances of differing interpretations for there to be a reason to regard the very structure of international law as threatened. Professor Charney

---

36 ICTY, Appeals Chamber, *The Prosecutor v. Duško Tadic*, Case No.: IT-94-1-A, judgment of 15 July 1999, Separate Opinion of Judge Shahabuddeen, para. 17.

37 *Case Concerning the Application of the Convention on the Prevention and Punishment of the Crime of Genocide (Bosnia and Herzegovina v Serbia and Montenegro)*, ICJ Judgment of 26 February 2007.

has shown in his extensive study of the practice of several international tribunals in core areas of international law that, generally, the different judicial bodies show a rather consistent practice.[38] Where this is not the case the divergence in view stems from the specifics of a certain subject matter and case at hand and incoherence in the structure of public international law itself, as both Judge Wolfrum and Judge Higgins have pointed out.[39]

3. Factual Hierarchy of Regimes

The second and third types of provisions on applicable law, i.e. provisions establishing a regime-specific hierarchy of norms and those limiting the applicable law, raise another problem that has so far been neglected. In those cases a factual hierarchy of regimes can arise. Three conditions have to be fulfilled to create a situation in which a factual hierarchy of regimes may come into play.

The first condition is that one factual situation is covered by two different regimes. Such "overlapping" regimes are fast becoming a common occurrence. Life cannot be compartmentalized neatly – and with the multiplication of legal regimes and the ever growing body of international law and number of regimes it can be no surprise that there are more and more conflicts between them.[40] The imposition of economic sanctions for security reasons or in order to enforce human rights may fall foul of economic law.[41] A government's imposition of a compulsory

---

[38] J. I. Charney, "Is International Law Threatened by Multiple International Tribunals?", *RdC* 271 (1998), 347.

[39] R. Wolfrum, "Konkurrierende Zuständigkeiten internationaler Streitentscheidungsinstanzen: Notwendigkeit für Lösungsmöglichkeiten und deren Grenzen", in: N. Ando et al. (eds.), *Liber Amicorum Judge Shigeru Oda*, 2002, 651, 656; R. Higgins, "A Babel of Judicial Voices? Ruminations from the Bench", *I.C.L.Q.* 55 (2006), 791.

[40] See e.g. J. Pauwelyn, *Conflict of Norms in Public International Law*, 2003; J. Neumann, *Die Koordination des WTO-Rechts mit anderen völkerrechtlichen Ordnungen*, 2002.

[41] See e.g. A. Giardina, "The Economic Sanctions of the United States against Iran and Libya and the GATT Security Exception", in: G. Hafner (ed.), *Liber amicorum Professor Ignaz Seidl-Hohenveldern in honour of his 80th birthday*, 1998, 219; C. M. Vázquez, "Trade Sanctions and Human Rights – Past, Present, and Future", *JIEL* 6 (2003), 797; P. Stirling, "The Use of Trade

licence on intellectual property may violate human rights obligations, international investment law or international patent law, namely the Paris Convention[42] or the TRIPS Agreement.[43] Security Council action under Chapter VII of the UN Charter may raise human rights concerns[44] and the potential conflicts between world trade law or regional trade agreements and environmental law have occupied legions of scholars.[45]

The second ingredient is that both overlapping regimes have a dispute settlement mechanism – be it a court, an arbitration tribunal, a reporting mechanism or another procedure.

Finally, the provision governing the applicable law of at least one of the tribunals must be of the second or third type, i.e. a provision establishing a regime-specific hierarchy of norms or one limiting the applicable law.

Where these conditions are fulfilled, the factual situation is subject to two possibly differing legal solutions. At least one tribunal will solve the legal question posed with a preference for the rules of its own regime, whereas the legal analysis of the situation under general international law (or under the other regime) may be different. The solution depends on which dispute resolution mechanism states make use of. The reason for this disconnect is that the norms on applicable law of one regime may establish a hierarchy between two regimes, but this hierarchy is relevant only for the dispute settlement system of that regime. It has no effect for any other tribunal – nor does it govern the

---

Sanctions as an Enforcement Mechanism for Basic Human Rights", *Am. U. Int'l L. R.* 11 (1996), 1.

42 Paris Convention for the Protection of Industrial Property.

43 Agreement on Trade-Related Aspects of Intellectual Property Rights. See e.g. J. Schneider, *Menschenrechtlicher Schutz geistigen Eigentums*, 2006, 55 et seq.; H. Hestermeyer, *Human Rights and the WTO. The Case of Patents and Access to Medicines*, 2007.

44 See e.g. C. Olivier, "Human Rights Law and the International Fight against Terrorism", *Nordic J Int'l L* 73 (2004), 399; E. de Wet, *The Chapter VII Powers of the United Nations Security Council*, 2004, 200 et seq.

45 See e.g. S. Charnovitz, "World Trade and the Environment: a Review of the New WTO Report", *Georgetown Int'l Env. L. R.* 12 (2000), 523; J. H. Knox, "The Judicial Resolution of Conflicts between Trade and the Environment", *Harvard Env. L. R.* 28 (2004), 1; R. H. Steinberg, "Trade-Environment Negotiations in the EU, NAFTA, and WTO", *AJIL* 91 (1997), 231; E. Brown Weiss (ed.), *Reconciling Environment and Trade*, 2001.

resolution of the conflict between regimes under general international law. The situation is entirely different from the hierarchy created under general international law, i.e. *jus cogens* (and possibly Art. 103 UN Charter). All tribunals and courts have to respect that hierarchy.

UNCLOS can be taken as an example of the "factual hierarchy": a decision delivered under Part XV UNCLOS has to regard norms of UNCLOS as superior to other norms of international law in cases of conflict. If the decision is not delivered under Part XV UNCLOS the outcome may be different as no such hierarchy exists under general international law.

The threat resulting from this aspect of the proliferation of international tribunals is that two conflicting legal orders are imposed on the states parties to a dispute. As Professor Wolfrum has stated in his article on the competing competences of international tribunals, this possibility is a logical consequence of the intentions of the states when setting up the regime.[46]

Where two conflicting legal orders are imposed on a state, it will have to make a choice which order to implement and which to disregard. Commonly, the state will then justify its disregard for one regime by arguing for the necessity of following the obligations imposed by the other, conflicting, regime. But which decision will a state follow? If it makes a rational choice the state will examine the consequences of disregarding the regime. Some regimes boast strong enforcement mechanisms with the possibility of sanctions; others are enforced by shaming states into compliance. Rationally, a state will follow the regime with the stronger enforcement mechanism. A hierarchy that is entirely different from the traditional notion of hierarchy in international law, namely *jus cogens*, arises from such conflicts: A factual hierarchy of regimes.

4. Solutions

Several approaches to how to counteract this factual hierarchy of regimes and how to prevent situations in which states have an incentive to

[46] R. Wolfrum, "Konkurrierende Zuständigkeiten internationaler Streitentscheidungsinstanzen: Notwendigkeit für Lösungsmöglichkeiten und deren Grenzen", in: N. Ando et al. (eds.), *Liber Amicorum Judge Shigeru Oda*, 2002, 651, 656.

uphold a regime with a strong enforcement mechanism (such as WTO law) over one with a weak enforcement mechanism (such as the ICCPR[47]) are conceivable.

The first solution that lends itself to the issue is to provide for specific rules regulating the relationship between the dispute settlement systems of different regimes. Thus Art. 2005 NAFTA[48] explicitly and in detail describes the relationship between NAFTA and GATT[49] dispute resolution, explaining when a party is allowed to resort to which of the two *fora*. However, the provision has to be drafted with appropriate care. The provision that states parties will not "submit a dispute concerning the interpretation or application of this Treaty to any method of settlement other than those provided for therein"[50] may not be sufficient, as Judge Wolfrum's Separate Opinion in the *Mox Plant* Case[51] illustrates. Even where different regimes overlap and the dispute is submitted to several tribunals for each regime the dispute remains a dispute concerning the application of that regime.

As an alternative, an appeal from specialized dispute resolution mechanisms to a more general dispute resolution mechanism, e.g. the ICJ, could be provided for.[52] Whereas the specialized body would have to rule under its own regime and give preference to the rules of that regime, the ICJ could apply the general international law rules on conflicts of norms and thereby reach an outcome that takes account of the general international law relationship between the two regimes. However, this solution is not now and probably will not be the law for a long time to come. The reason is simple: states entrench regimes and fix the applicable law for a reason. They want preference to be given to a

47 International Covenant on Civil and Political Rights.

48 The North American Free Trade Agreement.

49 General Agreement on Tariffs and Trade.

50 Art. 292 Treaty Establishing the European Community.

51 ITLOS, *The MOX Plant Case (Ireland v. United Kingdom)*, Case No. 10, Separate Opinion of Judge Wolfrum.

52 Guillaume suggested a procedure allowing the ICJ to rule on preliminary questions submitted by specialized international courts, G. Guillaume, *Speech by His Excellency Judge Gilbert Guillaume, President of the International Court of Justice, to the Sixth Committee of the General Assembly of the United Nations* (31 October 2001), available at http://library.lawschool.cornell.edu/cijwww/icjwww/ipresscom/SPEECHES/iSpeechPresident_Guillaume_6thCommittee_2001.htm.

set of rules, they want specialized regimes, why else would they establish such a preference? The factual hierarchy of regimes is a logical result of the decisions of the states that set up the regimes: why else would states endow one regime with a strong and the other with a weak enforcement mechanism?

This leaves another, softer and less clear approach as the only viable solution to the problem of "factual hierarchy": interpretation and cooperation.

According to Art. 31 (1) of the Vienna Convention on the Law of Treaties "[a] treaty shall be interpreted in good faith in accordance with the ordinary meaning to be given to the terms of the treaty in their context and in the light of its object and purpose." Together with the context a tribunal will, according to Art. 31 (3) (c), have to take into account "any relevant rules of international law applicable in the relations between the parties." The importance of this norm within the context of the often lamented fragmentation of international law has recently been stressed by Koskenniemi in his report for the ILC.[53] It can be illustrated by the famous WTO *Shrimp-Turtle* case in which the interpretation of Art. XX (g) GATT was at issue. Art. XX GATT exempts certain measures from compliance with the GATT regime if they fulfill the requirements of the *chapeau* of Art. XX GATT and pursue one of the listed policy goals. Art. XX (g) GATT names the "conservation of exhaustible natural resources" as one of these policy goals. The question the Appellate Body had to answer was whether this meant only non-living, e.g. mineral resources, or included living resources at well. Explicitly referring to other international treaties such as UNCLOS and the Convention on International Trade in Endangered Species of Wild Fauna and Flora (CITES), the Appellate Body held that living resources were included.[54] The case illustrates a convincing approach to how conflicts between different regimes can be avoided by interpreting one regime with

[53] M. Koskenniemi, *Fragmentation of International Law: Difficulties Arising from the Diversification and Expansion of International Law. Report of the Study Group of the International Law Commission*, UN Doc. A/CN.4/L.682 (13 April 2006); see also ILC, *Conclusions of the Work of the Study Group on the Fragmentation of International Law: Difficulties Arising from the Diversification and Expansion of International Law*, Yearbook of the ILC, 2006, vol. II, Part Two, paras. 17 et seq.

[54] Appellate Body Report, *United States – Import Prohibition of Certain Shrimp and Shrimp Products*, WT/DS58/AB/R, paras. 128 et seq. (12 October 1998).

the help of the provisions of another. It must be emphasized that such an approach is not prevented by the limitation of the applicable law of the tribunals of the regimes: the tribunals do not technically "apply" the law of the other regime. They merely use it as an aid in the interpretation of the laws of their own regime. To come back to the statement of the WTO Appellate Body cited above: one regime cannot be read "in clinical isolation" from the other.

In addition to using law stemming from regimes other than the one under which a tribunal was set up as an aid to interpreting the norms of its own regime, a tribunal should develop a relationship of "cooperation" with the tribunals of other regimes. It is hard to pinpoint what exactly such a relationship entails. The *Bundesverfassungsgericht* (German Constitutional Court) used the notion to describe its relationship with the ECJ[55] and Anne-Marie Slaughter develops a similar idea in her book on "A New World Order".[56] As the notion is particularly vague let me set out a number of tenets that I consider it to entail:

- Respect for the work of other tribunals, i.e. one tribunal may not simply discard or disregard findings of another international body on similar facts without discussion
- Cross-fertilization of jurisprudence, i.e. wherever possible one tribunal should follow the finding of another tribunal on questions of international law, particularly where the other tribunal is ruling on its own specialized regime
- Cross-fertilization of thought processes to prevent a regime-specific mindset from developing in which other values and goals are no longer taken into account

5. Consequences

The suggested approaches could alleviate some of the tension created by the proliferation of international tribunals; however, they cannot resolve the problem entirely. First of all, the development of some form of specialized, regime-specific philosophy within the dispute settlement mechanism of one regime cannot be prevented. Such a philosophy in-

---

55 BVerfGE 89, 155, 175 – Maastricht (see Leitsatz 7).

56 A.-M. Slaughter, *A New World Order*, 2004.

variably leads to conflicts between the findings of tribunals of different regimes. Secondly, regimes at times clash even though the judges did not succumb to any regime-specific tendencies. In those cases an outcome according to the suggested "factual hierarchy" cannot be prevented. But there is no reason to lament this fact as running counter to basic tenets of international law or even threatening the coherence of the international system. The clash between regimes is a logical consequence of states setting up different, and, at times, conflicting regimes of different strength. While we may, and at times certainly do, disagree with their judgment this is the law the states have made – incoherent as it at times is.

For the incoherences that remain we can take consolation from the fact that they are few. Too few to threaten the consistency of public international law and possibly just enough to provide food for thought for scholars of international law.

Genetic Resources of the Deep Sea – How Can They Be Preserved?

Doris König

"I don't know why I don't care about the bottom of the ocean but I don't." This quotation from a famous cartoon[1] probably reflects what many people think about the deep sea and its resources. Until quite recently, it was generally thought that in the "abyss", a cold and dark place in bottomless depths, life could not exist. It was not until 1977 that a marine science expedition discovered densely populated faunal communities along seabed hydrothermal vents 200 miles northwest of

[1] Quoted in: D. K. Leary, *International Law and the Genetic Resources of the Deep Sea*, 2007, 7 and note 1.

Ecuador's Galapagos Islands.[2] Little is still known about life in the deep sea, as humankind is just beginning to understand that it is a world with an amazing diversity of species adapted to extreme conditions. Nevertheless, the deep sea and its genetic resources are coming under increasing pressure from human activity. The discovery of rich biological communities, mineral deposits such as polymetallic sulphides and cobalt crusts, as well as methane hydrate deposits, has generated keen interest from marine scientists, the biotechnology and pharmaceutical industries, mining companies and the tourism sector.[3] While science and technology evolve rapidly, the legal and political regimes usually lag behind. They have to be adapted to deal with the new economic opportunities and ecological threats associated with these innovations.

This paper will focus on activities carried out with regard to genetic resources found in seabed areas *beyond* national jurisdiction. First, a very brief description of the main features of deep seabed ecosystems will be given, followed by an overview of the economic potential of deep-sea genetic resources and human activities threatening deep-sea biodiversity. In the second section, an existing legal gap will be identified with respect to commercially-oriented activities in respect of deep-sea genetic resources such as bioprospecting. Since there is no generally accepted definition of the term "bioprospecting", I will use here the definition given by the Secretariat of the Convention on Biological Diversity (CBD) and referred to in a recent study published by the United Nations University. Accordingly, bioprospecting is "the exploration of biodiversity for commercially valuable genetic and biochemical resources".[4] The legal analysis will concentrate on the provisions of the

---

[2] C. H. Allen, "Protecting the Oceanic Gardens of Eden: International Law Issues in Deep-Sea Vent Resource Conservation and Management", *The Georgetown Int'l Envtl. Law Review* 13 (2001), 563 et seq. (567); J.B. Corliss *et. al.*, "Submarine Thermal Springs at the Galapagos Rift", *Science* 203 (1979), 1073 et seq.

[3] Allen, see note 2, 565 et seq.; M. Baker/B. Bett/D. Billett/A. Rogers, "The Status of Natural Resources on the High-Seas, Part 1 - an Environmental Perspective", in: WWF/IUCN (eds.), *The Status of Natural Resources on the High-Seas,* 2001, 1 et seq. (17); J. Friedland, *Der Schutz der biologischen Vielfalt der Tiefseehydrothermalquellen – ein internationales Regime für die genetischen Tiefseeressourcen*, 2007 (upcoming soon), ch. 1, § 1, C.; J. Halfar/R. M. Fujita, "Precautionary Management of Deep-Sea Mining", *Marine Policy* 26 (2002), 103 et seq. (104).

[4] S. Arico/C. Salpin, *Bioprospecting of Genetic Resources in the Deep Seabed: Scientific, Legal and Policy Aspects*, UNU-IAS Report 2005, 15; with refer-

1982 UN Convention on the Law of the Sea (UNCLOS) and the 1992 Convention on Biological Diversity (CBD). In this respect, interesting insights can be found in a paper written by *Rüdiger Wolfrum* and *Nele Matz* which was published in the United Nations Yearbook in 2000.[5] In the third section, I will outline the legal and political activities currently taking place within the United Nations to close this legal gap. This article concludes with an overview of the various possible options for addressing the issue of deep-sea genetic resources and a preliminary evaluation of such options.

I. Genetic Resources of the Deep Sea – Their Economic Potential and Activities Threatening Their Preservation

1. Various Deep-Sea Ecosystems and Their Economic Potential

The world's oceans can be divided into various ocean realms, two of which are of particular interest in the present context: the realm of active geology and that of hidden boundaries. Areas of active and past volcanic activity, mainly the mid-ocean ridges and seamounts, comprise the realm of active geology. This area contains *hydrothermal vents* mainly found along mid-ocean ridges through which magma from the core of the earth emerges. Hydrothermal vents, often referred to as "black smokers" because of their intense fluid emissions from the ocean floor, support one of the highest densities of animal life on Earth. Approximately 500 species have been discovered around hydrothermal vents, but about 75% of vent species occur at only one site. Different oceans such as the Atlantic and Pacific Oceans play host to different biological communities.[6] Most remarkably, life in the vent ecosystems is based not on photosynthesis, but on chemosynthetic microbial pro-

---

ence to UN Doc. UNEP/CBD/COP/5/INF/7. See also M. Garson, "Biodiversity and Bioprospecting", in: N. Stoianoff (ed.), *Accessing Biological Resources, Complying with the Convention on Biological Diversity*, 2004, 17 et seq.

[5] R. Wolfrum/N. Matz, "The Interplay of the United Nations Convention on the Law of the Sea and the Convention on Biological Diversity", *UNYB* 4 (2000), 445 et seq.

[6] L. Glowka, "The Deepest of Ironies: Genetic Resources, Marine Scientific Research, and the Area", *Ocean Yearbook* 12 (1996), 154 et seq. (158); Leary, see note 1, 13 et seq.

cesses.[7] In other words, life develops from chemical energy rather than sunlight. All vents are characterised by extreme conditions, i.e. extremely high pressure due to the depths at which they are located, extremely high temperatures and pH values, and extreme salinity and toxicity due to the minerals that escape from the earth's crust. The main characteristic of species found at hydrothermal vents is their tolerance to these extreme conditions, a fact which makes them particularly attractive to chemical, pharmaceutical and biotech industries.[8] *Seamounts* are the remains of past geological activity. They are millions of years old, and they are characterised by active water circulation processes which result in a great richness of species, such as deep sea corals and sponges. They are also visited by several species of fish of commercial interest, such as swordfish, tuna, sharks, turtles and whales.[9] Recent studies indicate that there are more seamount species yet to be discovered than have been found so far.[10]

The so-called realm of hidden boundaries consists of unstable sediments of the continental slopes and of the sediments of the abyssal plain. This realm plays host to ecosystems known as *cold seeps*, soft-bottom areas where water, oil and gases seep out of the sediment. Again, microorganisms exist under extreme conditions caused by high pressure and high levels of toxicity. Unlike in hydrothermal vents, temperatures are moderate. Sometimes, cold seeps are associated with so-called "brine pools", i.e. lakes at the bottom of the ocean with an extremely high degree of salinity, mud volcanoes, and methane hydrates. These particular geological formations provide conditions in which various biological communities thrive.[11] Despite considerable ecological and biological differences between hydrothermal vents and cold seeps, the latter are of similar scientific and commercial interest because their

---

[7] J. F. Grassle, "Introduction to the Biology of Hydrothermal Vents", in: P. Rona *et al.* (eds), *Hydrothermal Processes at Seafloor Spreading Centers*, 1983, 665 et seq. (667); Halfar/Fujita, see note 3, 104; K. Sawyer, "Tauchfahrt zum Quell des Lebens", *Geo Wissen* 24 (1999), 54 et seq. (60 et seq.).

[8] Allen, see note 2, 584; Arico/Salpin, see note 4, 9 et seq.

[9] Baker/Bett/Billett/Rogers, see note 3, 24 et seq.; K. Gjerde, *Towards a Strategy for High Seas Marine Protected Areas, Proceedings of the IUCN, WCPA and WWF Experts Workshop on High Seas Marine Protected Areas, 15-17 January 2003, Malaga, Spain*, 5 et seq.

[10] Arico/Salpin, see note 4, 11.

[11] L. Glowka, "Genetic Resources, Marine Scientific Research and the International Seabed Area", *RECIEL* 8 (1999), 56 et seq. (57).

inhabitant species are also adapted to extreme conditions of depth and toxicity.[12]

Species found in deep seabed ecosystems, mentioned above, are not only of keen interest to marine scientific research, but they are also of considerable economic value. They offer huge potential for exploitation for commercial purposes. Industry sectors involved in the exploration of deep-sea genetic resources include biotechnology, waste treatment, agriculture, and the pharmaceutical and cosmetics industry.[13] These sectors are increasingly using biotechnology to develop new products. Early estimates of the commercial value of enzymes from high heat-loving microbes which could be applied in waste treatment, food processing, oil well services, paper processing and mining range from USD 600 million to USD three billion per year.[14] Today the role of biotechnology in the health care industry is steadily increasing. Pharmaceutical companies, for instance, enter into cooperation agreements with biotech companies, academic researchers, non-profit-making institutions, medical centres and foundations in order to develop new drugs. Innovative technologies, such as genomics – the study of genes and their functions – and bioinformatics – the application of information technologies to biodiversity studies and their applications – facilitate access to relevant information and are likely to reduce R & D costs.[15] It has to be pointed out that the ratio of potentially useful natural compounds to compounds already screened is higher in marine-sourced materials than in terrestrial organisms. Accordingly, marine genetic resources promise a higher probability of commercial success. Not surprisingly, all major pharmaceutical companies have marine biology departments. Estimates put worldwide sales of marine biotechnology-related products at USD 100 billion for the year 2000. It is, therefore, a safe guess that deep-sea genetic resources will be increasingly undergoing bioprospecting activities, and that the economic value of marine-sourced biotech products

---

12 Arico/Salpin, see note 4, 9.

13 Allen, see note 2, 583 et seq.; Arico/Salpin, see note 4, 25; Garson, see note 4, 19.

14 Allen, see note 2, 565; D. Anton, "Law for the Sea's Biological Diversity", *CJTL* 36 (1997), 341 et seq. (349) and L. Glowka, "Beyond the Deepest of Ironies: Genetic Resources, Marine Scientific Research and International Seabed Area", in: J.-P. Beurier/A. Kiss/S. Mahmoudi (eds), *New Technologies and Law of the Marine Environment*, 2000, 75 et seq. (79), with further reference.

15 Arico/Salpin, see note 4, 26.

will rise significantly in the next few years.[16] It should be kept in mind, though, that marine research in general, and deep-sea marine research in particular, is extremely expensive because of the high costs of the sophisticated technology needed for sampling and for laboratory investigation. The odds on commercial success are slim. For these reasons, research is increasingly conducted by multinational public research institutions and by public-private partnerships.[17] Almost all of the institutions involved come from industrial countries such as the United States, Australia and New Zealand, the EU Member States and Japan. This, of course, raises the question of benefit-sharing with the developing world which will be referred to later.

2. Activities Threatening the Preservation of Deep-Sea Biodiversity

Several human activities are increasingly threatening the preservation of deep-sea biodiversity. Among them are deep-sea fisheries, seabed mining, oil and gas exploration and exploitation, waste disposal and carbon sequestration, tourism, marine scientific research activities, and bioprospecting. The focus will be on the last two, because marine research and bioprospecting are the activities which currently most affect the deep-sea ecosystems, mentioned above.[18] What is the difference between those two? There is no commonly accepted definition of marine scientific research (MSR). The term is defined neither in UNCLOS nor in the CBD. A study prepared by the Secretariat of the CBD and the UN Division for Ocean Affairs and the Law of the Sea (UNDOALOS) on the relationship between the CBD and UNCLOS stated that "marine scientific research could be defined as an activity that involves collection and analysis of information, data or samples aimed at increasing humankind's knowledge of the environment, and is not undertaken with the intent of economic gain".[19]

---

[16] Arico/Salpin, see note 4, 27; Leary, see note 1, 158 et seq.

[17] H. Korn/S. Friedrich/U. Feit, *Deep Sea Genetic Resources in the Context of the Convention on Biological Diversity and the United Nations Convention on the Law of the Sea*, 2003, 19 et seq.; Arico/Salpin, see note 4, 27.

[18] L. Glowka, "Putting Marine Scientific Research on a Sustainable Footing at Hydrothermal Vents", *Marine Policy* 27 (2003), 303 et seq. (304); Leary, see note 1, 26 and 183.

[19] Study of the Relationship between the Convention on Biological Diversity and the United Nations Convention on the Law of the Sea with Regard to

Part of bioprospecting, as mentioned above, is also the collection of samples, information and data. It differs from marine scientific research in that it is undertaken with the aim of estimating the economic potential of the resource prior to commercialisation. Since both activities have the same object, namely collecting and analysing biological organisms, the distinction between them depends on the intention behind them and their purpose.[20] In theory, this distinction seems to be quite clear. In practice, however, the distinction is blurred because marine scientific research and commercial interests are closely related. Since sample collection on the deep seabed involves a high degree of skill and expensive technology, it usually relies on government funding. Sometimes it is funded by public-private partnerships to share the risk and cover the expense. Once the samples have been extracted from the deep sea, there is close cooperation between research institutions and industrial laboratories. Sometimes governments encourage research exchange between academic researchers and industry, or marine scientific researchers have signed consultancy contracts with certain biotech companies to share their data.[21] Generally speaking, the results of publicly funded research are openly published in scientific journals, whereas the results of privately funded research are kept confidential until after patent applications have been filed.[22] A future legal regime regulating these activities has to keep this close interrelationship between academia and industry in mind.

Both marine scientific research and bioprospecting activities can have an adverse environmental impact. Research vessels and the use of submersibles and remotely operated vehicles (ROVs) to extract samples can cause disturbance in the water column and on the deep seabed, especially with frequent visits and repeated sampling in the same areas.[23] Light, noise and heat associated with such research activities could cause stress to the biological organisms of the deep sea. Disturbance

---

the Conservation and Sustainable Use of Genetic Resources on the Deep Seabed, UN Doc. UNEP/CBD/SBSTTA/8/INF/3/Rev.1 (hereafter referred to as CBD-DOALOS Study).

20 Arico/Salpin, see note 4, 16; Glowka, see note 14, 81.

21 Examples are given by Leary, see note 1, 167 et seq.; Glowka, see note 14, 81 et seq.

22 Leary, see note 1, 168.

23 For the substantial impact of marine scientific research on the deep sea environment Allen, see note 2, 574 et seq. and Korn/Friedrich/Feit, see note 17, 19 et seq.

from sediment removal or spreading, the deposit of debris, chemical contamination or the introduction of alien species carried by underwater vehicles are even greater threats to deep-sea biodiversity. Such environmental impacts could lead to a decrease in population numbers or even the extinction of certain species. It has to be pointed out, though, that the environmental impact of marine scientific research is still unclear and more research is needed. Currently, only very few processes exist for considering the environmental impact of research activities when scientists plan research cruises.[24] Thus, an environmental impact assessment should become part of a future legal regime.

II. Current Legal Framework

Two international instruments are most relevant to the issue of the genetic resources of the deep sea: the UN Convention on the Law of the Sea and the Convention on Biological Diversity. Other instruments will be mentioned only in passing.

1. The United Nations Convention on the Law of the Sea

The UN Convention on the Law of the Sea (UNCLOS)[25] does not use the terms "biodiversity" or "genetic resources". Often referred to as the "Constitution for the Oceans", UNCLOS establishes a legal order for all activities in the oceans and promotes the conservation of their living resources and the protection and preservation of the marine environment.[26] Since this article focuses on the genetic resources of the deep sea beyond national jurisdiction, the legal analysis will be limited to Part XI of UNCLOS setting up a special regime for the Area and its resources, Part VII containing provisions on the legal regime of living resources of the High Seas, and Part XIII regulating marine scientific research.

---

[24] Report of the Secretary-General "Oceans and the Law of the Sea", UN Doc. A/60/63/Add.1 of 15 July 2005, 43 et seq.; Leary, see note 1, 189 et seq.

[25] United Nations Convention on the Law of the Sea, UN Doc. A/CONF.62/122 (1982), 1833 UNTS 397.

[26] Preamble of UNCLOS.

a) The Area and Its Resources

Under UNCLOS, the seabed and ocean floor and subsoil thereof beyond the limits of national jurisdiction have been designated as "the Area" (Article 1 para. 1 (1)). Part XI and the 1994 Implementing Agreement Relating to Part XI UNCLOS[27] establish a special legal regime for the Area. The Area and its resources are "the common heritage of mankind" (Article 136). A state can neither claim nor exercise sovereignty over any part of the Area or its resources, nor can it or any person appropriate any part thereof (Article 137 para. 1). The term "resources" is, however, confined to "all solid, liquid or gaseous *mineral* resources *in situ* in the Area or beneath the seabed, including polymetallic nodules" (Article 133 lit. a). Living marine resources are not included.

The International Seabed Authority (ISA) is the organisation through which the States organise and control all activities in the Area, which are to be carried out for the benefit of mankind (Article 140 para. 1). The ISA is to provide for the equitable sharing of financial and other economic benefits deriving from activities in the Area (Article 140 para. 2). At first glance, this would suggest that the ISA could regulate all activities in the Area, including marine scientific research and bioprospecting. The term "activities in the Area" is, however, very narrowly defined as "all activities of exploration for, and exploitation of, the resources of the Area" (Article 1 para. 1 (3)). From these provisions it can be inferred that the living resources of the deep seabed and its subsoil are not included in the specific legal regime for the Area. They are not part of the common heritage of mankind as elaborated in Part XI of UNCLOS.[28]

Does that mean that the ISA has no competence whatsoever to adopt regulations with regard to the preservation of deep-sea biodiversity and its genetic resources? The ISA's competence to regulate deep-sea mining includes the ability to adopt rules to prevent, reduce and control pollution of the marine environment (Article 145 lit. a) and to protect and preserve the natural resources of the Area and prevent damage to its

---

27 Agreement Relating to the Implementation of Part XI of UNCLOS of 10 December 1982, UN Doc. A/RES/48/263/Annex (48); ILM 33 (1994), 1309.

28 Allen, see note 2, 630; R. R. Churchill/A. V. Lowe, *The Law of the Sea*, 3rd ed., 1999, 239 and note 49; G. Dahm/J. Delbrück/R. Wolfrum, *Völkerrecht*, vol. I/2, 2nd ed., 2002, 410; R.-J. Dupuy/D. Vignes, *A Handbook on the New Law of the Sea*, vol. I, 1991, 594 et seq.; Wolfrum/Matz, see note 5, 451 et seq.

flora and fauna (Article 145 lit. b). In the context of the provisions mentioned above, these supplementary competences to regulate pollution and protect the deep-sea flora and fauna are limited to activities associated with mining. Accordingly, the ISA has adopted "Regulations on Prospecting and Exploration for Polymetallic Nodules" in 2000[29] and is currently working on "Draft Regulations on Prospecting and Exploration for Polymetallic Sulphides and Cobalt-rich Ferromanganese Crusts". Both Regulations provide that contractors are to make proposals for areas to be set aside and used exclusively as impact reference zones and preservation reference zones. "Impact reference zones" are areas to be used for assessing the effect of mining activities on the marine environment. "Preservation reference zones" are areas where mining is prohibited in order to assess any changes in the flora and fauna of the marine environment.[30] If the ISA designated such reference zones these areas would come close to marine protected areas.[31] Thus the ISA could contribute to the preservation of deep-sea biodiversity. It has to be noted, though, that the ISA has no mandate to prohibit or control activities other than those associated with mining. Consequently, the ISA has no regulatory and enforcement competences with regard to other activities on the deep seabed.[32]

b) The Freedom of the High Seas and Marine Scientific Research

Since Part XI is not applicable to marine living resources and their genetic components, they are covered by the high seas regime of Part VII UNCLOS.[33] The activities, mentioned above, may either fall under the

---

[29] UN Doc. ISBA/6/A/18 (2000). For details about the "Regulations on Prospecting and Exploration for Polymetallic Nodules" see E. D. Brown, *Sea-Bed Energy and Minerals: The International Legal Regime, Vol. 2, Sea-Bed Mining,* 2001, 152 et seq. and 398 et seq.; M. C. Wood, "International Seabed Authority: The First Four Years", *Max Planck UNYB* 3 (1999), 173 et seq.

[30] Regulation 31 (7) of the Nodule Prospecting Regulations viz. Regulation 33 (4) of the Draft Polymetallic Sulphide Prospecting Regulations.

[31] Leary, see note 1, 219 et seq., refers to "de-facto marine protected areas".

[32] Friedland, see note 3, ch. 2, § 6, B. V. 2. and ch. 5, § 16, B. I.; Leary, see note 1, 220; Wolfrum/Matz, see note 5, 455.

[33] Allen, see note 2, 628 et seq.; Korn/Friedrich/Feit, see note 17, 40 et seq.; N. Matz, "Marine Biological Resources: Some Reflections on Concepts for the Protection and Sustainable Use of Biological Resources in the Deep Sea", *Non-State Actors and Int. Law* 2 (2002), 279 et seq. (289).

freedom of scientific research (Article 87 para. 1 lit. f) or may be characterised as some other use encompassed by the freedom of the high seas. Accordingly, the deep-sea genetic resources are freely accessible. They are subject only to the reasonable use clause (Article 87 para. 2) and the general principles set out in Part XII dealing with the protection and preservation of the marine environment. The provisions on the management and conservation of marine living resources on the high seas are not appropriate though, because they are tailored to limiting the freedom of fishing and nothing else. They do not match the requirements for the management and preservation of deep-sea biodiversity and its genetic resources. Part VII of UNCLOS provides an inadequate framework for access to, conservation and management of deep-sea genetic resources beyond national jurisdiction.

Are there, nevertheless, any limitations on marine scientific research and bioprospecting under the high seas regime? Marine scientific research is regulated in Part XIII of UNCLOS. According to Articles 256 and 257, all States have the right to conduct marine scientific research in the Area and in the water column beyond the limits of the exclusive economic zone. This right is subject to some general principles set out in Article 240, *inter alia*, to have due respect for other legitimate uses of the sea and to protect and preserve the marine environment. Articles 242 to 244 spell out a duty to promote international cooperation in marine scientific research and actively to promote the flow of scientific data and information and the transfer of knowledge resulting from marine scientific research, to developing States in particular. As already mentioned, the term "marine scientific research" is not defined in UNCLOS. From Article 246 paras. 3 and 5 it can be inferred that the term comprises so-called pure scientific research, i.e. research undertaken to enhance humankind's knowledge of the marine environment, and so-called applied scientific research, i.e. research that is oriented towards commercial use. Bioprospecting could be characterised as applied scientific research, thus falling under Part XIII of UNCLOS.[34]

Even if one wants to distinguish between marine scientific research, which is generally open to publication and dissemination of its results, and bioprospecting, the results of which are usually kept confidential, it does not make much of a difference in the end. The obligations of States under Part XIII do not go much further than the general obligations which derive from the reasonable-use clause in Part VII. The same *cum grano salis* is true for marine scientific research in the Area which is also

[34] Wolfrum/Matz, see note 5, 456 et seq.

open to all States (Article 256 UNCLOS). According to Article 143 para. 1, which refers back to the provisions of Part XIII, it has to be carried out "exclusively for peaceful purposes and for the benefit of mankind as a whole". States parties are to promote international cooperation in marine scientific research in the Area by, *inter alia*, effectively disseminating the results of research and analysis when available, through the ISA or other international channels (Article 143 para. 3 lit. c). Accordingly, the ISA, which itself may conduct marine scientific research in the Area, is responsible for coordinating research activities and disseminating their results (Article 143 para. 2). As already mentioned, the ISA has, however, no competence to regulate or restrict marine scientific research in the Area because its mandate is limited to the regulation of activities associated with mining.[35]

In sum, the UNCLOS provisions on marine scientific research (Part XIII) aim predominantly at the distribution of jurisdictional powers between coastal States and States conducting research. They are not suitable for the management of marine genetic resources because they lack a protective component with regard to the object of research.[36] This is even more true for the provisions on the freedom of the high seas in Part VII. Under the UNCLOS regime, access to the genetic resources of the deep sea is free and it is up to each State to regulate marine scientific research and bioprospecting conducted by its nationals or by research vessels flying its flag. Since the common-heritage principle does not apply, there is no obligation to share benefits derived from deep-sea genetic resources.

2. The Convention on Biological Diversity

The provisions of UNCLOS must be read in conjunction with the provisions of the Convention on Biological Diversity.[37] Does the CBD fill

---

[35] Leary, see note 1, 209 et seq.; T. Scovazzi, "Mining, Protection of the Environment, Scientific Research and Bioprospection: Some Considerations on the Role of the International Sea-Bed Authority", *IJMCL* 19 (2004), 383 et seq. (384).

[36] Wolfrum/Matz, see note 5, 458 and 470; Korn/Friedrich/Feit, see note 17, 51 et seq.

[37] United Nations Convention on Biological Diversity, UN Doc. DPI/130/7 (1992), Treaty Doc. 20, 103rd Cong., 1st Sess. (1993), ILM 31 (1992), 818.

the gap left by UNCLOS with regard to the sustainable use of deep-sea genetic resources, the preservation of deep-sea biodiversity, and benefit-sharing? The CBD has three main objectives: the conservation of biological diversity, the sustainable use of its components and the fair and equitable sharing of the benefits arising out of the utilisation of genetic resources (Article 1). States parties must pursue the conservation of biodiversity by establishing a system of protection areas or areas where special measures need to be taken and promoting the protection of ecosystems, natural habitats and the maintenance of viable populations of species in natural surroundings (Article 8). To achieve these goals, the CBD provides for economic incentives. States with genetic resources may bargain access to them against the sharing of benefits derived from their use (Article 15, Arts 16 and 19). The underlying premise is that host States which will obtain part of the benefits have an interest in preserving biodiversity and in using genetic resources in a sustainable manner.[38]

The jurisdictional scope of the CBD is, however, limited to components of biodiversity found in areas within the limits of national jurisdiction (Article 4 lit. a). Accordingly, deep-sea genetic resources beyond national jurisdiction, i.e. on the high seas and in the Area, are excluded from direct conservation measures and benefit-sharing mechanisms. Nevertheless, the CBD applies to "processes and activities" carried out under the jurisdiction and control of a State party irrespective of where they take place (Article 4 lit. b). These processes and activities include marine scientific research and bioprospecting carried out in the Area. State parties to the CBD may regulate these activities in areas beyond national jurisdiction if they are conducted by their nationals or by ships flying their flags. It has to be noted, though, that an obligation to regulate can be assumed only if such processes and activities have or are likely to have a significant adverse impact on biodiversity (Article 8 lit. l in connection with Article 7 lit. c).[39]

The limited jurisdictional scope of the CBD is in conformity with UNCLOS provisions on State jurisdiction on the high seas and the

---

[38] B. Kellersmann, *Die gemeinsame, aber differenzierte Verantwortlichkeit von Industriestaaten und Entwicklungsländern für den Schutz der globalen Umwelt*, 2000, 211; Wolfrum/Matz, see note 5, 460 et seq.; R. Wolfrum, "The Convention on Biological Diversity: Using State Jurisdiction as a Means of Ensuring Compliance", in: R. Wolfrum (ed.), *Enforcing Environmental Standards: Economic Mechanisms as Viable Means?*, 1996, 372 et seq. (382).

[39] Arico/Salpin, see note 4, 38 and 56.

deep seabed. To date, no State party has regulated marine scientific research or bioprospecting carried out by its nationals or vessels in areas beyond its national jurisdiction.[40] In this respect, States parties are only required to cooperate directly or through competent international organisations for the conservation and sustainable use of biodiversity in these areas (Article 5). In sum, the CBD system of access to genetic resources and benefit-sharing is not applicable to deep-sea genetic resources in areas beyond national jurisdiction. Hence, the 2002 Bonn Guidelines on Access to Genetic Resources and Benefit-Sharing[41] cannot be applied either. Deep-sea genetic resources are, therefore, freely accessible under the CBD too, and their exploitation and use are unregulated. The CBD does not fill the gap left by UNCLOS.

At the Jakarta meeting in 1995, the Conference of the Parties (COP) requested the CBD Secretariat, in conjunction with the UN Division for Ocean Affairs and the Law of the Sea (DOALOS), to undertake a study of the relationship between the CBD and UNCLOS with regard to the conservation and sustainable use of genetic resources on the deep seabed.[42] This study, which was presented in 2003, came to the conclusion that neither UNCLOS nor the CBD provides a specific legal regime for commercially-oriented activities relating to marine genetic resources in the high seas and in the Area.[43]. It stressed the need to develop such a legal regime, and suggested three options for addressing the issue:

(1) maintaining the status quo and leaving the exploitation of deep seabed genetic resources unregulated;

(2) extending the UNCLOS regime of the Area to deep seabed genetic resources, which would entail an extension of the common-heritage principle and the competences of the ISA; and

40 Arico/Salpin, see note 4, 38; Leary, see note 1, 52.

41 Bonn Guidelines on Access to Genetic Resources and Fair and Equitable Sharing of the Benefits Arising Out of their Utilisation, Annex to COP Decision VI/24. See also C. Godt, „Von der Biopiraterie zum Biodiversitätsregime – Die sog. Bonner Leitlinien als Zwischenschritt zu einem CBD-Regime über Zugang und Vorteilsausgleich", *ZUR* 16 (2004), 202 et seq.

42 COP Decision II/10 „Conservation and Sustainable Use of Marine and Coastal Biological Diversity", para 12.

43 CBD-DOALOS Study, see note 19, para. 103.

(3) amending the CBD to bring deep seabed genetic resources within its framework.[44]

In addition, the study mentioned two more options which were not examined in detail, namely the establishment of Marine Protected Areas (MPAs)[45] on the high seas, and intellectual property rights as incentives for benefit sharing and sustainable management.[46] With regard to MPAs, it has to be pointed out that no State or international organisation has jurisdiction formally to establish such protected areas on the high seas. An international agreement in this respect would not be binding on third States (Article 34 VCLT).[47]

With regard to intellectual property rights (IPRs), it should be noted that this issue is extremely relevant in the context of the utilisation of marine genetic resources.[48] The granting of patents is important because they stimulate commercial innovation and ensure that those expending effort and cost to access deep-sea genetic resources will be rewarded for developing a new invention. In most national jurisdictions the patentability of biotechnology is now largely accepted.[49] Several international treaties are also relevant in this context. But these instruments lack a clear definition of what can be considered micro-organisms or resources suitable for patentability. Furthermore, as currently designed, patent classification systems and databases do not permit the tracking and identification of marine micro-organisms.[50] Therefore, issues for discussion within the World Intellectual Property Organisation (WIPO) and at the Doha Round concerning the Agreement on Trade-Related Aspects of Intellectual Property Rights (TRIPS) have been the patentability of biological inventions and new life forms, the interrelation of access to genetic resources and disclosure requirements in patent

---

44 CBD-DOALOS Study, see note 19, para. 72.

45 On the establishment of Marine Protected Areas see, in general K. Castringius, *Meeresschutzgebiete – Die völkerrechtliche Zulässigkeit mariner Natura 2000-Gebiete*, 2006; D. Czybulka/P. Kersandt, *Rechtsvorschriften, rechtliche Instrumentarien und zuständige Körperschaften mit Relevanz für marine Schutzgebiete in der Ausschließlichen Wirtschaftszone und auf Hoher See des OSPAR-Konventionsgebiets*, 2000, and Gjerde, see note 9.

46 CBD-DOALOS Study, see note 19, para. 120 et seq.

47 Wolfrum/Matz, see note 5, 468.

48 Glowka, see note 6, 174 et seq.

49 Leary, see note 1, 171 et seq.

50 Arico/Salpin, see note 4, 42 et seq. and 56.

applications, and intellectual property aspects of genetic resources and equitable benefit-sharing arrangements.[51] These discussions, aiming at an adaptation of the relevant treaties have not yet been concluded.

III. Current Activities within the United Nations

In recent years the General Assembly of the United Nations has annually addressed issues relating to the conservation and sustainable use of marine ecosystems and biodiversity, both within and beyond national jurisdiction. In 1999, it established an *Open-Ended Informal Consultative Process* (ICP)[52] to undertake annual reviews in oceans affairs. At its fifth meeting in 2004, the ICP heard a presentation on the types of uses of deep seabed biological resources including bioprospecting and discussed their legal status. It became clear that the issue was highly contentious. Conflicting views ranged from regarding deep-sea genetic resources as the common heritage of mankind which ought to be dealt with under the regime for the Area to upholding the freedom of marine scientific research on the high seas and maintaining the *status quo*.[53] At its 59th session in 2004, the General Assembly established an *Ad hoc Open-ended Informal Working Group* to study issues relating to the conservation and sustainable use of marine biological diversity beyond areas of national jurisdiction.[54] The Secretary-General was requested to report on these issues in order to assist the Working Group in preparing its agenda. This report came to the conclusion that new measures and regulatory mechanisms should be considered and that the legal status of the deep-sea genetic resources and the nature of the activities relating to them should be clarified.[55]

The *Ad hoc Open-ended Informal Working Group* held its first meeting in February 2006. Again conflicting views on the status of deep-sea ge-

---

[51] See for more details the 2005 Report of the Secretary-General, see note 24, 73 et seq.; Arico/Salpin, see note 4, 41 et seq.; Leary, see note 1, 172 et seq.

[52] UN Doc. A/RES/54/33 of 24 November 1999; the 2007 annual ICP meeting will focus on marine genetic resources.

[53] Report on the work of the United Nations Open-ended Informal Consultative Process on Oceans and the Law of the Sea at its fifth meeting, UN Doc. A/59/122.

[54] UN Doc. A/RES/59/24.

[55] 2005 Report of the Secretary-General, see note 24, 76, paras. 314 and 315.

netic resources and the need for a new regime to regulate their exploration and exploitation were offered. Whereas some delegations were in favour of expanding the mandate of the ISA and establishing a benefit-sharing mechanism, others suggested that the issue could be addressed through the development of guidelines, codes of conduct, and impact assessment.[56] In the summary of trends prepared by the Co-Chairpersons, it was stated that there is a need to study and determine whether there is a governance gap in marine areas beyond national jurisdiction. The Working Group concluded that further discussion will be needed in order to clarify how deep-sea genetic resources should be regulated and whether new tools are required, including the consideration of access and benefit-sharing.[57]

IV. Options

The analysis of UNCLOS and the CBD has revealed that currently there is no adequate legal regime for the conservation of deep-sea marine biodiversity and the sustainable use of its genetic resources. Therefore, maintaining the *status quo* is not an option. On the contrary, the lack of clear legal provisions on access to deep-sea genetic resources might be a deterrent to future researchers and investors. In addition, it has to be kept in mind that the preservation of biological diversity and its components is a prerequisite for any future marine scientific research or bioprospecting activity. Open access usually leads to over-exploitation and the ensuing degradation of the resource. This phenomenon is called "tragedy of the commons" and, with a view to high seas fisheries, it should be avoided. Finally, the "first come, first served" approach favours a small number of States which have the technology and financial resources to access deep-sea genetic resources. Other States, and developing countries in particular, would be left out.[58] Consequently, there is a need for a new legal regime which should take into account that biological diversity has an intrinsic value and that its conservation is the

56 Report of the Ad Hoc Open-ended Informal Working Group to study issues relating to the conservation and sustainable use of marine biological diversity beyond areas of national jurisdiction, UN Doc. A/61/65 of 20 March 2006, 18 et seq.

57 Ibid., Annex I, 22, paras. 11 and 12.

58 For more details see Arico/Salpin, see note 4, 58.

"common concern of humankind".[59] For this reason, private appropriation of deep-sea genetic resources under the high seas freedoms regime does not seem to be adequate.[60] In view of the contribution genetic resources could make to the advancement of scientific knowledge and human welfare, access to deep-sea genetic resources should be linked to the publication and dissemination of research results and to benefit-sharing deriving from their commercialisation. It should be noted that both Part XI of UNCLOS and the CBD are based on the underlying idea of access in exchange for benefit-sharing. The next two options mentioned in the CBD-DOALOS study are an expansion of Part XI of UNCLOS to include deep seabed genetic resources or an amendment to the CBD.

1. Amendment to the CBD

The CBD and the Bonn Guidelines provide a legal framework regulating access to terrestrial and marine genetic resources and benefit-sharing, including the transfer of technology and exchange of information. Issues discussed in CBD *fora* are also of relevance to deep seabed genetic resources. The problem is, however, that the CBD conservation approach is based on national sovereignty. Accordingly, access and benefit-sharing are regulated in bilateral agreements between the host State and the user State. As mentioned already, the philosophy behind this system is the assumption that a host State which participates in benefit-sharing will, in its own interest, adopt all measures necessary to preserve biodiversity in areas under its jurisdiction and ensure the sustainable use of its genetic resources. This state-centred model does not work in areas beyond national jurisdiction. An adaptation of this model to such areas seems not to be possible. It would entail the establishment of a central institution which would authorise access to deep-sea genetic resources, adopt rules on the conservation of deep-sea marine ecosystems, and make the necessary arrangements for benefit-sharing and the transfer of technology. A CBD institution endowed with such competences would, however, be inconsistent with the current provisions of UNCLOS and customary law. According to Article 22 para. 2 CBD,

---

59 See the Preamble of the Convention on Biological Diversity.

60 Anton, see note 14, 361; Arico/Salpin, see note 4, 53 et seq.; E. Canal-Forgues, "Les Ressources Génétiques des Grands Fonds Marins ne relevant d'aucune Juridiction Nationale", *ADM* 8 (2003), 99 et seq. (107 et seq.).

the implementation of the CBD has to be consistent with the rights and obligations of States under the law of the sea. In cases of conflict, therefore, the law of the sea prevails. For these reasons, an amendment or the adoption of a Protocol to the CBD does not seem to be a promising option.

2. Expansion of Part XI of UNCLOS to Deep Seabed Genetic Resources

The second option, i.e. the expansion of the common heritage regime of the Area to deep seabed genetic resources, seems to be more promising. Article 133 UNCLOS could be broadened and the genetic resources of the deep sea be added to the definition of "resources" in the Area.[61] There is no convincing reason – other than self-interest – why new uses of the living resources of the deep seabed which are in the interest of humankind as a whole should not also be covered by the common heritage principle. This includes – as with regard to mineral resources – the authorisation of activities relating to the exploration and exploitation of marine genetic resources, conservation and environmental protection measures, and benefit-sharing agreements. In addition, it should be made clear that the extension of the common heritage principle would refer not only to organisms which are found on the ocean floor and subsoil thereof, but also to all organisms which are dependent on deep-sea ecosystems and not suitable for human consumption.

To bring the deep seabed genetic resources within the ambit of UNCLOS by an expansion of Part XI would have several advantages. In its Part XII UNCLOS already provides a comprehensive framework for environmental protection. So there is already in place a structure for the international supervision of the conservation and sustainable use of resources. Moreover, even the creation of detailed rules for the conservation of the genetic resources of the deep sea under the UNCLOS regime would be possible. The Implementation Agreement Relating to Part XI of UNCLOS could be used as a model for a new agreement implementing UNCLOS as regards the genetic resources of the Area. This "would not waste effort on reinventing the wheel".[62]

---

[61] E. Mann-Borgese, *The Oceanic Circle: Governing the Seas as a Global Resource*, 1998, 170 et seq.

[62] Anton, see note 14, 368; Korn/Friedrich/Feit, see note 17, 45.

The international institution needed to manage the deep-sea genetic resources is already in place. An expansion of the ISA's mandate would allow the mineral and genetic resources of the deep seabed to be managed in an integrated manner. This makes sense, because mineral resources such as polymetallic sulphides and cobalt crusts are found at hydrothermal vent sites and on seamounts where unique deep-sea ecosystems exist.[63] Furthermore, this might lead to better coordination and international respect for marine environmental issues.[64] Another point in favour of this option is the fact that the ISA has accumulated expertise with regard to deep-sea biodiversity, because one of its tasks is the effective protection of the marine environment. The Authority already closely cooperates with marine scientific researchers and coordinates research activities. To facilitate research efforts and to disseminate their results, the ISA has established databases on species to be found in potential mining areas, their distribution and gene flow, and it promotes the standardisation of relevant environmental data and information.[65]

Nevertheless, there are some arguments against an expansion of the ISA's mandate. It has been pointed out that the ISA's main task is to promote and facilitate the exploration and exploitation of the deep-sea mineral resources.[66] These activities threaten the genetic resources of the deep seabed. In addition, the criticism has been made that the Regulation on Polymetallic Nodules and the Draft Regulation on Polymetallic Sulphides, mentioned above, are insufficient, because they do not adequately implement elements of modern environmental law, such as the precautionary principle and the ecosystem approach.[67] One of the main arguments against an expansion of the ISA's mandate focuses on the structural impediments based on the composition of the ISA Council. The Council consists of 36 Member States, 18 of which represent major consumers and major exporters of minerals found on the deep seabed, major investors in deep seabed mining, and developing countries repre-

---

[63] Scovazzi, see note 35, 408 et seq.; S. N. Nandan, The International Seabed Authority and the Governance of High Seas Biodiversity, Prepared for the Workshop on the Governance of High Seas Biodiversity, 16-20 June 2003, Cairns, Australia, 4 and 7, available at http://www.highseasconservation.org/documents/nandan.pdf.

[64] Matz, see note 33, 298.

[65] For more details see the 2005 Report of the Secretary-General, see note 24, 69 et seq.; Nandan, see note 63, 5 et seq.

[66] Leary, see note 1, 210; Matz, see note 33, 297.

[67] Leary, see note 1, 212 et seq.

senting special interests. The other 18 members are elected according to the principle of equitable geographical distribution. This structure ensures that no decisions can be made against the will of one the recognised interest groups.[68] Not surprisingly, the ISA was designed to accommodate deep seabed mining interests. If its mandate were extended to the management of deep-sea genetic resources, its structure and composition would have to be adapted to this new task. Such adaptations are not impossible, but difficult to achieve. An amendment to UNCLOS, a Protocol or another implementing agreement is likely to be time-consuming and very difficult to negotiate, since some States do not want any change at all. This option is, therefore, at best a medium- to long-term approach.[69]

3. Short-Term Measures

Since there is a need to act soon, short-term measures should have priority. They could comprise voluntary codes of conduct developed by researchers, a code of conduct for marine scientific research and prospecting in the deep seabed elaborated by the ISA[70], or the adoption of guidelines by the General Assembly. Voluntary actions by marine researchers in particular would be an appropriate way to minimize research conflicts and to conserve the genetic resources of the deep seabed. The InterRidge[71] Biology Working Group has already submitted a draft code of conduct for the sustainable use of hydrothermal vent sites[72] which could be used as a model by other research institutions. Voluntary codes of conduct and guidelines are, however, not legally binding and cannot be enforced. Nevertheless, they could be used as temporary measures until a binding regime was negotiated.[73] Their adoption should, therefore, be strongly encouraged.

---

[68] Leary, see note 1, 220 et seq.

[69] Working Group Report, see note 56, 15, para. 55.

[70] Nandan, see note 63, 4 et seq.

[71] InterRidge is an international scientific initiative concerned with facilitating international and multi-disciplinary research associated with mid-ocean ridges; see http://interridge.org.

[72] For details of the InterRidge Code of Conduct see Glowka, see note 18, 311 and Leary, see note 1, 196 et seq.

[73] Arico/Salpin, see note 4, 59.

The success of any voluntary system such as a code of conduct is intimately related to the process by which it is developed. It is therefore very important that all the key stakeholders are involved in the process of the creation of non-binding rules which may have an impact upon their activities. Furthermore, the creation of incentives is important to promote the application of voluntary codes. For example, institutions funding marine scientific research could agree to make grants of money upon the demonstrable application of a code of conduct by the grantee.[74] Moreover, in order to implement voluntary codes, States whose nationals or vessels conduct research activities in the deep sea should adopt legislation relating to and require environmental impact assessments for research projects and bioprospecting ventures.

V. Résumé

About ten years ago, *Lyle Glowka* from the International Union of Conservation of Nature and Natural Resources (IUCN) started what could be called a wake-up call. He drew attention to the fact that, although genetic resources may be the Area's most immediately exploitable and lucrative resource, they are not mentioned in UNCLOS and no international mechanism to ensure their fair and equitable utilisation exists. To raise public awareness, he called this unsatisfactory situation "the deepest of ironies".[75] Could this irony – as he hoped – be transformed into one of the greatest opportunities for humankind? Deep-sea genetic resources are still openly accessible, and because of their immense economic potential research activities, including bioprospecting, will increase. So will adverse environmental impacts deriving from such activities. Now, ten years later, the situation could be called critical, but not hopeless. After discussion in various international *fora*, there seems to be a clear sense that threats to deep-sea biodiversity and the utilisation of deep-sea genetic resources need to be managed in a more effective and equitable way. The establishment of the *Ad hoc Open-ended Informal Working Group* by the General Assembly to discuss the options and to work on an appropriate international management regime is a step in the right direction.

---

[74] This is suggested by Glowka, see note 18, 311.

[75] Glowka, see note 6, 155.

An agreement implementing UNCLOS as regards the genetic resources of the deep sea seems to be the most promising option. Since the elaboration of new legal rules takes a lot of time, in the meantime priority should be given to short-term measures. In addition to voluntary codes of conduct developed by the scientific community, the ISA or the General Assembly should also adopt internationally agreed guidelines or codes of conduct. States under whose jurisdiction and control research and bioprospecting are conducted should adopt legislation to regulate such activities in areas beyond national jurisdiction. Last but not least, it has to be pointed out that an international regime should be negotiated soon. The larger the vested interests of the biotechnology and other industries get, the more difficult will international negotiations become.

The Liability Annex to the Protocol on Environmental Protection to the Antarctic Treaty

*Silja Vöneky**

* The author took part in the negotiations of the Liability Annex as Legal Adviser of the German Delegation since 2001. All views defended in this article are however her personal views and do not necessarily represent the opinions of the German Delegation.

I. Introduction

When the Antarctic Treaty Consultative Meeting (ATCM) adopted the Liability Annex[1] in June 2005, all delegations expressed their joy and gratitude that after 13 years[2] the discussions and negotiations had come to an end. The compromise agreed upon by the members of the Antarctic Treaty System would not have been possible without the work of Rüdiger Wolfrum,[3] especially taking into account the complexity of the questions and the array of different interests at issue.

However, when I refer to the work done by Rüdiger Wolfrum this does not suggest that he is responsible for any shortcomings of or lacunae in the existing Liability Annex. There are many differences between the existing Annex and Rüdiger Wolfrum's draft, the so-called Eighth Offering.[4] The most striking one is that the Eighth Offering aimed to formulate a comprehensive legal regime covering and regulating 'the liabil-

---

1 Annex on Liability Arising from Environmental Emergencies (Annex VI) to the Protocol on Environmental Protection to the Antarctic Treaty, Measure 1 (2005) – Annex, cf. Final Report of the Twenty-Eighth Antarctic Treaty Consultative Meeting, Antarctic Treaty Secretariat (ed.), Stockholm, 6-17 June 2005, 63; http://www.ats.aq/uploaded/ANNEXVI.pdf (last visit in March 2007).

2 The preparation for the negotiations of a Liability Annex started at the ATCM in Venice, November 1992, cf. F. Francioni, "Liability For Damage to the Common Environment: The Case of Antarctica", *RECIEL* 3 (1994), 223; A. Aust/J. Shears, "Liability for Environmental Damage in Antarctica", *RECIEL* 5 (1996), 312.

3 Cf. Final Report of the Twenty-Eighth Antarctic Treaty Consultative Meeting, Antarctic Treaty Secretariat (ed.), Stockholm, 6-17 June 2005, para. 128, available at http://www.ats.aq/28atcm/reportes.php (last visit in March 2007); Rüdiger Wolfrum was Chair of the Group of Legal Experts on the work undertaken to elaborate an annex or annexes on liability for environmental damage in Antarctica from 1993 till 1998. The Group of Legal Experts was established by the XVII ATCM in Venice (paras. 37 to 40 Final Report). The XXI ATCM asked this Group to 'prepare a written report on the work undertaken to elaborate an annex or annexes and [to] outline the results achieved (...)', cf. XXII ATCM/Working Paper (WP) 1, April 1998, 1 et seq.

4 The deliberations of the Group took place on the basis of 'Offerings' prepared by the Chairman. The final 'Eighth Offering' is Part of the XXII ATCM/Working Paper (WP) 1, April 1998, 19 et seq. Concerning the history of negotiations after the Eighth Offering under the chairmanship of Don MacKay (New Zealand), see D. Shelton, "ATCM XXIII – Discussion on Liability Annex", *Environmental Policy and Law* 29 (1999), 178.

ity for *damage* arising from activities in the Antarctic Treaty area'.[5] On the contrary, the Annex as it stands now covers only liability if an operator 'fails to take prompt and effective response action to environmental emergencies arising from its activities' (Article 6 Liability Annex (LA)). This means that the Annex follows a much more limited approach, and one of the main areas of dispute between the state parties right up to the end of the negotiations was whether this approach was sufficient to fulfil the obligation of the Protocol on Environmental Protection to the Antarctic Treaty (EP).[6] The Environmental Protocol states that

> '[c]onsistent with the objectives of this Protocol for the comprehensive protection of the Antarctic environment and dependent and associated ecosystems, the Parties undertake to elaborate rules and procedures relating to the liability for damage arising from activities taking place in the Antarctic Treaty area and covered by this Protocol.' (Article 16).[7]

In this paper I try to show and to explain, firstly, what made the negotiations of a liability annex in Antarctica so delicate and what may be a possible yardstick by which to measure the new Annex; secondly, why there is a need for a liability annex and the general rules of international law are not sufficient; and thirdly, I outline the main features of the Annex as it stands now as well as its main shortcomings.

I do not focus on a comparison of this Liability Annex with other liability treaties for the protection of the environment. I will rather elaborate whether the Annex is a sufficient liability regime with regard to the special circumstances, legal and environmental ones, which can be found in Antarctica. As I took part in the negotiations of the Annex,

---

5 Article 2 Eighth Offering, see note 4; emphasis added by the author.

6 The discussion whether a step-by-step approach as advocated by the United States or a comprehensive approach as supported by Germany and other like minded states should be followed started right from the beginning of the discussions in the Working Group, cf. D. J. Bederman/S.P. Keskar, "Antarctic Environmental Liability: The Stockholm Annex and Beyond", *Emory International Law Review* 19 (2005), 1383, 1387 et seq.; D. Vidas, "The Protocol on Environmental Protection to the Antarctic Treaty: A Ten-Year Review", in: O. Schram Stokke/O.B. Thommessen (eds), *Yearbook of International Cooperation on Environment and Development* 2002/2003, 51, 57.

7 1991 Protocol on Environmental Protection to the Antarctic Treaty, ILM 30 (1991), 1455. Emphasis added by the author.

I will try to give an insight into which rules were most contested between state parties.

II. Setting the Scene

1. Unique Features of Antarctica and the Antarctic Environment

There are special and unique features of Antarctica and the Antarctic environment:[8]

> 'Antarctica is one of the most beautiful places on earth – a spectacular wilderness of snow, ice and rock, teeming with wildlife. (...) The vast numbers of penguins, seals and seabirds – nearly all unafraid of humans – are unmatched anywhere else in the world.'[9]

In plainer language, Antarctica is a huge continent with an area of 14.2 million sq km, representing nine per cent of the earth's landmass.[10] Being surrounded by the Southern Ocean, the ocean south 60 degrees South Latitude, it is the earth's most isolated continent. The Southern Ocean is the largest contained ecosystem on the planet connecting the Atlantic, Pacific and Indian Oceans and comprising nearly ten per cent of the world's oceans.[11]

If we look at the environment of Antarctica we have to keep in mind that 99.6 per cent of the continent is covered by permanent ice and snow,[12] which may be up to 4.7 km thick.[13] Its snow and ice contains over 85 per cent of the world's fresh water reserves. It acts as a cold sink for the entire southern hemisphere.[14] If the Antarctic ice sheet melts, the

---

[8] Z. Keyuan, „Environmental Liability and the Antarctic Treaty System", *Singapore Journal of International & Comparative Law* 2 (1998), 596, 618.

[9] J. Rubin (ed.), *Antarctica*, 3rd edition 2005, 5.

[10] That is 1.5 times the size of the United States, cf. CIA, The World Factbook, cf. https://www.odci.gov/cia/publications/factbook/geos/ay.html#Intro (last visit in March 2007).

[11] D. Walton, in: J. Rubin (ed.), see note 9, 130.

[12] Walton, see note 11, 135 et seq.

[13] Rubin, see note 9, 84 et seq.

[14] Walton, see note 11, 139.

world's oceans will rise by up to 60 m.[15] Hence disturbances of this ecosystem may have enormous implications on the world climate.[16]

Beside this Antarctica has a rich wildlife: Antarctic birds are spectacular in size, number and habit. Six species of seals are found in the Antarctic Area. The Southern Ocean also has a rich marine life: different species of whales and different kinds of fish, squid and krill can be found.[17] However, it is not only a particularly beautiful environment; it is at the same time an ecosystem with very little capacity to regenerate, i.e. a very fragile one.[18]

2. Human Impacts on the Antarctic Environment

There are certainly several different kinds of *indirect* human impacts and threats to the Antarctic Environment.[19] The three main sources of *direct* environmental impact – and these a liability annex should cover – are, first, scientific research and support activities, second, tourism, and, third, fishing. Antarctica has no native human population, but there are around 40 permanently manned scientific stations, which means that there are 4.000 scientific and support staff in summer and 1.000 in winter.[20] 30 airstrips belong to these stations.[21]

With regard to tourism one has to note that the numbers of tourists are steadily rising.[22] The total estimates for the 2006-2007 season are 37.900

---

15 Keyuan, see note 8, 596.

16 C. Langenfeld, „Verhandlungen über ein neues Umwelthaftungsregime für die Antarktis – Innovationen für ein Internationales Haftungsrecht“, *NUR* 16 (1994), 338, 345; R. Puri, *Antarctica A Natural Reserve*, 1997, 25 et seq.

17 J. Cooper, in: Rubin (ed.), see note 9, 105 et seq.; Walton, see note 11, 130 et seq.

18 Langenfeld, see note 16, 341.

19 Keyuan, see note 8, 596, 618.

20 Aust/Shears, see note 2, 312, 314.

21 See the Antarctic Flight Information Manual (AFIM), www.comnap.aq (last visit in March 2007).

22 The number of tourists going ashore doubled during the last three years. See Information Paper (IP) 86, IAATO Overview of Antarctic Tourism 2005-2006 Antarctic Season, ATCM XXIX, 12-23 June 2006, Appendix B, 1992-2007 Antarctic Tourist Trends – Landed, 18.

visitors, 27.500 of whom went ashore.[23] Moreover, the capacity of tourist vessels has increased significantly. Today ships going to Antarctica can carry up to 3.000 people.[24] Thus, it is not mining or drilling for oil – as some once feared – but tourism that has become Antarctica's growth industry[25] with a volume of around 300 Million[26] Euro per season.[27]

Besides scientific research and tourism one has to mention that krill, fish and squid are fished commercially and caught in large numbers in Antarctic waters.[28]

---

[23] IP 86, see note 22, 23. This takes place during the short four month Antarctic summer season, from November till February. Tourists mainly visit areas where wildlife is concentrated, hence they increase the risk to plants and animals. The large number of people making frequent visits to a few popular sites intensifies cumulative long-term effects, see Rubin, note 9, 9, 101. For an overview of the legal aspects of tourism in Antarctica see K. Bastmeijer/R. Ruora, "Regulating Antarctic Tourism and the Precautionary Principle", *AJIL* 98, 2004, 763 et seq.; R. Wolfrum/S. Vöneky/J. Friedrich, "The Admissibility of Land-Based Tourism in Antarctica under International Law", *ZaöRV/HJIL* 65 (2005), 735 et seq.

[24] Cf. IP 86, see note 22, Appendix C, 19, 21. United Kingdom submitted a draft Resolution on limiting landings from large ships in at the ATCM in 2006; according to this states should take a precautionary approach and refrain from allowing vessels carrying more than 500 passengers from making landings in Antarctica. Because of the view of some state parties that more analysis on potential environmental impacts is required to inform such decisions the ATCM did not adopt this Resolution.

[25] T.G. Bauer, *Tourism in the Antarctic – Opportunities, Constraints, and Future Prospects*, 2001, 4 et seq.

[26] This is a rather cautious estimation based on 8.000 Euro for a journey times 38.000 visitors (2006-2007 season, see note 22, 23); some of the journeys, however, are much more expensive.

[27] There is only very limited land-based infrastructure for tourism. However a draft Resolution tabled by United Kingdom and supported by a number of states, inter alia Germany, limiting permanent non-governmental infrastructure in Antarctica and recommending that 'Parties should refrain from authorising permanent land based facilities in Antarctica that are not in support of national Antarctic science programmes or associated with a Government operator' (version of 21 June 2006) was not adopted during the ATCM XXIX, 12-23 June 2006 in Edinburgh.

[28] Rubin, ibid., 92, 96 et seq.; Antarctic fisheries in 2003-04 (1 July-30 June) reported landing 136,262 metric tons; cf. CIA, The World Factbook, see note 10.

To sum up, one has to state that an effective liability annex should cover at least these three kinds of human activities (research, tourism and fisheries) and has to cover the whole continent and the Southern Ocean which are ecologically particularly vulnerable, and which are, at the same time, ecologically especially important to preserve. This is certainly not an easy task.

3. Special Legal Features

The task of negotiating an effective liability regime becomes even more challenging if one takes into account the special legal features concerning Antarctica.

a. Legal Status of Antarctica

First of all, there is the problem of the legal status of Antarctica. Antarctica is neither a so-called common space outside national jurisdiction nor clearly under the sovereignty of particular states: seven claimant states,[29] claim territorial sovereignty in Antarctica. The 39 non-claimant states – as for instance Germany, the United States and Russia – however, do not recognize the legal validity of the claims,[30] because – according to them – the traditional requirements for the acquisition of territory are not fulfilled.[31] The Antarctic Treaty (AT)[32] itself does not solve the problem of territorial claims; it only 'freezes' but does not deny all territorial claims. It thereby safeguards the legal positions taken by claimant and non-claimant parties by saying that '[n]o acts (…) taking place while the present Treaty is in force shall constitute a basis for asserting, supporting or denying a claim to territorial sovereignty in Antarctica or create any rights of sovereignty in Antarctica' (Article 4 AT).

---

[29] United Kingdom, Norway, Australia, France, New Zealand, Chile and Argentina.

[30] These states have made no claims to Antarctic territory although Russia and the United States have reserved the right to do so.

[31] R. Wolfrum/U.D. Klemm, "Antarctica", in: R. Bernhardt (ed.), *Encyclopedia of Public International Law (EPIL)*, Vol. I, 1992, 173.

[32] Antarctic Treaty, UNTS Vol.402 No.5778, 71-85.

b. Legitimacy of Rules in the Antarctic Treaty Area

A further problem is the one of legitimacy of rules in the Antarctic Treaty area. Although this is not the central topic of this paper some remarks have to be made.

The Antarctic Treaty is open to accession by any state which is a member of the United Nations or by any other state which may be invited to accede to the treaty (Article 13 (1) AT). However, only the so-called *consultative parties* have the right to participate fully in the consultative meetings and to approve measures and decisions to change and develop the Antarctic Treaty system. Consultative parties are – apart from the original twelve signatories[33] – only those parties that demonstrate their interest in Antarctica by 'conducting substantial scientific research activity' in Antarctica (Article 9 AT).

'Conducting substantial scientific research activity' means in practice the establishment of a scientific station or the dispatch of a scientific expedition (Article 9 (2)). It is evident that a scientific station or a scientific expedition entails the expenditure of major financial efforts. Hence not every state can become a consultative party in practice. Antarctic science is very expensive science: the German Alfred-Wegener-Institute doing research in Antarctica has an annual budget of 100 Mio Euro.[34] Thus, it is not surprising that today there are 46 parties to the treaty, but only 28 of them are consultative parties.[35]

With regard to the legitimacy of rules and standards adopted by the consultative parties it might be a problem that they are binding on every state party and have an effect on an area which is unique in the world and important to the world climate. To put it differently: the

---

[33] Argentina, Australia, Chile, France, New Zealand, Norway, United Kingdom, Belgium, Japan, South Africa, Soviet Union (now Russia) and the United States.

[34] Cf. http://www.awi-bremerhaven.de/AWI/index-d.html (last visit in March 2007); Walton, see note 11, 129.

[35] Cf. http://www.ats.aq (last visit in March 2007); Consultative Parties are Argentina, Australia, Belgium, Brazil, Bulgaria, Chile, China, Ecuador, Finland, France, Germany, India, Italy, Japan, Korea ROK, Netherlands, New Zealand, Norway, Peru, Poland, Russian Federation, South Africa, Spain, Sweden, Ukraine, United Kingdom, United States and Uruguay. Non-Consultative Parties are (inter alia) Estonia, Hungary, Romania, Slovakia, Colombia, Cuba, Papua New Guinea, Guatemala.

rules and standards affect the whole of mankind but they are laid down by a kind of 'exclusive' class of parties.

My remarks should not be misunderstood. I am certainly *not* saying that those states are right, which – as for instance the United States in 1948 and later on Malaysia did[36] – argue that Antarctica should be brought under the auspices of the United Nations. This is because the two-class[37] party system has its merits: states which have no direct knowledge of the very particular circumstances in that region should not participate in decision-making on Antarctica.[38]

However I think one nevertheless has to see that the Antarctic Treaty system has a kind of deficit with regard to its *input legitimacy*[39] because of its two class party system.[40] Therefore the consultative parties are under a special obligation and have a special responsibility to ensure that the output legitimacy of the rules of the Antarctic Treaty system is unquestioned. This means that the consultative parties have to make very sure that they adopt rules which are not solely in their own interest but in the interest of all mankind.

---

[36] In 1948 the United States proposed the establishment of an international regime for Antarctica, either in form of a United Nations trusteeship or of a condominium of the claimants and the United States; the reasons behind this were to avoid conflicts between Argentina and the United Kingdom and to ensure the freedom of scientific research, cf. Wolfrum/Klemm, see note 31, 173, 174.

[37] Correctly speaking it is a three-class system as the original signatories are permanent consultative parties, independent of their research activities (Article 9 AT).

[38] Wolfrum/Klemm, see note 31, 173, 176.

[39] For the concept of input and output legitimacy, see F.W. Scharpf, *Demokratietheorie zwischen Utopie und Anpassung*, 1970, 21 et seq.; F.W. Scharpf, *Governing in Europe: Effective and Democratic?*, 1999, 6 et seq.: The input concept is the traditional participation based model of legitimacy; the output concept stresses the results of rule making.

[40] In this regards it makes no difference that the population of the consultative parties represents about 80 % of the world's population and NGOs and expert groups are allowed to take part and do take part in the negotiations at the ATCM. For instance COMNAP (Council of Managers of National Antarctic Programmes, http://www.comnap.aq/), ASOC (Antarctic and Southern Ocean Coalition of NGOs, http://www.asoc.org/) and IAATO (International Association of Antarctic Tour Operators, http://www.iaato.org/); for the involvement during the negotiations of the liability annex see for instance Shelton, see note 4, 178; Bederman/Keskar, see note 6, 1383, 1388.

This special obligation is accepted by the states parties themselves. Right at the beginning, in the preamble to the Antarctic Treaty, they accept the interest of all mankind as a yardstick and they use it themselves as underlying legitimacy for the treaty system in referring several times to the interest and progress of all mankind. The Treaty states: 'Recognizing that it is in the interest of all mankind that Antarctica shall continue for ever to be used for peaceful purposes (...)'.[41] This is a commitment which is also decisive with regard to new rules in this treaty system.

Now the crucial question remains: Which kinds of rules are in the interest of all mankind? An ultimate justification and determination would certainly be beyond the scope of this paper, but I think most of you and most of the states parties would agree that (first) the protection of the Antarctic environment is in the interest of all mankind, because of its uniqueness and because damages to this environment could significantly change the global environment. Besides this, there are good reasons for arguing that (second) it is the promotion of scientific research in Antarctica that is in the interest of all mankind. The reason behind such a position is that scientific research in Antarctica in many cases contributes to recognizing or solving global environmental problems.[42] The most obvious examples are studies on the depletion of the ozone layer,[43] the measurement of changes in greenhouse gases,[44] research on the world sea level and patterns of currents in the world's oceans,[45] which can be done in Antarctica but nowhere else. That scientific research is in the interest of all mankind is recognized by the parties to the Antarctic Treaty as well.[46] On the contrary it is hard to see how the promotion of tourism or the protection of fishing is an interest of all mankind. These are rather singular interests of a very limited

---

41 See as well paras. 4 and 5 preamble AT.

42 Walton, see note 11, 128; Keyuan, see note 8, 596.

43 It was a project undertaken in Antarctica which monitored the stratospheric ozone and which provided 1985 evidence of the increasing rate of ozone destruction and resulted in the international agreements to ban CFCs as the Montreal Protocol; cf. Walton, see note 11, 142.

44 Walton, see note 11, 143.

45 Research in the Southern Ocean is part of the World Ocean Current Experiment, which is attempting to measure current patterns for all the oceans in order to improve models for predicting climate change, Walton, see note 11, 130.

46 Cf. Preamble para. 4 AT.

number of states parties. The Antarctic tourism industry – for instance – is mainly based in North America, Europe and Australia.[47]

According to this line of argument it has to be the protection of the environment without preventing scientific research which provides the yardstick for a liability annex to be measured against.

III. The Need for a Liability Annex

One may imagine the following scenario: a ship was chartered by a German expedition team, the expedition was approved by Germany, it started its journey to Antarctica but was stuck in the ice of the Antarctic Sea Area, the ship was damaged and caused an oil spill.[48] What is the legal situation if the Liability Annex does not come into force?

1. Rules of the Antarctic Treaty System

The rules of the Antarctic Treaty System, apart from the Liability Annex, do not help to solve such a case. The Antarctic Treaty of 1959 lays

---

[47] Antarctic tourism industry is based mainly in the United States, Netherlands, Norway, United Kingdom, Germany, France, Canada and Australia; cf. Apendix A, IP 86, see note 22, 13. During the 2005-2006 season there cruised 47 operators/charterers in Antarctica, cf. ibid., IP 86, 5.

[48] Similar incidents happened for instance in 1989, when the Argentine supplier ship Bahia Paraiso ran aground off the northern tip of Antarctic Peninsula and spilled 250.000 gallons of diesel fuels stored on board; cf. Keyuan, see note 8, 596, 598 with further references. 2002 a German expedition team was stuck in the Antarctic ice and in February 2007 a Norwegian tourism ship and, only two weeks later, a Japanese whaling ship were stuck. Luckily there was no environmental damage caused by the last three incidents, cf. FAZ 16.02.07; Spiegel Online, 01.02.2007 and 15.02.2007, http://www.spiegel.de/reise/aktuell/0,1518,463650,00.html and http://www.spiegel.de/panorama/0,1518,466498,00.html (last visit in March 2007); Information Paper 119 (Chile), XXX Antarctic Treaty Consultative Meeting, New Delhi 30 April to 11 May 2007 (Grounding of Vessels on Deeption Island and the M/N Nordkapp Incident); Working Paper 37 rev. 1 (Norway), XXX Antarctic Treaty Consultative Meeting, New Delhi 30 April to 11 May 2007 (The M/S Nordkapp Incident); Information Paper 40 (New Zealand), XXX Antarctic Treaty Consultative Meeting, New Delhi 30 April to 11 May 2007 (Fire on Board the Japanese Whaling Vessel Nisshin Maru).

down three main principles: that Antarctica is to be used for peaceful purposes only (Article 1); that international cooperation in scientific research in Antarctica is to be promoted (Article 2) and that the Antarctic environment is to be preserved.[49] However it does not include any liability clause. The same is true for other conventions of the Antarctic Treaty System, the Convention for the Conservation of Antarctic Seals of 1972 (CCAS) and the Convention for the Conservation of Antarctic Marine and Living Resources of 1980 (CCAMLR).[50] The purpose of the CCAS is to limit the vulnerability of seals to commercial exploitation, the purpose of the CCAMLR is to foster the conservation and prudent management of krill fishery resources in the Southern Ocean.

There is only one convention in the Antarctic Treaty System that entails rules of liability. It is the Convention on the Regulation of Antarctic Mineral Resource Activities (CRAMRA) of 1988.[51] This is often overlooked, probably because the Convention did not come into force and will never come into force, as France and Australia have decided not to ratify it.[52] Moreover, the liability rule covers only cases of an operator undertaking Antarctic mineral resource activities (Article 8 CRAMRA).[53] Hence nothing can be found to apply to our case.

The same is true for the Protocol on Environmental Protection to the Antarctic Treaty of 1991 (EP) which was negotiated after the failure of CRAMRA. Its ambitious aim is the 'comprehensive protection of the Antarctic environment and dependent and associated ecosystems' (Article 2 EP). According to its core regulations, if an activity is likely to have more than minor or transitory impacts, environmental impact assessments must be prepared by the state parties (Annex I EP). In more general terms it is stated that activities in the Antarctic Treaty area have to be planned and conducted so 'as to limit or avoid adverse impacts on

---

49 Wolfrum/Klemm, see note 31, 173, 174. So it is expressly stated that any nuclear explosions in Antarctica and the disposal of radioactive waste is prohibited (Article 5); and that state parties are obliged to formulate measures regarding the preservation and conservation of living resources in Antarctica (Article 9 (1) lit. f AT).

50 ILM 19 (1980), 841.

51 ILM 27 (1988), 859.

52 Bederman/Keskar, see note 6, 1383, 1385; D.J. Bederman, "Theory on Ice: Antarctica in International Relations", *Virginia Journal of International Law* 39 (1999), 467, 478.

53 For further discussion of the liability regime of CRAMRA, see Keyuan, see note 8, 596, 600.

the Antarctic environment and dependent and associated ecosystems' (cf. Arts 2, 3, 8 (2), 13 EP). This means that the Protocol stipulates a clear duty effectively to prevent adverse impacts on the Antarctic environment. The Protocol does not include substantive rules with regard to liability issues. Article 16 of the Protocol states only – as mentioned before – that the parties 'undertake to elaborate rules and procedures relating to liability for damage arising from activities taking place in the Antarctic Treaty area and covered by this Protocol'.

2. Liability Treaties and Rules of General International Law

If the existing rules of the Antarctic Treaty System do not help to solve our case, the question remains whether other liability treaties, or at least rules of general international law, apply. But here again the answer must be in the negative. Neither international treaties nor general rules of international law are sufficient.

It is a well established rule of international law that every international wrongful act – i.e. an action or omission that is attributable to a state and constitutes a breach of an international obligation of a state – entails the international responsibility[54] of that state.[55] Hence as states are – according to the Environmental Protocol – obliged effectively to prevent damage to the Antarctic environment the failure to do so would incur liability.

However when we look at our case – a ship with an expeditions team is stuck in the ice of the Antarctic Sea Area, it is damaged by the ice and causes an oil spill – the first question is whether any state violated its duty to protect the Antarctic environment? It is not forbidden to go to Antarctica to do scientific research. On the contrary, in numerous provisions scientific research is granted privileges by the Antarctic Treaty

---

54 For the differentiation between state responsibility and liability, C. Hoss, "State Responsibility, Liability and Environmental Protection", in: R. Wolfrum/C. Langenfeld/P. Minnerop (eds), *Environmental Liability in International Law*, 2005, 455: Liability, contrary to responsibility, arises out of harm alone, i.e. a breach of international obligation need not be established in order to obtain reparation; see as well Keyuan, see note 8, 596, 622.

55 Arts 1, 2 ILC Articles on Responsibility of States for Internationally Wrongful Acts, 2001, Report of the ILC on the Work of its Fifty-Third Session, UN GAOR, 56th Sess., Supp. No 10, at 43, UN Doc. A/5610, available at http://www.un.org/law/ilc (last visit in March 2007).

System (Article 2 EP: '(...) Antarctica (...) devoted to peace and science'). Thus, normally one cannot assume that a state which gives a permit to an expedition violates a duty only because the ship is damaged by ice shelves in the Antarctica. Sea ice poses the most common threat to polar navigation.[56]

Even if we assume for the sake of argument that a state had violated its duty to protect the environment there is another problem with regard to the general rules of state liability. It is the common view that general international law does not yet provide for the possibility of claims relating to environmental damage *per se*. According to such view liability would cover only damage to or loss of property of a third party, loss of life of or personal injury to a third party, and loss or impairment of an established use, if such damage directly resulted from damage to the Antarctic environment.[57] Sometimes this is disputed and it is said that environmental or ecological damage as such can be seen as a sort of immaterial or moral[58] damage,[59] and immaterial or moral damage is seen as damage for which the state responsible is under the obligation to make full reparation (i.e. restitution, compensation or satisfaction).[60]

56 '(...) most environmental damage is caused by lawful acts that have had adverse effects on the environment', Francioni, see note 2, 223.

57 R. Wolfrum, *Convention on the Regulation of Antarctic Mineral Resource Activities*, 1991, 93; R. Wolfrum/P. Minnerop, "Elements of Coherency in the Conception of International Environmental Law", in: Wolfrum/Langenfeld/Minnerop (eds), see note 55, 495, 503: 'There is no state practice to establish that 'ecological damage' as such would be a compensable loss. The term is rather broad and there are so far not sufficient elements to concretize this kind of damage'; G. Dahm/J. Delbrück/R. Wolfrum, *Völkerrecht*, Vol. I / 2, 2nd edition 2002, 502.

58 Article 31 ILC Articles on State Responsibility.

59 S. Erichsen, *Der ökologische Schaden im Umwelthaftungsrecht*, 1983, 138; Hoss, see note 55, 482; for a different view see G. Dahm/J. Delbrück/R. Wolfrum, *Völkerrecht*, Vol. I / 3, 2nd edition 2002, 977 ff.

60 See for instance Arts 31, 34 et seq. ILC Articles on State Responsibility: Injury includes any damage, whether material or moral, caused by the internationally wrongful act of a state (Article 31 (2)). The existence of immaterial damages in international law has been disputed at the beginning, but is now widely accepted, cf. Hoss, see note 55, 475. UN Security Council Res. 687 (3 April 1991) the Resolution covering the Iraq-Kuwait conflict includes within its definition of 'damage', the environmental damage and the depletion of natural resources; see UN Doc. S/RES/687 (1991), para. 16.

But even if we agree and state that environmental damage is a compensable loss, there is the particular problem that Antarctica is neither a so-called common space outside national jurisdiction nor clearly under the sovereignty of certain states. As indicated above, the Antarctic Treaty 'freezes' but does not deny all territorial claims.[61] Thus, the question is which state could be entitled to claim that a state should make full reparation for the immaterial environmental damage: which are the injured states?[62] Is it the state community as a whole or the consultative parties of the Antarctic Treaty system? Or is there a single (third) state entitled to invoke the responsibility,[63] as the obligation breached is owed to a group of states and is established for the protection of a collective interest of the group?[64] The same questions arise if there is environmental damage taking place on the high seas in the area of the Antarctic Treaty system.[65]

Besides which state is entitled to invoke responsibility is not the only question to be asked. It is also questionable how it could be possible to value the damage to the environment: is the damage to the environment equivalent to the costs of clean up measures? Even more difficult is the case where clean up measures are not possible; irreparable damage is very likely in Antarctica, where heavy weather is frequent. Who should pay whom how much if there is environmental damage which cannot be cleaned up? These questions cannot be solved properly by reference to the general rules concerning the responsibility of states for internationally wrongful Acts. Although the rules of the ILC exist everything is heavily disputed and would need further clarification with regard to the special situation appertaining to Antarctica and Antarctic waters. The same is true for the ILC Principles on the Prevention of Transboundary Harm from Hazardous Activities of 2001, which deal only

---

[61] Article 4 AT.

[62] Cf. Article 42 ILC Articles on State Responsibility.

[63] For this view see J. Charney, "Third State Remedies for Environmental Damage to the World Common Spaces", in: F. Francioni/T. Scovazzi (eds), *International Responsibility for Environmental Harm*, 1991, 149.

[64] Cf. Article 48 ILC Articles on State Responsibility.

[65] See Article 6 AT; according to this rule the rights of any state under international law with regard to the high seas within the treaty area are not affected.

with transboundary harm and general state duties concerning prevention, cooperation and implementation.[66]

The same problems exist with respect to other international treaties concerning questions of environmental liability. Although there are several conventions covering liability in connection with oil pollution damage to the marine environment, as for instance the International Convention on Civil Liability for Oil Pollution Damage of 1992 (CLC),[67] the scope of those conventions is limited and they apply exclusively to pollution damage caused in the territory, including the territorial sea and the exclusive economic zone of a state party (for instance Article 2 CLC). As – because of the disputed status of Antarctica – there are no coastal states and territorial seas, those conventions are not *per se* applicable in Antarctica between state parties. One could argue only that the Civil Liability Convention applies with regard to liability issues between claimant states and only concerning those parts[68] of Antarctica where those states claim territorial rights.[69]

All this makes it obvious that there is a need for a liability annex covering Antarctica and the Southern Ocean. The question however remains, what do we gain from the Annex as it stands now? Is the Annex fostering the interest of all mankind, and hence does it meet the threshold of a

---

[66] Available at http://untreaty.un.org/ilc/texts/instruments/english/draft%20articles/9_7_2001.pdf (last visit in March 2007).

[67] Available at http://www.admiraltylawguide.com/conven/civilpol1969.html (last visit in March 2007).

[68] Australia, Chile, and Argentina claim Exclusive Economic Zone (EEZ) rights or similar over 200 nm extensions seaward from their continental claims, but like the claims themselves, these zones are not accepted by other countries and "frozen" by the Antarctic Treaty; cf. CIA, The World Factbook, see note 10.

[69] Cf. N. Krüger, *Anwendbarkeit von Umweltschutzverträgen in der Antarktis*, 2000, 213. The same is true for other Conventions, for instance the International Convention on Civil Liability for Bunker Oil Damages. C. Langenfeld/P. Minnerop, "Environmental Liability Provisions in International Law", in: Wolfrum/Langenfeld/Minnerop (eds), see note 55, 3, 21; Article 235 Law of the Sea Convention refers to general international law with regard to possible liability on the part of the contracting states. A similar problem arises in regard to the ILC 2006 Draft Principles on the Allocation of Loss in the Case of Transboundary Harm arising out of Hazardous Activities, available at http://untreaty.un.org/ilc/texts/instruments/english/draft%20articles/9_10_2006.pdf (last visit in March 2007); these include important features but apply to transboundary damage only

special output legitimacy? Are the rules protecting the environment without preventing scientific research?

IV. Main Features and Main Shortcomings

1. Scope

As indicated above, contrary to Rüdiger Wolfrum's Eighth Offering,[70] the Liability Annex (LA) does not regulate the whole gamut of environmental damage but only questions of environmental emergencies (Article 1 LA). An environmental emergency – according to the definition in the Annex – is (only) 'any accidental event that has occurred, having taken place after the entry into force of this Annex, and that results in, or imminently threatens to result in, any significant and harmful impact on the Antarctic environment' (Article 2 lit. b LA). This means that, first, events without a significant and harmful environmental impact are not covered by the liability regime. This threshold is common to liability treaties as they shall not cover minor events.[71] However, only 'accidental' events are covered, and all events that are intentionally damaging to the environment are not included. This is certainly a decisive limitation on the scope of the Annex. With regard to the aim of protecting the environment it seems unconvincing. During the negotiations several states argued against this limitation, but there was no agreement amongst states to delete the word 'accidental'. It will be shown later why perhaps this restriction can be overcome by interpretation.[72]

---

70 See note 4.

71 A similar rule is included in the Eighth Offering Article 3 (1a); there it has to be more than minor or transitory/significant and lasting; see generally Wolfrum/Minnerop, see note 57, 495, 501. There are no agreed international standards which establish a general threshold for environmental damage which triggers liability; in recent state practise, however, the significance of harm has been a decisive factor (cf. Article 2 of the European Liability Directive 2004/35/CE, OJ 2004, L 143, 56). For the discussions of the ATCM Working Group in 1999 on this topic, see Shelton, see note 4, 178, 179. For a crucial view on the 'significant and harmful' criterion, Bederman/Keskar, see note 6, 1383, 1391.

72 See infra part IV. 4.

It is another limitation that the impact on associated and dependent ecosystems is irrelevant according to the definition of environmental emergencies. The only matter that is decisive is the impact on the Antarctic environment itself. This means that impacts outside the geographical limits of Antarctica and Southern Ocean, for instance impacts on fishes migrating to subtropical regions are not covered by the Annex.[73] This is a much more limited approach than that of the Environmental Protocol where it is stated that the 'parties commit themselves to the comprehensive protection of the Antarctic environment and *dependent and associated ecosystems*'[74] (Article 2 EP).[75]

There is another unconvincing limitation of the scope of the Annex. According to its Article 1, the Annex expressly covers scientific research programmes and tourism, including tourist vessels entering the Antarctic Area. Yet, it does not include fishing and other vessels cruising in the Southern Ocean.[76] As fishing vessels are the third potential major source of environmental pollution by accidental events this seems to me to be an example of where the output legitimacy of the Annex is weakened.[77] Certainly it was a major concern of many states during the negotiations to include such vessels, but the important interests of other states meant that no consensus could be reached.[78] It is only small comfort that, according to its Article 13, the Annex can be amended to include fishing vessels or other activities (Article 1 LA).[79]

---

[73] See Langenfeld, see note 16, 338, 339.

[74] Emphasis added by the author; liability rules protecting dependent and associated ecosystems were part of the Eighth Offering (Article 3 (1a)) and CRAMRA (Article 1 (15)).

[75] Some states proposed already 1999 to exclude damage to associated and dependant ecosystems from the liability regime, cf. Shelton, see note 4, 178, 179.

[76] *E contrario* Article 1 LA.

[77] For a similar view Francioni, see note 2, 223, 225 et seq.

[78] To the debate, cf. Final Report 28th ATCM, see note 3, para. 101 et seq.; Bederman/Keskar, see note 6, 1383, 1389 et seq.

[79] Art 1 LA states: '(...) It shall also apply to environmental emergencies in the Antarctic Treaty area which relate to other vessels and activities as may be decided in accordance with Article 13'.

2. Prompt and Effective Response Action

Before dealing with the core regulation on liability one must remark on the obligation to take prompt and effective response action which is laid down in detail in the Annex and is the basis for the liability regime. According to Article 5 LA the states are obliged to require its operators to take prompt and effective response action to environmental emergencies if the emergencies arise from the activities of those operators. In our case with the ship and the German expedition team, this would mean that Germany is obliged to require from its operator[80] – i.e. the natural or juridical person which organised the expedition in Germany and the activities of which were authorised by Germany – prompt and effective response action.

However here again one can find major limitations on these duties: Firstly, the definition of response actions is rather narrow. Response actions are only 'reasonable measures (...) to avoid, minimise or contain the impact of that environmental emergency, which to that end may include clean up in appropriate circumstances (...)' (Article 2 lit. f LA). Hence response actions, contrary to what was proposed by some state, as for instance Germany, do not include restorative or restoration measures and only *may* include cleaning up.[81]

Secondly, 'reasonable' response actions are only those which are 'appropriate, practicable, proportionate and based on the availability of objective criteria and information', including risks to the Antarctic environment and to human life and safety, but also 'technological and economic feasibility' (Article 2 lit. e (iii) LA). This means that for an evaluation of whether there is a duty to take response action the 'technological and economic feasibility' of the action may be decisive. This

---

[80] Operator is defined as 'any natural or juridical person, whether governmental or non-governmental, which organizes activities to be carried out in the Antarctic Treaty area. An operator does not include a natural person who is an employee, contractor, subcontractor, or agent of, or who is in the service of, a natural or juridical person, whether governmental or non-governmental, which organizes activities to be carried out in the Antarctic Treaty area, and does not include a juridical person that is a contractor or subcontractor acting on behalf of a State operator', see Article 2 (c) LA. There was right from the beginning little disagreement over the inclusion of state and non-state actors in the definition of operator, see Shelton, see note 4, 178, 179.

[81] However some delegations were concerned even with this inclusion of clean-up measures, cf. Final Report 28th ATCM, see note 3, para. 106.

seems to be a very doubtful criterion, if we look at the aim of the Annex to prevent and minimise the impact of environmental emergencies.

Thirdly, there is an even more important limitation which concerns the right of third parties to take response action (Article 5 (2) and (3) LA). According to this a third party is only *encouraged* and not obliged to take response action, in the event that an operator does not take prompt and effective response action;[82] and a third party shall *not* take response action

> 'unless a threat of significant and harmful impact to the Antarctic environment is imminent and it would be reasonable in all the circumstances to take immediate response action, or the Party of the operator has failed within reasonable time to notify the Secretariat of the Antarctic Treaty that it will take the response action itself, or where that response action has not been taken within a reasonable time after such notification' (Article 5 (3) lit. b LA).

This rule establishes a very high threshold. There is a great danger that this threshold is preventing effective response action by third parties. However, here again a state party was not willing to withdraw from its position. It is therefore an example of the rules of the Annex missing a special output legitimacy and of singular state interests overriding the common good.

3. Core Regulation on Liability

Article 6 LA provides for strict operator liability and states that an operator that fails to take prompt and effective (reasonable) response action to an environmental emergency arising out of its activities is liable to pay the costs of the response action to such party or parties that undertook the necessary response action.[83]

Hence, the question of who is liable is solved: it is the operator who did not act, although he was obliged to act. In our case this is the natural or juridical person, whether governmental or non-governmental, which organised the expedition. Furthermore, the question to whom the money has to be paid is solved: it is the party that undertook the neces-

---

[82] For a critical view see as well Bederman/Keskar, see note 6, 1393.

[83] Strict liability of the operator is laid down as well in Article 8 (2) CRAMRA and Article 3 bis Eighth Offering. In general see A. Watts, *International Law and the Antarctic Treaty System*, 1992, 196.

sary response action. Finally, the question how much must be paid is also solved: the operator has to pay the costs of the reasonable response action. Although this system of strict liability of the operator leads only to an indirect protection of the environment[84] from the point of view of environmental protection it seems to be a straightforward solution as it avoids all problems of defining environmental damage and the question how to measure it.

The possibilities of enforcement of operator liability are also straightforward: if a *non-state operator* caused the accident, a party that has taken response action may bring an action against that operator in the courts of a party where the operator is incorporated or has its principal place of business or his or her habitual place of residence, or – if there is no such party – in the courts of the party where the activities were organised (Article 7 (1) LA) – in our case in German courts.[85] However if a *state operator* caused the environmental emergency the dispute between the state parties is to be resolved by the dispute settlement procedure of the Protocol (Articles 18, 19, 20 EP), i.e. negotiation, inquiry, mediation, conciliation and lastly arbitration (Article 7 (4) LA). This seems at first glance not as effective; but one has to be realistic that only by negotiation, mediation and inquiry can such inter state conflicts be solved.

There is another, much more problematic and at the same time very likely scenario. This is where there is an environmental emergency but nobody takes any response action. It is the question how to deal with unrepaired environmental damage. As this is a typical case given Antarctic weather conditions it would be a major loophole to exclude such damage from the system of liability.[86] For those cases the Annex differ-

---

84 The environmental damage *per se* is not decisive for the liability.

85 Such actions have to be brought within three years after the response action or of the date on which the party knew or had to know the identity of the operator; in no event must this be later than 15 years after the commencement of the response action (Article 7 (1) LA). It is important to note that it was the common understanding that actions according to Article 7 (1) LA could only be brought by state parties; hence the attribution of jurisdiction to domestic courts pursuant to Article 7 (1) does not relate to civil and commercial matters under EC Regulations; Statement of Member States of the European Union, cf. Final Report 28th ATCM, see note 3, 643.

86 See Article 5 bis Eighth Offering.

entiates again between state operators and non-state operators.[87] When a *state operator* caused the emergency it is liable to pay the costs of the response action, which it should have undertaken, into a fund established by the Annex.[88]

The crucial question is how this rule can be implemented. How does one know what the 'costs of the response action, which should have been undertaken' are? The solution in the Annex has some explosive force. The costs of response action to be paid by a state operator into the fund are to be approved by the ATCM by means of a Decision (Article 7 (5) lit. b LA). As decisions can only be adopted if there are no objections by a consultative party, this means that the consultative party – in our case Germany – whose state operator is liable can determine or veto the amount which has to be paid. In the end, if the consultative parties cannot reach an agreement, the arbitration procedure of the Protocol applies (Article 7 (5) lit. a LA).

It is obvious that this clause was very much disputed. I agree with the view of many state parties that it would have been preferable if the state party of the state operator had been excluded from the decision making process. Yet, consensus could not be reached on this as other states feared that they would be faced with liability claims in uncertain amounts. I do not think that this fear was justified. As every decision of the consultative parties would have been a precedent for the future valuation of unrepaired damages, and as every state is in the position where it may be the next that has to pay for unrepaired damage caused by its state operators, this would have had the effect of reasonable self-limitation.

The case of operator liability where nobody took response action is also a difficult question to solve if a *non-state operator* is involved. The Annex states in Article 6 (2) lit. b that a non-state operator is liable (only) to pay the amount of money that reflects 'as much as possible' the costs

---

[87] Article 6 (2) lit. a, b LA. This clause is intended to encompass three situations: where no response action had been taken; where response action had been taken but it was not prompt; where response action had been taken but it was not effective; cf. Final Report 28th ATCM, see note 3, para. 109.

[88] According to Article 12 LA the Secretariat of the Antarctic Treaty will maintain and administer a fund for the reimbursement of the reasonable and justified costs incurred by a party in taking response action. In contrast to the Convention on Civil Liability, see note 67, however, there is no guaranteed financial source. A Fund was established as well by Article 8 (7) (iii) CRAMRA and Article 10 Eighth Offering.

of response action that ought to have been undertaken. These are to be paid to the party to which that operator belongs. But the party shall make only 'best efforts to make a contribution to the fund, which at least equals the money received from that operator'. This means that with regard to non-state operators the duty to pay the money into the fund is already softened by the wording of the Annex. As regards implementation each party shall ensure that there is an enforcement mechanism under domestic law with respect to the liability of any of its non-state operators (Article 7 (3) LA).[89] This soft version was accepted as a compromise in the final weeks of negotiations as some states, especially those with a federal structure, made it plain that they have inner state problems transferring money into an international fund, if this money was paid by the operator not as direct compensation for environmental damage but rather had a punitive aspect.[90]

4. Exemptions, Limits and Immunity

For an overall assessment of the liability regime, one has to take into account exemptions from and limits of liability. There are five exemptions from the liability regime (Article 8). There is no liability if the environmental emergency was caused

(1) by an act or omission necessary to protect human life or safety;

(2) by an event constituting in the circumstances of Antarctica a natural disaster of an exceptional character, which could not have been reasonably foreseen;[91]

(3) by an act of terrorism;

(4) by an act of belligerency against the activities of the operator;[92] or

---

[89] Here it is first of all decisive which party authorised the activities of the operator; subsidiary where the operator is incorporated or its principal place of business or the habitual place of residence is. There exists the time limit of 15 years after becoming aware of the environmental emergency. For the rules of the Eighth Offering, cf. Krüger, see note 69, 218.

[90] Final Report 28th ATCM, see note 3, 108. In both cases (state or non-state operator) the quantification of the liability is not related to the extent of the damage, but rather to the costs of the response action which should have been undertaken.

[91] This is a limited exemption taking in account the special climatic circumstances in Antarctica.

(5) if an environmental emergency resulted from reasonable response action taken by an operator pursuant to the rules of the Annex.

In general these are typical exemptions from liability, which can be found also in other liability treaties. That there is no liability where an environmental emergency was caused by reasonable response action is a necessary limitation, as otherwise there would be no incentive for parties to carry out response action.[93] However, the exemption of emergencies caused by an act of terrorism is rather new and was under discussion until the end of the negotiations, as the term 'terrorism' is broad and no specific definition exists in the Annex itself.[94] Most states would have preferred to delete or to limit this exemption. In CRAMRA for instance an exemption is made only for those acts of terrorism which are 'directed against the activities of the operator, against which no reasonable precautionary measures could have been effective'.[95] In view of the aim to protect the environment such a limited exemption would be preferable. But here again a state party was not willing to withdraw from its position. In the end it was at least agreed that the operator asserting an exemption would have the burden of proof of it.[96]

Even more problematic with regard to the effectiveness of the Annex is the sovereign immunity rule of Article 6 (5). There it is stated that notwithstanding that a party is liable the sovereign immunity under international law of warships, naval auxiliaries, or other ships or aircraft owned or operated by a party and used for the time being on government non-commercial service is not affected by the Annex. This is a common clause of environmental protection treaties covering sea areas.[97] However there is a particular drawback with regard to Antarctica

---

[92] See for similar provisions Article 32 and 236 UNCLOS, Article 11 Annex IV EP; for further discussion cf. S.N. Simonds, "Conventional Warfare and Environmental Protection: A Proposal for International Legal Reform", *Stanford Journal of International Law* 29 (1992), 195; Francioni, see note 2, 223, 227.

[93] Similar Bederman/Keskar, see note 6, 1383, 1397.

[94] Final Report 28th ATCM, see note 3, para. 112.

[95] Article 8 (4) lit. b CRAMRA.

[96] Article 8 states: 'An operator shall not be liable (...) if it proves that the environmental emergency was caused by (...)'. See as well Final Report 28th ATCM, see note 3, para. 112.

[97] See as well Article 11 Annex IV to the Protocol on Environmental Protection to the Antarctic Treaty: Prevention of Marine Pollution.

as a majority of ships and aircraft in Antarctica, especially those of expedition teams, are owned or operated by states.[98]

Regimes with strict liability clauses often include express limits which lay down the maximum amount for which each operator may be liable. This amount depends in this Annex, if an event involves a ship, on its tonnage, starting at one million SDR (Article 9 LA).[99] For other emergencies the maximum amount is three million SDR, i.e. the equivalent of 4.5 million US Dollars. If one thinks that these numbers are to low, as some state parties did,[100] one has to keep in mind that, firstly, the consultative parties are required to review these limits every three years (Article 9 (4) LA). Secondly, there is an exception to these limits (Article 9 (3) LA). Liability shall not be limited if it is proved that the environmental emergency resulted from an act or omission of the operator, committed with the intent to cause such emergency or recklessly and with knowledge that such emergency would probably result. It is a question of interpretation how this last clause fits together with the scope of the Annex, where environmental emergencies are defined as 'accidental events'. It seems convincing to argue that, because of the wording of Article 9 (4) LA, at least some intentional events are covered by the Annex, irrespective of the rather narrow definition of environmental emergencies in Article 2.[101] During the negotiations it was expressly stated that this clause was intended to ensure that 'the limits of liability were only excluded in the most serious circumstances of culpability; that is where the harm was either done intentionally or with such recklessness and knowledge that it almost equated to intention'.[102]

---

98 Bederman/Keskar, see note 6, 1383, 1395; Keyuan, see note 8, 596, 626.

99 SDR are Special Drawing Rights as defined by the International Monetary Fund; 1 million SDR is the equivalent to 1.5 million US-Dollar. There was no date for conversion of SDR into national currency specified; however parties should provide a method for ascertaining the date of SDR conversion in their national laws implementing the Annex with regard to actions of Article 7 LA, cf. Final Report 28th ATCM, see note 3, para. 118.

100 Cf. Final Report 28th ATCM, see note 3, para. 116; COMNAP had provided figures for land-based and sea-based emergencies based on an analysis of worst-case scenarios in 2003, cf. Final Report of the 25th ATCM, Warsaw, 10-20 September 2002, para. 83, available at http://www.ats.aq/25atcm/index.htm (last visit in March 2007).

101 See as well S. Addison-Agyei, "The Liability Annex: One important but hopefully not final step", *Environmental Policy and Law*, 2007 (forthcoming).

102 Final Report 28th ATCM, see note 3, para. 117.

At first glance it seems incomprehensible why such limits are needed, as the Annex already contains certain exemptions from liability and has a limited scope.[103] However, blunt criticism would omit the fact that it is a very important practical feature of a functioning liability regime that there is a duty to maintain adequate insurance for operators.[104] Otherwise the duty to pay for the costs of clean up measures can easily become an empty shell if the operator does not have the means to pay a large amount of money.

5. Insurance

A duty to obtain insurance is laid down in Article 11 of the Annex. In practice no insurance would be applicable if there were no limits of liability laid down in the Annex. In the end, one has to say that the insurance obligation is crucial for the reduction of the risk of damage to the Antarctic environment: an insurance company probably will impose checks on the insured operator; besides other parties are more likely to take response action voluntarily if they know that the operator is insured. Hence one has to conclude that the limits of liability, as they are the precondition to obtaining insurance, indirectly promote environmental protection.

It is a drawback in the Annex, however, that the duty to obtain insurance is also limited. It does not cover the likely event that nobody takes response action. Parties are not obliged to require insurance to cover this type of liability (Article 11 (2) LA).[105] The reason behind this is that in cases of an environmental emergency where nobody took any response action, the amount of money which has to be paid to the fund is not clear and is punitive in character. It was therefore disputed by some states whether one could obtain insurance for such cases at all. It was not possible for the insurance industry experts who actively participated in the discussion of the Annex to dispel these doubts.[106] In my

---

[103] The Eighth Offering sets a liability limitation only for non-state operators, see as well Krüger, see note 69, 219.

[104] Delegations agreed that a limit on liability was necessary for the reason to allow insurance markets to operate to cover risks of environmental damages at certain levels, cf. Bederman/Keskar, see note 6, 1383, 1399.

[105] 'Each Party *may* require its operators to maintain adequate insurance (...)'; emphasis added by the author.

[106] Final Report 28th ATCM, see note 3, 120.

opinion the limited duty to obtain insurance in such cases reduces the effect of the Annex in cases where no response action was undertaken. Even if considerable damage to the environment were to be caused, if the operator does not have the financial capacity to pay an adequate amount of money liability is nothing more than an empty shell. However, as indicated above the yardstick by which to measure a special output legitimacy is not just the protection of the environment. At the same time scientific research must not be made impossible. Indeed it was one of the greatest concerns of scientists during the negotiations that they would be bound by a duty to insure their expeditions and that this would mean too great financial burden. In this regard one could justify the decision to make insurance discretionary with regard to the category of unrepaired damages. Moreover, because of the strongly felt concerns of the scientific community state parties have been given the right to insure themselves in respect of their state operators, including those carrying out activities in the furtherance of scientific research (Article 11 (3) LA).

6. The Fund

As indicated above it is the Fund which plays an important role with regard to the reimbursement of the costs which should have been incurred by a party in taking response action where nobody takes such action. Besides, the Fund is important for reimbursement if the identity of the operator responsible cannot be ascertained or the operator is not subject to the provisions of the Annex; the latter being the case where there is no link between the operator and a state party, i.e. no party authorised the operator, as the rules of the Antarctic Treaty have no effect *erga omnes* (Article 2 lit. d LA *e contrario*). The Fund is also important for reimbursement in cases of unforeseen failure of the relevant insurance company to pay and where an exemption from liability applies (Article 12 (3) LA). The problem however remains that any proposal for reimbursement must be approved by the ATCM[107] and the money paid into the Fund depends on cases of unrepaired damage and voluntary contributions.[108]

---

[107] It was generally accepted that there should not be an automatic right to receive reimbursement from the fund, and that the ATCM would retain the discretion in all cases, cf. Final Report 28th ATCM, see note 3, para. 123.

[108] Bederman/Keskar, see note 6, 1383, 1403.

7. State Liability

According to Article 10 LA state liability is limited. A state party shall be liable for the failure of a non-state operator to take response action to the extent that that party did not take appropriate measures within its competence – this means the adoption of laws and regulations, administrative actions and enforcement measures – to ensure compliance with the Annex.[109] Although these conditions will rarely be met, and in all other cases there is no state liability for non-state operators,[110] it means that, at least theoretically, a state can be responsible for the misconduct of a non-state operator, without controlling its activities which might be seen as broadening the concept of state liability.

V. Conclusion

It is true that the rules of the Annex are not revolutionary. Elements can be found in CRAMRA and other liability regimes. But this is not decisive. Taking into account that there is a certain deficiency of input legitimacy and that there is a commitment in the Antarctic Treaty in this regard, the rules adopted by the consultative parties of the Antarctic Treaty have to have a special output legitimacy as these parties are privileged in adopting rules for an area which is of concern to all mankind. It is crucial whether the Liability Annex is in the interest of all mankind.

It seems at least that it is a first step in the right direction. As shown, there is an urgent need for a liability annex as no other international rules apply adequately. And in a very specific field, in cases of environmental emergencies, this Annex sets out some reasonable rules. The fact that operators have to pay the costs of response action or an equivalent amount, if no response action was taken, is not unreasonable and reinforces the precautionary principle for the protection of the environment incorporated in the Environmental Protocol to the Antarctic Treaty. This is true although the rules of the Annex provide for only indirect protection of the environment, as it is not the environmental damage which is decisive but the costs of the response action. However it is also clear that this is not a comprehensive liability annex covering every case

---

[109] The Eighth Offering was more limited, cf. Krüger, see note 69, 220.

[110] For a review of the regulations in CRAMRA on civil and state liability, cf. Francioni, see note 2, 223, 225.

of environmental damage in Antarctica. With regard to cases of unrepaired damage it is very much for the state parties to ensure that liability does not become an empty shell.

There were some other chances which were not seized, for instance to include fishing vessels and other ships cruising in Antarctica, intentional damage, or the protection of dependent and associated ecosystems. Furthermore it is very doubtful whether it is in the interest of all mankind if the indirect protection of the environment by the Liability Annex steps back behind the achievements of the Environmental Protocol, which already covers – for instance – all sorts of ships and dependent and associated ecosystems.

As the liability regime sets minimal standards, it does not in any relevant way prevent scientific research activities. In my opinion the same result could have been reached – and this would have been a better way to achieve a legitimate set of norms – if there had been broader liability rules and at the same time limited special exemptions to operators doing scientific research had been given.[111] In the Annex as it stands there are special rules which cover state operators. However not every expedition team necessarily counts as a state operator. The German Alfred Wegener Institute for instance is financed by the state (Bund and Länder) but is nevertheless an independent research institute. It is certainly even more problematic in this respect that there is not even a definition of who or what is a state operator.

Finally, I agree with the state parties and NGOs that this Liability Annex is better than nothing. Therefore, I hope that the Annex comes into effect soon and will be approved by all consultative parties.[112] However I think that what Max Weber calls the '*Legitimitätsglaube*', the belief that a normative order is a legitimate one,[113] needs to be strengthened

---

111 Some Latin American States and Germany sought a preferential liability regime for scientific activities at the beginning of the negotiations, cf. Shelton, see note 4, 178, 179. However it would not have been reasonable, in regard to an effective liability regime, to include a broad or general exemption from liability covering all scientific research; this however was suggested by SCAR (Scientific Committee on Antarctic Research) during the negotiations; cf. Final Report 28th ATCM, see note 3, para. 113.

112 Measure 1 (2005) para. ii, cf. Final Report 28th ATCM, see note 3, 61: 'The Annex become effective upon the date on which this Measure has been approved by all Consultative Parties entitled to attend the XXVIIIth Antarctic Treaty Consultative Meeting.'

113 M. Weber, *Wirtschaft und Gesellschaft*, 1925, Erster Teil, Kapitel 1.

by a further step and a second, more far reaching, liability annex. The Annex has too many lacunae as it stands now. Therefore I welcome the fact that the state parties have at least decided not later than 2010 to take a decision in '(...) the establishment of a time-frame for the resumption of negotiations to elaborate further rules and procedures as may be necessary relating to liability for damage (...)'.[114] This again is very 'soft' wording and there is no obligation to adopt a second annex. But it is again a further step in the right direction.

---

[114] Decision 1 (2005) para. 2, cf. Final Report 28th ATCM, see note 3, 333.

Annex VI to the Protocol on Environmental Protection to the Antarctic Treaty – Liability Arising From Environmental Emergencies (Excerpts)

Article 1
Scope

This Annex shall apply to environmental emergencies in the Antarctic Treaty area which relate to scientific research programmes, tourism and all other governmental and non-governmental activities in the Antarctic Treaty area for which advance notice is required under Article VII (5) of the Antarctic Treaty, including associated logistic support activities. Measures and plans for preventing and responding to such emergencies are also included in this Annex. It shall apply to all tourist vessels that enter the Antarctic Treaty area. It shall also apply to environmental emergencies in the Antarctic Treaty which relate to other vessels and activities as may be decided in accordance with Article 13.

Article 2
Definitions

[...]

(b) "Environmental emergency" means any accidental event that has occurred, having taken place after the entry into force of this Annex, and that results in, or imminently threatens to result in, any significant and harmful impact on the Antarctic environment;

(c) "Operator" means any natural or juridical person, whether governmental or non-governmental, which organizes activities to be carried out in the Antarctic Treaty area. An operator does not include a natural person who is an employee, contractor, subcontractor or agent of, or who is in the service of, a natural or juridical person, whether governmental or non-governmental, which organizes activities to be carried out in the Antarctic Treaty area, and does not include a juridical person that is a contractor or subcontractor acting on behalf of a State operator;

(d) "Operator of the Party" means an operator that organizes, in that Party's territory, activities to be carried out in the Antarctic Treaty area, and:

   (i) those activities are subject to authorization by that Party for the Antarctic Treaty area; or

(ii) in the case of a Party which does not formally authorize activities for the Antarctic Treaty area, those activities are subject to a comparable regulatory process by that Party.

The terms "its operator", "Party of the operator", and "Party of that operator" shall be interpreted in accordance with this definition;

(e) "Reasonable", as applied to preventative measures and response action, means measures or actions which are appropriate, practicable, proportionate and based on the availability of objective criteria and information, including:

(i) risks to the Antarctic environment, and the rate of its natural recovery;

(ii) risks to human life and safety; and

(iii) technological and economic feasibility;

(f) "Response action" means reasonable measures taken after an environmental emergency has occurred to avoid, minimize or contain the impact of that environmental emergency, which to that end may include clean-up in appropriate circumstances, and includes determining the extent of that emergency and its impact;

[...]

Article 6
Liability

1. An operator that fails to take prompt and effective response action to environmental emergencies arising from its activities shall be liable to pay the costs of response action taken by Parties pursuant to Article 5 (2) to such Parties.

2. (a) When a State operator should have taken prompt and effective response action but did not, and no response action was taken by any Party, the State operator shall be liable to pay the costs of the response action which should have been undertaken, into the fund referred to in Article 12.

(b) When a non-State operator should have taken prompt and effective response action but did not, and no response action was taken by any Party, the non-State operator shall be liable to pay an amount of money that reflects as much as possible the costs of the response action that should have been taken. Such money is to be paid directly to the fund referred to in Article 12, to the Party of that operator or to the Party that enforces the mechanism referred to in Article 7(3). A Party receiving such money shall make best efforts to make a contribution to the fund referred to in Article 12 which at least equals the money received from the operator.

3. Liability shall be strict.

[...]

Article 11
Insurance and Other Financial Security

1. Each Party shall require its operators to maintain adequate insurance or other financial security, such as the guarantee of a bank or similar financial institution, to cover liability under Article 6 (1) up to the applicable limits set out in Article 9 (1) and Article 9 (2).
2. Each Party may require its operators to maintain adequate insurance or other financial security, such as the guarantee of a bank or seminal financial institution, to cover liability under Article 6 (2) up to the applicable limits set out in Article 9 (1) and Article 9 (2).
3. Notwithstanding paragraphs 1 and 2 above, a Party may maintain self-insurance in respect of its State operators, including those carrying out activities in the furtherance of scientific research.

[...]

The Strange Case of Human Rights and Intellectual Property: Is There a Way to Reconcile Dr. Jekyll with Mr. Hyde?

*Karen Kaiser**

> "My provision of the salt, which had never been renewed since the date of the first experiment, began to run low. I sent out for a fresh supply and mixed the draught; the ebullition followed, and the first change of colour, not the second; I drank it and it was without efficiency."
>
> Robert Louis Stevenson, *The Strange Case of Dr. Jekyll and Mr. Hyde and Other Tales of Terror*, Penguin Books, 2002, 69 et seq.

* The author wishes to thank Russell A. Miller for his constant support.

I. Introduction

The relationship between human rights and intellectual property has much in common with Robert Louis Stevenson's novel *The Strange Case of Dr. Jekyll and Mr. Hyde*. Intellectual property, like Dr. Jekyll, has a dual personality. On the one hand, it is protected as a human right on the international level under Article 27 para. 2 of the Universal Declaration of Human Rights (hereinafter UDHR)[1] and Article 15 para. 1 lit. c of the International Covenant on Economic, Social and Cultural Rights (hereinafter ICESCR).[2] Both provisions recognize the right of everyone "to benefit from the protection of the moral and material interests resulting from any scientific, literary or artistic production of which he [or she] is the author." On the other hand, intellectual property is protected as a private right[3] in intellectual property treaties that have laid down specific legal entitlements for owners of patents, plant varieties, trade marks, industrial designs, and geographical indications, as well as for owners of copyright and related rights.[4] The two concepts, intellectual property as a human right and intellectual property as a private right, are drastically different in character and scope. Thus, human rights, including the human right of the author, are casually regarded as "good," like Stevenson's Dr. Jekyll; intellectual property rights tend to be perceived as "evil", and have been regarded by some human rights bodies with the same anguish as Mr. Hyde was by his fellow citizens.[5]

The paper delves briefly into the topic by discussing why and where human rights and intellectual property rights intersect. Approaching the subject from an intellectual property perspective, the paper then argues that the main intellectual property organizations, the World Intel-

---

1 A/RES/217 A (III) of 10 December 1948.

2 993 UNTS 3.

3 See e.g. the 4th paragraph of the preamble of the Agreement on Trade-Related Aspects of Intellectual Property Rights (1869 UNTS 299; hereinafter TRIPS Agreement): "Recognizing that intellectual property rights are private rights".

4 See, within WIPO, in particular the Paris Convention for the Protection of Industrial Property (828 UNTS 305; hereinafter Paris Convention) and the Berne Convention for the Protection of Literary and Artistic Works (1161 UNTS 3; hereinafter Berne Convention), and within the WTO the TRIPS Agreement.

5 See *infra* B. 2. a. and b.

lectual Property Organization (hereinafter WIPO) and the World Trade Organization (hereinafter WTO), should become more receptive to human rights concerns and examine whether and how they can do so.

II. Intersections between Human Rights and Intellectual Property Rights

1. Reasons for Intersection

Why do human rights and intellectual property rights intersect? At least in the continental European tradition, the origin of intellectual property rights can be traced back to human rights. Influenced by John Locke's argument that property is a natural right and derived from labour,[6] the concept of property was gradually enlarged to include intellectual property as the product of an individual person's scientific, literary or artistic labour. In France, the patent and copyright revolutionary laws of 1791 and 1793 explicitly recognized the specific legal entitlements for owners of patents and copyright to be part of the human right to property.[7] However, it took more than a century for the idea of a human right to intellectual property to emerge on the international plane. It was first taken up by the American Declaration of Rights and Duties of Man[8] and, later, at the instigation of the French and Latin American delegates, by the UDHR and the ICESCR.[9]

---

6 J. Locke, *Second Treatise of Government*, 1690, Chapter V.

7 J. Schmidt-Szalewski, "Die theoretischen Grundlagen des französischen Urheberrechts im 19. und 20. Jahrhundert", *GRUR Int.* 1993, 187-194, at 187, with further references.

8 *AJIL Supplement* 43 (1949), 133, Article 13.

9 P. K. Yu, "Reconceptualizing Intellectual Property Interests in a Human Rights Framework", *Michigan State University College of Law, Legal Studies Research Paper Studies*, Research Paper No. 04-01, 5-20. See for the drafting history of Article 27 para. 2 UDHR and Article 15 para. 1 lit. c ICESCR also J. Schneider, *Menschenrechtlicher Schutz geistigen Eigentums*, 2006, 56-86. The human right to intellectual property is equally recognized in Article 1 of the Protocol to the Convention for the Protection of Human Rights and Fundamental Freedoms (ETS No. 9), Article 14 para. 1 lit. c) of the Additional Protocol to the American Convention on Human Rights in the Area of Economic, Social and Cultural Rights (OASTS No. 69) and Article II-77 of the Treaty Establishing a Constitution for Europe (OJ C 310 of 16 December 2004, 1).

Despite this historical context, the tension between human rights and intellectual property rights is a relatively recent phenomenon. For several decades neither regime saw the other as aiding or threatening its sphere of influence or opportunities for expansion.[10] While the human rights regime concentrated on the elaboration and codification of legal norms and the enhancement of compliance mechanisms after World War II, the intellectual property regime gradually expanded to include new subjects and rights, in particular taking into account new technological developments, through the Berne, Paris and other conventions.

Three events caused the human rights community to overcome the historical separation that existed between the fields and to take a closer look at intellectual property.[11] First, in the early 1990s human rights bodies of the United Nations (hereinafter UN) increasingly dealt with the rights of indigenous peoples, an area of concern that had been neglected to that point.[12] Secondly, the entry into force of the TRIPS Agreement in 1995 created a link between intellectual property and trade. Thirdly, developed countries, in particular the United States, in the late 1990s began to conclude bilateral and regional TRIPS-plus treaties with developing countries.[13] TRIPS-plus treaties contain rules more stringent than those found in the TRIPS Agreement and require developing countries to implement the TRIPS Agreement before the end of transition periods or require them to accede to or conform to the requirements of other intellectual property treaties.

---

[10] L. R. Helfer, "Human Rights and Intellectual Property: Conflict or Coexistence?", *Minnesota Intellectual Property Review* 5 (2003), 47-61, at 51.

[11] *Ibid.*, at 52.

[12] R. Wolfrum, "The Protection of Indigenous Peoples in International Law", *ZaöRV* 59 (1999), 369-382, at 375 et seq.

[13] See e.g. M. P. Pugatch, "The International Regulation of IPRs in a TRIPS and TRIPS-Plus World", *Journal of World Investment & Trade* 6 (2005), 431-465; M. El-Said, "The Road from TRIPS-Minus, to TRIPS, to TRIPS-Plus", *Journal of World Intellectual Property* 8 (2005), 53-65. The conclusion of TRIPS-plus treaties is also part of the new trade policy of the European Union, see Communication from the Commission to the Council, the European Parliament, the European Economic and Social Committee and the Committee of Regions, Global Europe: Competing in the World, COM(2006) 567 final of 4 October 2006, at 10.

2. Areas of Intersection

It shall now be illustrated how these developments bridged the gap between the fields. If we focus on human rights in general, and not on discrete human rights, such as the right to health,[14] the right to food,[15] the right to education and the freedom of expression,[16] there are two main areas of intersection with intellectual property: first the protection of cultural heritage and traditional knowledge of indigenous peoples; and, secondly, the general relationship between human rights, the TRIPS Agreement and TRIPS-plus treaties.

a. Protection of Cultural Heritage and Traditional Knowledge of Indigenous Peoples

From an intellectual property perspective, much of the cultural heritage and traditional knowledge of indigenous peoples was treated as part of the public domain, either because it did not meet established subject matter criteria for protection, or because the indigenous peoples did not endorse private ownership rules. Relegated to the public domain, indigenous peoples' traditional knowledge could be exploited by outsiders who could use it as the basis for patents, copyrights and plant variety rights.[17]

The UN human rights bodies have taken a sceptical view of intellectual property rights,[18] especially where they operate to disadvantage indigenous peoples. The Draft Principles and Guidelines for the Protection of the Heritage of Indigenous Peoples demand that national laws should

---

[14] See, with regard to the right to health, H. Hestermeyer, *Human Rights and the WTO, The Case of Patents and Access to Medicines*, 2007; C. Herrlich, *Internationale Menschenrechte als Korrektiv des Welthandelsrechts*, 2005.

[15] See, with regard to the right to food, H. M. Haugen, *The Right to Food and the TRIPS Agreement*, 2005.

[16] See, with regard to the freedom of expression, M. D. Birnhack, "Copyrighting Speech: A Trans-Atlantic View", in: P. L. C. Torremans (ed.), *Copyright and Human Rights*, 2004, 37-62.

[17] See e.g. M. Leistner, "Traditional Knowledge", in: S. von Lewinski (ed.), *Indigenous Heritage and Intellectual Property*, 2004, 49-149, at 56-58; A. von Hahn, *Traditionelles Wissen indigener und lokaler Gemeinschaften zwischen geistigen Eigentumsrechten und der public domain*, 2004.

[18] Helfer, see note 10, at 53 et seq.

provide the means for indigenous peoples to prevent, as well as obtain damages for, "the acquisition, documentation or use of their heritage without proper authorization of the traditional owners."[19] Although such means would fit within the intellectual property system, existing intellectual property rights owned by others and based upon traditional knowledge might be called into question to the extent that national laws had retrospective effect.[20] Another provision is arguably inconsistent with the TRIPS Agreement[21] because it requires national laws to deny third parties the ability to obtain "patent, copyright or other legal protection for any element of indigenous peoples' heritage" that does not also provide for "sharing of ownership, control, use and benefits" with "traditional owners."[22] It might conflict with Arts 27 para. 1 and 29 of the TRIPS Agreement in so far as the conditions of patentability are limited to novelty, inventiveness and industrial applicability and as the disclosure requirements regulated in Article 29 are exclusive.

The Draft UN Declaration on the Rights of Indigenous Peoples is less specific in its view of intellectual property rights than the Draft Principles and Guidelines for the Protection of the Heritage of Indigenous Peoples. It recognizes the right of indigenous peoples to "maintain, control, protect and develop their intellectual property" over their "cultural heritage, traditional knowledge, and traditional cultural expressions"[23] and, similar to the Draft Principles and Guidelines, requires States to provide for "redress through effective mechanisms" with respect to the "cultural, religious and spiritual property taken without

---

[19] Revised Text of the Draft Principles and Guidelines for the Protection of the Heritage of Indigenous Peoples, E/CN.4/Sub.2/2000/26 of 19 June 2000, Annex I, para. 23 lit. b.

[20] R. J. Coombe, "Intellectual Property, Human Rights & Sovereignty: New Dilemmas Posed in International Law by the Recognition of Traditional Knowledge and the Conservation of Biodiversity", *Indiana Journal of Global Legal Studies* 6 (1998), 59-115, at 71 (footnote 50).

[21] N. Pires de Carvalho, "Requiring Disclosure of the Origin of Genetic Resources and Prior Informed Consent in Patent Applications Without Infringing the TRIPS Agreement: The Problem and the Solution", *Washington University Journal of Law & Policy* 2 (2000), 371-401, at 386-389.

[22] See note 19, para. 23 lit. c.

[23] Revised Draft Declaration, A/C.3/61/L.18/Rev.1 of 20 November 2006, Annex, Article 31.

their free, prior and informed consent or in violation of their laws, traditions and customs."[24]

b. Relationship between Human Rights, the TRIPS Agreement and TRIPS-plus Treaties

The TRIPS Agreement and TRIPS-plus treaties intersect with human rights for at least two reasons. First, because of the possibility of imposing trade sanctions, the WTO's dispute settlement system is more stringent than the UN human rights compliance system.[25] The International Covenant on Civil and Political Rights (hereinafter ICCPR)[26] and the ICESCR require no more than that states report periodically on their progress in achieving the rights in the two treaties.[27] These reports are then reviewed by the Human Rights Committee and the Committee on Economic, Social and Cultural Rights (hereinafter CESCR). In addition, the Human Rights Committee has the capacity to adjudicate individual complaints under the (First) Optional Protocol of the ICCPR.[28] However, neither the recommendations made on the basis of the state reports nor the Human Rights Committee's decisions on individual complaints are binding on states.[29] In contrast, the reports by the panels and the Appellate Body are, once they have been adopted by the Dispute Settlement Body, not only binding on the parties involved.[30] If they are not implemented, the injured party may either seek compensation or request authorization from the Dispute Settlement Body to suspend the application of concessions and other obligations entered into, for example, under the TRIPS Agreement. The imbalance in the way compliance with human rights and intellectual property rights is se-

---

24 *Ibid.*, Article 22 para. 2.

25 Helfer, see note 10, at 54 et seq.

26 999 UNTS 171.

27 Article 40 ICCPR; Arts 16 and 17 ICESCR.

28 999 UNTS 302.

29 Article 5 para. 4 of the Optional Protocol of the ICCPR.

30 P.-T. Stoll and F. Schorkopf, *WTO – World Economic Order, World Trade Law*, 2006, para. 267; J. Jackson, "The Dispute Settlement Understanding: Misunderstandings on the Nature of Legal Obligation", *AJIL* 91 (1997), 60-64, at 63 et seq.

cured leads to a factual hierarchy of compliance systems.[31] Compliance with human rights could, in the end, be subordinated to compliance with the TRIPS Agreement in areas where the two regimes overlap.

Secondly, the TRIPS Agreement and TRIPS-plus treaties have serious consequences for developing countries. On the one hand, implementation has proven slow, costly and a source of domestic opposition.[32] The transition period granted to least-developed countries under Article 66 para. 1 of the TRIPS Agreement had to be extended twice.[33] On the other hand, both the TRIPS Agreement and TRIPS-plus treaties fail to deal with the right to enjoy the benefits of scientific and cultural progress that is in the interest of developing countries and is equally protected under Article 27 para. 2 UDHR and Article 15 para. 1 lit. c ICESCR. One way to give effect to this right would be to facilitate technology transfer to developing countries. Under Article 66 para. 2 of the TRIPS Agreement, developed countries have agreed to provide incentives to their enterprises and institutions for the purpose of promoting and encouraging technology transfer to least-developed countries. As this provision is, however, silent on the extent to which developed countries have to exert themselves, it may be difficult to establish a violation in WTO dispute settlement proceedings.[34] The Council on Trade-Related Aspects of Intellectual Property Rights (hereinafter TRIPS Council) has, therefore, called on developed countries to submit annual reports on the implementation of Article 66 para. 2 of the TRIPS Agreement.[35] However, like the compliance mechanism under the ICCPR and the ICESCR, the recommendations made by the TRIPS Council on the basis of these reports are not binding.

---

[31] H. Hestermeyer, "Where Unity is at Risk: When International Tribunals Proliferate", in this volume, 123-140, at 134 et seq.

[32] J. H. Reichman, "The TRIPS Agreement Comes of Age: Conflict or Cooperation with the Developing Countries?", *Case Western Reserve Journal of International Law* 32 (2000), 441-470.

[33] Extension of the Transition Period under Article 66.1 for Least-Developed Country Members, IP/C/40 of 30 November 2005; Extension of the Transition Period under Article 66.1. for Least-Developed Country Members for Certain Obligations with Regard to Pharmaceutical Products, IP/C/25 of 1 July 2002.

[34] D. Gervais, *The TRIPS Agreement – Drafting History and Analysis*, 2nd ed. 2003, para. 2.514.

[35] Implementation of Article 66.2 of the TRIPS Agreement, IP/C/28 of 20 February 2003.

In the beginning, UN human rights bodies developed an antagonistic approach to the TRIPS Agreement.[36] Resolution 2000/7 of the Sub-Commission on the Promotion and Protection of Human Rights on Intellectual Property and Human Rights, for example, stresses that "actual or potential" conflicts between the TRIPS Agreement and human rights exist, since the "implementation of the TRIPS Agreement does not adequately reflect the fundamental nature and indivisibility of all human rights, including the right of everyone to enjoy the benefits of scientific progress and its applications, the right to health, the right to food and the right to self-determination."[37] These conflicts include, *inter alia*, "impediments to the transfer of technology to developing countries, the consequences for the enjoyment of the right to food of plant variety rights and the patenting of genetically modified organisms, 'bio-piracy', [...] and restrictions on access to patented pharmaceuticals and the implications for the enjoyment of the right to health."[38] Aware of the factual hierarchy of compliance systems, Resolution 2000/7 asserts that states must give priority to human rights over the TRIPS Agreement.[39] Later resolutions, reports and statements of UN human rights bodies follow the same line of reasoning.[40] The UN High Commissioner for Human Rights, moreover, emphasizes the public interest

---

36 Helfer, see note 10, at 55.

37 E/CN.4/Sub.2/RES/2000/7 of 17 August 2000, para. 2.

38 *Ibid.*, preambular para. 11.

39 *Ibid.*, para. 3. See for further analysis of this resolution D. Weissbrodt and K. Schoff, "A Human Rights Approach to Intellectual Property Protection: The Genesis and Application of Sub-Commission Resolution 2000/7", *Minnesota Intellectual Property Review* 5 (2003), 1-46.

40 See for the year 2001 alone, *inter alia*, Report of the Secretary-General, Intellectual Property Rights and Human Rights, E/CN.4/Sub.2/2001/12 of 14 June 2001; Progress Report submitted by J. Oloka-Onyango and D. Udagama, Globalization and its Impact on the Full Enjoyment of Human Rights, E/CN.4/Sub.2/2001/10 of 2 August 2001; Sub-Commission on the Promotion and Protection of Human Rights, Resolution 2001/21, Intellectual Property and Human Rights, E/CN.4/Sub.2/RES/2001/21 of 16 August 2001; and Committee on Economic and Social Rights, Substantive Issues Arising in the Implementation of the International Covenant on Economic, Social and Cultural Rights, Follow-up to the Day of General Discussion on Article 15.1 (c), Statement on Human Rights and Intellectual Property, E/C.12/2001/15 of 15 December 2001.

in access to new knowledge and innovations,[41] laid down in Article 15 para. 1 lit. a and b ICESCR, and opposes the adoption of TRIPS-plus standards[42].

This antagonistic approach is startling when it is recalled that intellectual property is also a human right and, thus, part of the system. Accordingly, the tone became more conciliatory in 2005 when the CESCR issued General Comment No. 17[43] on the right of everyone to benefit from the protection of the moral and material interests resulting from any specific, literary or artistic production of which he or she is the author (hereinafter human right of the author) and tried to shed light on the relationship between the intellectual property clauses of the ICESCR and the remaining human rights. Three of the CESCR's statements are relevant to this context. First, the scope of protection of the human right of the author is not confined to copyright, as the wording suggests and as has been argued before,[44] but includes all intellectual property rights that protect creations of the human mind, i.e. patents, plant varieties, industrial designs, and copyright.[45] In contrast, intellectual property rights that protect distinctive signs, such as trade marks and geographical indications, are excluded from the scope of protection. Secondly, some of the specific legal obligations deduced from the human right of the author overlap with several provisions in intellectual property treaties, notably with the reproduction right and moral rights clauses in the Berne Convention, the right of communication to the public in the WIPO Copyright Treaty and the WIPO Performances and Phonograms Treaty, and the enforcement provisions of

---

41 Report of the High Commissioner, The Impact of the Agreement on Trade-Related Aspects of Intellectual Property Rights on Human Rights, E/CN.4/Sub.2/2001/13 of 27 June 2001, para. 61.

42 *Ibid.*, para. 69.

43 E/C.12/GC/17 of 12 January 2006.

44 See e.g. T. Oppermann, "Geistiges Eigentum: Ein "Basic Human Right" des Allgemeinen Völkerrechts. Eine deutsche Alternative innerhalb der International Law Association (ILA)", in: A. Weber (ed.), *Währung und Wirtschaft – Das Geld im Recht, Festschrift für Prof. Dr. Hugo J. Hahn zum 70. Geburtstag*, 1997, 447-464, at 455.

45 See note 43, para. 9. See also P. Buck, *Geistiges Eigentum und Völkerrecht*, 1994, 227.

the TRIPS Agreement.[46] These commonalities suggest that states can satisfy their obligations by ratifying intellectual property treaties.[47] States have regularly referred to such treaties to demonstrate compliance with the human right of the author.[48] Thirdly, the mere ratification of intellectual property treaties is, however, not enough, as states are obliged to strike a balance between the human right of the author and other human rights.[49] In striking this balance, states should, according to the CESCR, make use of the opportunity to exclude inventions from patentability under Article 27 para. 2 of the TRIPS Agreement, whenever their commercialization would jeopardize the achievement of human rights.[50]

III. Opening Intellectual Property to Human Rights Concerns

1. Reasons for Urging Intellectual Property's Receptiveness

WIPO and the WTO must challenge the prevailing sceptical and antagonistic approaches of UN human rights bodies to intellectual property rights. If the two main intellectual property organizations do not become more receptive to human rights concerns, UN human rights bodies may stigmatize intellectual property rights as violating human rights in general. Worse, they may also overlook opportunities to use intellectual property as a means to protect human rights, for example with regard to the rights of indigenous peoples to cultural heritage and

---

46 Arts. 6 and 9bis of the Berne Convention; Article 8 of the WIPO Copyright Treaty (36 ILM 65); Article 10 of the WIPO Performances and Phonograms Treaty (36 ILM 76); Arts. 41-51 and 61 of the TRIPS Agreement.

47 L. R. Helfer, "Towards a Human Rights Framework for Intellectual Property", Vanderbilt University Law School Public Law and Legal Theory, Working Paper Number 06-03, at 14.

48 See e.g. Third Periodic Report: Cyprus, Implementation of the International Covenant on Economic, Social and Cultural Rights, E/1994/104/Add.12 of 6 June 1996, para. 420.

49 See note 43, para. 35.

50 *Ibid.* See for further analysis of General Comment No. 17 H. M. Haugen, "General Comment No. 17 on 'Authors' Rights'", *Journal of World Intellectual Property* 10 (2007), 53-69.

traditional knowledge.[51] A one-sided opening up of UN human rights bodies to intellectual property that is not reciprocated by the intellectual property regime may, furthermore, negatively influence the success of existing intellectual property treaties as the generation of anti-intellectual property norms increases the likelihood of inconsistent obligations for states.[52] Developing countries that have problems implementing intellectual property treaties may use these anti-intellectual property norms to abstain from further implementation or to reopen negotiations.

Last but not least, the future work of WIPO and the WTO may be hampered should they fail to become more receptive to human rights concerns. Even if the majority of anti-intellectual property norms are non-binding legal instruments, they require a certain interpretation of the relationship between human rights and intellectual property that must be taken into account in the future development of the intellectual property system.[53] Therefore, it is in the interest of intellectual property organizations to participate as early as possible in the process of generating norms that address the relationship between human rights and intellectual property in order to achieve a well-balanced compromise.

2. Justifying Intellectual Property's Receptiveness: Limited Mandates

The assumption that intellectual property organizations should become more receptive to human rights concerns raises the question: do the mandates of WIPO and the WTO allow them to do so? International organizations are bound to and limited by their constituent treaties with regard to their functions.[54] While the UDHR and the ICESCR refer to authors' "moral and material interests" in their "scientific, literary

---

51 D. R. Downes, "How Intellectual Property Could Be a Tool to Protect Traditional Knowledge", *Columbia Journal of International Law* 25 (2000), 253-282.

52 L. R. Helfer "Regime Shifting: The TRIPs Agreement and New Dynamics of International Intellectual Property Lawmaking", *Yale Journal of International Law* 29 (2004), 1-83, at 58.

53 *Ibid.*, at 61.

54 M. Ruffert, „Zuständigkeitsgrenzen internationaler Organisationen im institutionellen Rahmen der internationalen Gemeinschaft", *AVR* 38 (2000), 129-168, at 156 et seq.

or artistic production[s]," direct references to human rights appear neither in the constituent treaties of WIPO and the WTO nor in the major intellectual property treaties administered by them.

However, as far as WIPO is concerned, the function "to promote the protection of intellectual property throughout the world," provided by Article 3 of the Convention Establishing the World Intellectual Property Organization (hereinafter WIPO Convention),[55] may be interpreted broadly. It may include areas where human rights and intellectual property rights intersect, as long as the focus is on the generation of new intellectual property protection standards. This is the case with regard to the protection of indigenous peoples' cultural heritage and traditional knowledge. WIPO may discuss and develop rules on how the protection of traditional cultural expressions and traditional knowledge can be improved within the intellectual property system. By doing so, it may take human rights concerns into account.

Yet, areas of intersection are not embraced by WIPO's function "to promote the protection of intellectual property," if the intersection between human rights and intellectual property rights calls for non-proprietary approaches to promoting human innovation and creativity. This is the case with regard to WIPO's Development Agenda.[56] The core of the agenda is the proposal for a Treaty on Access to Knowledge that includes several provisions on limitations and exceptions to copyright and related rights and on exclusion from patentable subjects as well as measures to enhance the "knowledge commons" and to promote open standards and control anticompetitive practices.[57] Bearing in mind that intellectual property organizations ought to become more receptive to human rights concerns, the WIPO Convention could be read in conjunction with the agreement between WIPO and the UN[58] designating WIPO as a specialized agency.[59] According to Article 1 of this agreement, WIPO's function would not be restricted to the generation

---

55 828 UNTS 1749.

56 Proposal by Argentina and Brazil for the Establishment of a Development Agenda for WIPO, WO/GA/31/11 of 27 August 2004.

57 Draft of 9 May 2005, <http://www.cptech.org/a2k/a2k_treaty_may9.pdf> (last visit: 15 March 2007).

58 Agreement between the United Nations and the World Intellectual Property Organization, <http://www.wipo.int/treaties/en/agreement/pdf/un_wipo_agreement.pdf> (last visit: 15 March 2007).

59 Helfer, see note 47, at 28.

of new intellectual property standards. WIPO would, moreover, be responsible for "promoting creative intellectual activity and facilitating the transfer of technology [...] to developing countries in order to accelerate economic, social and cultural development."

The WTO does not seem to be equally amenable as WIPO to becoming more receptive to human rights concerns. The Preamble to the Agreement Establishing the World Trade Organization (hereinafter WTO Agreement)[60] mentions as an objective the economic development of developing countries, but not the protection and furtherance of human rights.[61] However, several provisions of the TRIPS Agreement could be used as a gateway to introducing human rights. These provisions include Arts 7, 8, 27 and 73 of the TRIPS Agreement. Arts 7 and 8 provide that intellectual property rights should, *inter alia*, "contribute to [...] the transfer [...] of technology [...] and to a balance of rights and obligations" and that Members may lay down measures "necessary to protect public health and nutrition." In the Doha Ministerial Declaration, Arts 7 and 8 were singled out as having special importance in the review of the TRIPS Agreement.[62] An argument could, therefore, be made that these provisions have higher legal status than mere policy statements, not only for the current review, but also for the interpretation of the TRIPS Agreement in the context of WTO dispute settlement proceedings.[63] Article 27, which was mentioned by the CESCR in General Comment No. 17,[64] allows for exclusions from patentability of inventions in the interest of the protection of *ordre public* (para. 2) as well as in medical and biotechnological fields (para. 3). Article 73 contains exceptions referring to the protection of the national security interests of a Member. In contemporary international law, the term "security" is no longer understood as the mere safeguarding of a state or person against the danger of armed conflict, but has been broadened by inter-

---

60 1867 UNTS 3.

61 A. von Bogdandy, "Preamble WTO Agreement", in: R. Wolfrum, P.-T. Stoll and K. Kaiser (eds), *WTO – Institutions and Dispute Settlement*, 2006, para. 15.

62 WT/MIN(01)/DEC/1 of 20 November 2001, para. 19.

63 Gervais, see note 34, at 2.80 and 2.85. See, in this context, R. Okediji, "Toward an International Fair Use Doctrine", *Columbia Journal of Transnational Law* 39 (2000-2001), 75-175; R. Howse, "The Canadian Generic Medicines Panel: A Dangerous Precedent in Dangerous Times", *Journal of World Intellectual Property* 3 (2000), 493-507.

64 See note 50.

pretation to include human rights concerns.[65] In his report "In Larger Freedom," former UN Secretary-General Kofi Annan draws attention to the mutual interdependence of security and human rights. "[D]evelopment, security and human rights go hand in hand" and "reinforce each other."[66] The threats to security in the 21st century include "poverty, deadly infectious disease and environmental degradation".[67] The interdependence of security and human rights is further emphasized by the increasing use of composite words such as "food security"[68] and "health security."[69]

In addition, Article IX:3 of the WTO Agreement authorizes the political organs to waive obligations under the TRIPS Agreement "in exceptional circumstances" and Article 3.2 of the Dispute Settlement Understanding (hereinafter DSU)[70] calls upon the dispute settlement organs to interpret the TRIPS Agreement "in accordance with customary rules of interpretation of public international law," i.e. the Vienna Convention on the Law of Treaties (hereinafter VCLT).[71]

3. Methods of Making Intellectual Property Regimes More Receptive

How may WIPO and the WTO become more receptive to human rights concerns, even if to different degrees?

a. Formal Methods

First, both organizations make use of formal methods. Such methods consist of cooperation between intellectual property organizations and

---

65 Hestermeyer, see note 14, at 58 et seq.

66 In Larger Freedom: Towards Development, Security and Human Rights for All, Report of the Secretary General, A/59/2005 of 21 March 2005, paras 14 and 16.

67 *Ibid.*, para. 78.

68 See e.g. K. Mechlem, "Food Security and the Right to Food in the Discourse of the United Nations", *European Law Journal* 10 (2004), 631-648.

69 See e.g. R. J. Cook, "Human Rights Dimensions of Health Security", *ASIL Proceedings* 97 (2003), 101-106.

70 1869 UNTS 401.

71 1155 UNTS 331.

other entities, in particular human rights organizations; and institutionalization within intellectual property organizations.

Cooperation includes the granting of observer status and establishment of formal and informal cooperation agreements.[72] Human rights concerns may influence decisions to grant observer status and, thereby, enlarge the circle of possible candidates. The latest version of the Draft Declaration on the Rights of Indigenous Peoples, for example, recognizes the right of indigenous peoples to participate in decision-making in matters that would affect their rights.[73] Human rights concerns may also influence the use of experts in WTO dispute settlement proceedings. Panels have consistently sought expert advice from WIPO on the interpretation of intellectual property treaties incorporated into the TRIPS Agreement by Arts 2 para. 1, 9 para. 1 and 35.[74] Other panels could follow this example and request expert advice from human rights organizations on the interpretation of human rights norms that intersect with intellectual property. The Dispute Settlement Body could, moreover, select a member of the Human Rights Committee or the CESCR for service on a panel.[75] While it is true that members of these two human rights bodies have neither "served on or presented a case to a panel" nor "taught or published on international trade law or policy," the list of possible panellists in Article 8 para. 1 DSU is not exhaustive.

Institutionalization refers to the establishment of subsidiary committees within intellectual property organizations dealing with human rights and intellectual property rights. One prominent example within WIPO is the Intergovernmental Committee on Intellectual Property, Genetic Resources, Traditional Knowledge and Folklore which collaborates, *inter alia*, with indigenous peoples.[76] The WTO has also established committees dealing with cross-cutting systemic issues, such as, for example, the Committee on Trade and Environment.

---

[72] See for the cooperation agreement UN-WIPO, note 58, and for the cooperation agreement UN-WTO, Exchange of Letters Constituting a Global Arrangement on Cooperation (WTO-UN), 1889 UNTS 589.

[73] See note 23, Article 18.

[74] See e.g. *United States – Section 110 (5) of the US Copyright Act*, WT/DS160/R of 15 June 2000, Attachment 4.

[75] F. M. Abbott, "The Future of the Multilateral Trading System in the Context of TRIPS", *Hastings International and Comparative Law Review* 20 (1997), 661-682, at 671.

[76] <http://www.wipo.int/tk/en/igc/> (last visit: 15 March 2007).

The mutual exchange of ideas fostered by these formal methods is of special importance as compromises between human rights and intellectual property rights are difficult to achieve. On the one hand, human rights claim a certain "moral superiority" over intellectual property rights. On the other hand, human rights norms are only vaguely drafted and depend on interpretation, while intellectual property rights are very explicit.

b. Substantive Methods

Cooperation and institutionalization are complemented by two substantive approaches to making intellectual property regimes more receptive to human rights concerns: the creation of new – binding and non-binding – legal instruments and the broad and human rights consistent interpretation of general legal terms, exceptions and flexibility clauses contained in existing legal instruments. New binding legal instruments could be framework and policymaking conventions that provide a basis for future normative development. A possible example within WIPO could be the Access to Knowledge Treaty[77] exploring hitherto unknown non-proprietary approaches to intellectual property. New non-binding legal instruments could be used as points of reference in a range of national, regional and international policy discussions and standard-setting processes. An example within WIPO could be the Draft Provisions for the Protection of Traditional Cultural Expressions and for the Protection of Traditional Knowledge.[78] According to these provisions, states may combine different forms of protection: intellectual property protection, if necessary with appropriate adaptations; *sui generis* protection; and other protection available under national law (unfair competition, unjust enrichment, access and benefit-sharing, etc.) as well as under customary and indigenous law.

Eventually, the broad and human rights consistent interpretation of existing legal instruments could give more precise guidance on how to implement international standards without creating distinct obligations. Examples, this time within the WTO, are the Doha Declaration on the

---

[77] See note 57.

[78] Revised Provisions for the Protection of Traditional Cultural Expressions/Expressions of Folklore: Policy Objectives and Core Principles, WIPO/GRTKF/IC/9/4 of 9 January 2006, Annex; Revised Provisions for the Protection of Traditional Knowledge: Policy Objectives and Core Principles, WIPO/GRTKF/IC/9/5 of 9 January 2006, Annex.

TRIPS Agreement and Public Health[79] and the subsequent waiver of Article 31 lit. f and h of the TRIPS Agreement[80] and could – at least in the future – be the consideration of human rights within the dispute settlement system. Article 3 para. 2 DSU refers to Article 31 para. 3 lit. c VCLT, and, thus, to "any relevant rules of international law applicable in the relations between the parties." The dispute settlement organs might, therefore, opt for an evolutionary interpretation of general legal terms, exceptions and flexibility clauses in accordance with human rights, provided that they do not "add or diminish the rights and obligations" laid down in the TRIPS Agreement and provided that the human rights rules in question apply between the parties. Although – strictly speaking – only legal instruments fall within the definition of "rules," the dispute settlement organs could follow the example set by the Appellate Body in the *US – Shrimp* case and also take into account non-binding legal instruments, for example General Comment No. 17 on the human right of the author. In the *US – Shrimp* case, the Appellate Body held that "exhaustible natural resources" in Article XX lit. g of the GATT 1994[81] was an evolutionary concept to be "read by a treaty interpreter in the light of contemporary concerns [...] about the protection and conservation of the environment."[82] As these concerns were reflected in "modern international conventions *and* declarations,"[83] it also considered non-binding legal instruments, such as Agenda 21 and the Rio Declaration on Environment and Development.[84]

---

[79] WT/MIN(01)/DEC/2 of 20 November 2001.

[80] Implementation of Paragraph 6 of the Doha Declaration on the TRIPS Agreement and Public Health, WT/L/540 of 2 September 2003. See on the legal qualification of this decision as a waiver R. Wolfrum, "Article IX WTO Agreement", in: R. Wolfrum, P.-T. Stoll and K. Kaiser (eds), *WTO – Institutions and Dispute Settlement*, 2006, para. 33.

[81] General Agreement on Tariffs and Trade, 1867 UNTS 187.

[82] *United States – Import Prohibition of Certain Shrimp and Shrimp Products*, WT/DS58/AB/R of 12 October 1998, para. 129.

[83] *Ibid.*, para. 130. Emphasis added by the author.

[84] *Ibid.*, para. 168.

4. Evaluation

How can the chances of improving the receptivity of the main intellectual property organizations to human rights concerns be evaluated? First of all, an unequal distribution of possibilities and limits must be remarked on. While WIPO has more possibilities and can actively become more receptive to human rights concerns, the WTO is confronted with more limits and can react only passively. Why is this so? As a UN specialized agency, WIPO belongs to the UN family in which responsibilities for different subject matter areas are shared.[85] The WTO, on the contrary, is an independent international organization and is focused on the particular subject area of world trade. The founding members of the WTO deliberately decided to leave human rights to specialized organizations and bodies.

Another limitation will be whether WIPO, and especially the WTO, exhaust the scope of their mandates with regard to the areas of intersection between human rights and intellectual property. Although the Doha Ministerial Declaration instructed the TRIPS Council to examine the relationship between the TRIPS Agreement and the protection of traditional knowledge and folklore,[86] members could not achieve consensus on any of the contentious issues.[87] Unconstrained by consensus, WIPO, therefore, seems to be better suited than the WTO to addressing the protection of indigenous peoples' cultural heritage and traditional knowledge within the intellectual property system, and striking the balance between intellectual property rights and the right to access to knowledge. In the long run, non-binding legal instruments, such as the Draft Provisions for the Protection of Traditional Cultural Expressions and for the Protection of Traditional Knowledge,[88] may prove to be more successful than binding legal instruments. The proposed Access to Knowledge Treaty, if adopted, will not succeed if it is ratified only by developing countries and if the number of ratifications falls under the one of the major intellectual property treaties. If WIPO failed

---

[85] H. G. Schermers and N. M. Blokker, *International Institutional Law*, 4th edition 2003, § 1691.

[86] See note 62.

[87] The Protection of Traditional Knowledge and Folklore, Summary Issues Raised and Points Made, IP/C/W/370/Rev.1 of 9 March 2006.

[88] See note 78.

and cross-concessions became relevant, the WTO could reappear on the stage and serve as a forum of last resort.[89]

However, only the WTO can soften the effects of its compliance system and destroy fears with regard to the factual hierarchy of compliance systems. It cannot extend its mandate without the consent of its members, but it can and should make more use of the above-described formal and substantive methods to facilitate its increased receptivity to human rights concerns. The TRIPS Council could, for example, reconsider pending applications for observer status, such as the application submitted by the Secretariat of the Convention on Biological Diversity,[90] a body that has shown a strong interest in traditional knowledge. It could, moreover, continue and intensify the trend towards broadly interpreting general legal terms, exceptions and flexibility clauses in order to take account of human rights concerns. But we have to be realistic. Due to the absence of explicit linkages, the establishment of a Committee on Trade and Human Rights is highly unlikely.[91] The reason is that there are considerably fewer linkage references in the legal texts in the case of trade and human rights than in the case of trade and the environment. As the WTO is a member-driven organization and very much dominated by the "Quads," the four biggest trading members, it is equally doubtful whether the dispute settlement organs would dare to interpret the TRIPS Agreement in accordance with human rights rules. The United States is, after all, not party to the ICESCR.

IV. Conclusion

Despite the commonalities that I described in the beginning, intellectual property rights have not yet superseded human rights in the same way that Mr. Hyde came to possess Dr. Jekyll. The persistent mistrust with which intellectual property rights meet results from a misunderstanding

---

89 F. M. Abbott, "Distributed Governance at the WTO-WIPO: An Evolving Model for Open-Architecture Integrated Governance", *JIEL* 3 (2000), 63-81, at 70.

90 International Intergovernmental Organizations, Requests for Observer Status in the Council for TRIPS, IP/C/W/52/Rev.11 of 27 May 2005.

91 G. Sampson, "Is There a Need for Restructuring the Collaboration Among the WTO and UN Agencies so as to Harness Their Complementarities?", *JIEL* 7 (2004), 717-727, at 725 et seq.

of their worth and adaptability. Intellectual property rights certainly are not "evil" enough to be "killed." Even if they were, the abandonment of intellectual property rights would not be a viable means. For, as Stevenson's novel teaches us, Mr. Hyde cannot be killed without sacrificing Dr. Jekyll at the same time. The abandonment of intellectual property rights would ultimately lead to the abandonment of the human right of the author.

Although there are several areas of intersection between human rights and intellectual property rights, a cure-all for Dr. Jekyll's schizophrenia has not yet been found. For the time being, WIPO and the WTO as the main intellectual property organizations serve as a kind of laboratory in which different individual conflicts are solved on a case-by-case basis. The different solutions found through that process may give indications of how to relax the relationship between human rights and intellectual property rights in the future and, in the end, lead Dr. Jekyll to the antidote.

The Struggle for Minority Rights and Human Rights: Current Trends and Challenges

Rainer Grote

I. Introduction

Even at the beginning of the 21st century, important issues concerning the protection of minority rights in international law still remain unresolved. This is somewhat surprising since historically the protection of minorities in international law has a much longer tradition than the protection of individual human rights, which is essentially an "invention" of the post-war period. Every major peace treaty in Europe from that of Westphalia onwards has contained provisions for the protection of religious minorities.[1] In the course of the 19th century this protection

[1] P. Thornberry, *International Law and the Rights of Minorities*, 1991, 25 et seq.; N. Lerner, "Religious Human Rights under the United Nations", in: J.D. van der Vyver/J. Witte Jr. (eds.), *Religious Human Rights in Global Perspective*, 1996, 83; R. Grote, „Die Religionsfreiheit im Spiegel völkervertraglicher Vereinbarungen zur politischen und territorialen Neuordnung", in: R. Grote/T.

was extended to ethnic groups, culminating in the minority treaty system established at the Versailles peace conference after the First World War under which many of the States in Central, Eastern and South Eastern Europe which had been newly created or had had their boundaries redrawn as a result of the war pledged to safeguard essential rights of the religious and ethnic minorities living within their boundaries.[2] These treaties were placed under the supervision of the League of Nations, and disputes arising out of them could be referred by the League Council to the Permanent Court of International Justice for an advisory opinion. In a number of advisory opinions the Court laid the foundations of an international jurisprudence on minority rights by elaborating on the purposes of the protection system and on the basic characteristics of the groups protected by it.[3]

Several decades later minority protection in international law seems to be still in its infancy. While there are some widely recognized international standards which are of relevance to the protection of minorities, the normative and institutional framework is in many ways considerably weaker than that established after the First World War. Article 27 of the UN Covenant on Civil and Political Rights (UNCCPR), which is generally considered to be the linchpin of the international protection of minorities in the post-war era, speaks of the "rights of persons belonging to ethnic, religious or linguistic minorities", not of the rights of minorities as such. With this approach it has set a standard for other international instruments in the field of minority protection which have been adopted since, most notably the – non-binding – UN Declaration on the Rights of Persons belonging to National or Ethnic, Religious

---

Marauhn (eds.), *Religionsfreiheit zwischen individueller Selbstbestimmung, Minderheitenschutz und Staatskirchenrecht – Völker- und verfassungsrechtliche Perspektiven*, 2001, 3 et seq.

[2] F. Capotorti, *Study on the Rights of Persons Belonging to Ethnic, Religious and Linguistic Minorities*, 1979, 16 et seq.; Thornberry, see note 1, 38 et seq.; H. Rosting, "Protection of Minorities by the League of Nations", *AJIL* 17 (1923), 641 et seq.

[3] These included the opinion in the *Minority Schools in Albania* case (PCIJ [1935], Series A/B No. 64), in which the Court pointed out that the main purpose of the protection of minorities established under the League System, i.e. the preservation of the distinguishing characteristics of the minorities, warranted the application of a substantial, as opposed to a merely formal, concept of equality. For a list of the different advisory opinions by the PCIJ relating to various aspects of minority protection under the League System see Capotorti, note 2, 24 footnote 43.

and Linguistic Minorities[4] and the European Framework Convention for the Protection of National Minorities.[5] None of these instruments tries to define the groups which qualify as minorities and thus stand to benefit, if only indirectly, from the protection offered by them. Nor is any of them subject to the supervision and interpretation of an international court. The Human Rights Committee has a conditional right to review individual petitions for violation of the Covenant's substantive provisions, including Article 27, but the overall context in which it is placed ensures that the main focus of the Committee's review activities will remain firmly on individual rights. The Advisory Committee under the European Framework Convention is confined to evaluating the reports submitted by the States Parties for the adequacy of the measures taken with regard to the principles set out in the Convention and is thus not in a position to test and clarify the legal substance of those principles in individual cases. Not surprisingly, the international courts and tribunals, including the ICJ, have had even less to say on the matter. This shows that, although minority rights have attracted renewed attention in the decade following the end of the cold war,[6] the basic terms and legal parameters of this debate seem to have remained virtually unchanged.

If one tries to identify the causes for this rather unsatisfactory state of affairs, one has to start with the changed historical and political context in which the debate on minority rights takes place today. The disrepute into which the manipulation and abuse of minority rights namely by Nationalist Germany in the years preceding the Second World War had brought the whole system convinced many that such rights constituted

[4] A/RES/47/135 of 18 December 1992.

[5] CETS No. 157 (1995).

[6] This renewed interest in the protection of minorities as an indispensable means to prevent and to check ethnic and civil strife in multi-ethnic countries and territories was documented by the adoption of the UN Declaration on the Rights of Persons Belonging to National or Ethnic, Religious and Linguistic Minorities in 1992 and the drafting of new instruments at the regional, especially at the European level. But this period also witnessed the emergence of other forms and institutions of minority protection. Minority rights were explicitly made part of the conditions which the successor states of Yugoslavia had to meet in order to be recognized by the European Community, and the CSCE (later OSCE) established a High Commissioner on National Minorities in 1992. For a survey of developments during this period see S. Krasner, *Sovereignty – Organized Hypocrisy*, 1999, 98 et seq.

an unacceptable threat to national sovereignty and domestic stability.[7] The Universal Declaration of Human Rights of 1948 had nothing at all to say about minority rights,[8] setting an important precedent for the human rights discussion in the years to come. Moreover, a number of states opposed the recognition of such rights as a matter of principle because they deemed the perpetuation of fixed group identities associated with these rights as incompatible with their definition of themselves as immigrant societies or "melting pots" or with important constitutional principles like the indivisible character of the Republic.[9]

But there are also a number of important conceptual issues which appear far from settled although they are indispensable to establishing a firm basis for an effective system of international minority protection. Some of these issues will be discussed in the next section.

II. Conceptual Issues

1. Group Rights vs. Individual Rights

One of the most important and difficult conceptual issues in contemporary debate about minority protection concerns the relationship between minority rights as group rights on the one hand and individual rights on the other. In general, it has been difficult to justify the need for specific group rights in the light of the individualist rights discourse which has dominated most of the debate on the protection of human rights in the post-war era. Within this liberal tradition of human rights doctrine two different stands of thinking on group rights can be distinguished.

The first view considers group rights as by their very nature incompatible with individual rights. According to this doctrine, the preservation of fixed group identities which the granting of minority rights tries to ensure is inherently inimical to the personal autonomy the effective

---

[7] S. Poulter, "The Rights of Ethnic, Religious and Linguistic Minorities", *EHRLR* 2 (1997), 254 et seq.

[8] On the debate concerning this issue in the Assembly and the Third Committee see Thornberry, note 1, 133 et seq.; Capotorti, note 2, 27.

[9] See the detailed account of the arguments advanced by the different states in the debate on the concept of "minorities" within the meaning of Article 27 ICCPR by Thornberry, note 1, 154 et seq.

protection of which is at the very core of human rights protection as it has developed after the Second World War. An integral part of this autonomy is the freedom of each individual to determine to which group he or she wants to belong or not belong. Minority rights tend to obscure or even to deny the autonomy of the members of the group by focusing on the group's identity as such and by turning it into an object of protection in its own right. However, it is widely recognized today that the dichotomy between individual rights and collective rights thus created is a false one. While there is certainly a bias towards the individual as the ultimate beneficiary of human rights in liberal human rights doctrine it cannot simply be equated with one of the more extreme streams of liberal thought which focuses on the individual as an isolated, largely self-sufficient human being free of any social or community constraint.[10] On the contrary, the prevailing view today is that of the individual as a social being who in many situations can make meaningful use of his or her human rights only in interaction or in community with others. This approach leaves considerable room for the development of the human personality in association with others, as long as the voluntary nature of the relevant association is maintained. It is this view which is supported by the wide interpretation given by international and national human rights jurisprudence to the right to free association which protects not only the right of individuals to establish an association and to become members of it, but also the right of the association freely to pursue the purposes for which it was founded.[11] In a similar vein, courts and monitoring bodies have readily accepted the collective dimension of fundamental rights like the freedom of religion by extending their protection to practices and institutions which are as relevant to the identity of the group as such as they are to the liberty of their members, for example by recognizing the importance of special slaughtering practices to the free exercise of certain religious beliefs.[12]

---

[10] John Packer, "Problems in Defining Minorities", in: D. Fottrell/B. Bowring (eds.), *Minority and Group Rights in the New Millenium*, 1999, 243, who traces this isolationist view of the individual to a peculiar strand in American liberal thinking most brilliantly exemplified by the work of Henry David Thoreau.

[11] E.g., European Court of Human Rights Series A 44, § 39 – *National Union of Belgian Police Case.*

[12] See, e.g., European Court of Human Rights, Reports 2000-VII, 231, § 76 – *Cha'are Shalom ve Tsedek*.

A second objection to the acceptance of group rights is based on more pragmatic considerations. Its supporters argue with the dynamic character of human rights protection which, they say, has been extended over the last few decades to a point where they cover all relevant concerns which in former times were discussed under the heading of minority or group rights. They point particularly to the inclusive concepts nowadays associated with the right to equality and the prohibition of discrimination. The principle of non-discrimination is of particular relevance here, because it is, as in the UN Covenant, often formulated in such an open-ended way as to allow for the inclusion of additional prohibited grounds of differential treatment through interpretation by the competent courts and treaty bodies in the light of changing circumstances. But the prohibition of discrimination has proved flexible not just with regard to the prohibited grounds of discrimination. In many cases it has also proved flexible enough to accommodate the need for affirmative action to redress past injustices and to achieve substantive – as opposed to formal – equality for members of groups which historically have been the victims of particularly severe oppression and discrimination. An example at the UN level is the Convention on the Elimination of all Forms of Racial Discrimination (CERD) which in Articles 1 and 2 specifically and explicitly allows for measures to be taken for the purpose of securing adequate advancement of certain racial or ethnic groups or individuals in order to ensure to such groups or individuals equal enjoyment of their human rights. Such broadly conceived rights to equality and non-discrimination, it is argued, are sufficient to cover those needs and concerns advanced by the proponents of minority rights which deserve protection.[13] The example of the black population in the US may be used to illustrate this approach: while blacks in the US would certainly qualify as a minority worthy of special protection in accordance with most views and definitions proposed on the subject, the black civil rights movement never seems to have seriously viewed their plight in terms of lack of sufficient minority rights, but rather in terms of the need to pursue and intensify their struggle for *equal* rights.

However, this view is convincing only if one assumes that all that minorities want, and all that they are entitled to expect, is equal access to the rights and opportunities of the other groups in society, namely those of the dominant or majority culture. While this assumption may

---

[13] N. Rodley, "Conceptual Problems in the Protection of Minorities: International Legal Developments", International Human Rights Quarterly 17 (1995), 48 et seq. (at 64/65).

have a high degree of plausibility for some societies and the groups living within those societies, it may be less suitable for others. Tribal societies and their members, for example, may have a very different view of the relationship between the individual and the group from societies and groups which have long lived under the influence of modern life. Minority protection in international law, however, must be able to cover a wide variety of groups and minorities, ranging from the tribes in the Amazon basin or Papua New Guinea which have only recently emerged from the Stone Age to groups which have for long been used to living in dynamic, multi-cultural societies. What at least some of these groups want is to preserve their traditional ways of life and to remain distinct from the dominant society rather than to integrate fully within it. This preference cannot be met with rights to equality or the principle of non-discrimination, even if broadly conceived.[14] If the wish of a minority group and its members to choose freely between assimilation or preservation as a distinct group is not to be denounced as illegitimate, it must be possible to grant it some measure of legal protection. Minority rights in this view cannot be limited to the right of the relevant group not to be discriminated against, even if formulated in the most peremptory terms, but must include a number of additional guarantees designed to allow the group to preserve and protect the elements on which its collective identity is based.

Empirical evidence tends to support the view that the recognition of group rights can in certain situations be an adequate and even an indispensable instrument to promote the welfare of certain vulnerable groups and their members. Historically, industrialized countries have been prepared to recognize particular rights, such as the right to collective bargaining, accorded to trade unions in their capacity as organizations representing the economic interests of workers which were independent of the individual rights of workers. These union rights were seen at the time, and still continue to be seen, as necessary instruments for promoting the welfare of the relevant sector of the population, which obviously could not be secured to the extent necessary by the contractual freedom of individual workers or by protective legislation alone.

The real issues concerning the recognition of group rights or collective rights are thus whether certain rights should be enjoyed exclusively by groups and which rules apply where there is conflict between a group

---

[14] E. Heinze, "The Construction and Contingency of the Minority Concept", in: Fottrell/Bowring, note 10, 40.

right and the individual rights of one or several of its members. The answer to the first question depends on the nature and the content of the relevant right. For example, the right to the establishment and maintenance of certain educational facilities in which the language and culture of the minority group in question are taught can be achieved only as a group right, and therefore should be formulated as such. The right to free access to existing institutions of such kind, on the other hand, is by necessity an individual right which accrues to each member of the relevant group. Similarly, the determination of a conflict between group rights and individual rights depends on the context of the conflict and the nature of the clashing rights. E.g., a group's right to communal property with regard to ancestral lands must necessarily prevail over the conflicting property rights of individual group members, since any other solution would undermine the protective function of the institution of communal property. Conversely, the rights of the individual to physical integrity and the free development of his or her personality may well establish limits to certain forms of group or tribal jurisdiction and the way in which it has traditionally been exercised. Like any other rights, group rights are neither absolute nor totally unlimited, but have to be balanced with competing (individual or collective) rights or the public interest in cases of conflict.

2. Definition of Minorities

One of the most vividly discussed and seemingly intractable problems in the debate about minority rights concerns the definition of minorities. Such a definition appears desirable from a theoretical as well as from a practical perspective. From a theoretical point of view it is highly problematic to define the content of a right without having a clear idea to whom the right thus defined is to apply. With regard to the effective implementation of minority rights the lack of a clear definition raises the prospect of a multitude of unfounded claims to minority rights and endless controversies about the legitimacy of claimants and the full scope of their rights.[15] Nevertheless it has proved exceedingly difficult in practice to achieve a substantial degree of consensus on any definition of minority. Not only have governments been reluctant to tie their hands through the acceptance of a binding international definition of minorities which may reduce their freedom in pursuing their own

---

[15] Packer, see note 10, 225 et seq.

priorities in this sensitive field of domestic policy; the advocates of minority rights have equally been reluctant to accept any definition which is too precise and could thus make the future extension of the protective regime to other vulnerable groups more difficult.

A number of important proposals attempting to define the concept of minority have nevertheless been made by experts and human rights bodies. One of the most influential was that submitted by the Special Rapporteur of the UN Subcommittee on the Prevention of Discrimination and the Protection of Minorities, Francesco Capotorti, in his study of the rights of people belonging to minority groups, which relied on four criteria for the delimitation of minorities: the numerical inferiority of the group concerned to the rest of the population; its subordinate position; ethnic, religious or linguistic characteristics which distinguish the group from the rest of the population; and a sense of solidarity within it, directed towards the preservation of the group's culture, tradition, religion or language. Crucially, Capotorti limited the definition to groups whose members possessed the nationality of the State in which they lived.[16] On this last point, he has not been followed by the Human Rights Committee which in its – contested – General Comment 23 asserted that Article 27 of the UNCCPR also covers people who are not citizens or permanent residents of the State responsible for the alleged violation of Article 27.[17]

A similar definition to Capotorti's was contained in Recommendation 1201 (1993) of the Parliamentary Assembly of the Council of Europe on the adoption of an Additional Protocol on the rights of national minorities to the European Convention on Human Rights (ECHR).[18] The definition in Article 1 of the proposed Protocol followed Capotorti's proposal in so far as it limited the concept of minority to people who are resident in the host state and are citizens of it, i.e. to *national* minorities. Two more elements of the definition – the display of distinctive ethnic, cultural, religious or linguistic characteristics and the concern to preserve that which constitutes the common identity of the group, including its culture, traditions, religion or language – are also clearly reminiscent of Capotorti's definition. However, the draft protocol added two further elements of its own which clearly narrowed the

16 Capotorti, see note 2, 95.

17 CCPR/C/21/Rev.1/Add.5, General Comment No. 23, Observation 5.1.

18 Text available on http://assembly.coe.int/Mainf.asp?link=/Documents/AdoptedText/ta93/EREC1201.htm.

scope of the definition in comparison to Capotorti's: The group concerned must be "sufficiently representative" (although smaller in number than the rest of the population) and it must maintain "longstanding, firm and lasting ties" with the state. The latter requirement was incorporated in the definition in order to exclude members of the so-called "new minorities", particularly immigrants, from the protection of the Protocol.[19] In its report to the Committee of Ministers on the matter the Steering Committee of Human Rights noted, however, that there was no consensus among experts and member states on the interpretation of the term "national minorities." The proposed Protocol to the ECHR was never adopted. Nevertheless, in its Recommendation 1492 (2001) the Parliamentary Assembly of the Council of Europe reaffirmed its view that the Draft Protocol contained "the most acceptable definition at European level of a 'national minority'".[20]

The proposed definitions have been criticised for pragmatic as well as for conceptual reasons. At the conceptual level, the criticism has focused on the attempt to define minorities by reference to some alleged essential or 'organic' link between their members, namely on the basis of their shared ethnic, cultural and linguistic characteristics. According to this line of argument, none of the categories used to "classify" people and to determine their group identity can be understood as merely reflecting an "objective" reality which exists independently of the human mind. Categorizations based on some allegedly unalterable facts like, in particular, racial classifications have invariably been shown to lack any proper biological or other foundation. Categorizations have therefore to be seen as social constructions which are conceived and applied in order to satisfy certain political or social needs. As social constructions they are subject, in varying degrees, to cultural relativism and historical contingency. This suggests that any definition of the concept of minorities has to be constantly adapted in order to reflect changing social realities. It thus cannot be regarded as exhaustive or exclusive, but only as

---

[19] A similar approach was followed by the European Charter for Regional and Minority Languages of 5 November 1992 (CETS No. 148) which defines in Article 1 the protected regional or minority languages as languages "traditionally used within a given territory of the State", expressly excluding the languages of "migrants".

[20] Available on http://assembly.coe.int/Mainf.asp?link=/Documents/AdoptedText/ta01/EREC1492.htm.

an incomplete attempt to characterize social entities which are constantly in flux.[21]

The practice has side-stepped the issue by simply not including a definition in the relevant international instruments at all. While this may be tolerable in the UN Declaration on the Rights of Persons Belonging to National or Ethnic, Religious and Linguistic Minorities, which has no legally binding character, it is more problematic in the case of the European Framework Convention for the Protection of National Minorities, which imposes a number of legal obligations on the Member States. The drafters of the Convention were unable to reach consensus even on the minimal definition contained in the draft protocol to the ECHR and followed a "pragmatic approach" by elaborating provisions mainly of a programmatic character for which, it was claimed, a definition would not be needed.[22] Nor have the States Parties been able to agree on a common approach in the application of the Convention.[23] A number of States Parties have added to their instruments of ratification declarations concerning the scope of the Convention. While some of them have defined the term "national minority" by using abstract criteria borrowed from national[24] or international law[25], others have specifically named the minorities which in their view fall within the scope of the

---

21 For a full development of this argument see Heinze, note 14, 45 et seq.

22 Packer, see note 10, 236/237.

23 For an overview of the treatment of the definition issue in the application of the Convention see H.-J. Heinze, "Article 3", in: M. Weller (ed.), *The Rights of Minorities in Europe – A Commentary on the European Framework Convention on the Protection of National Minorities*, 2005, 111 et seq.

24 For example Austria ("those groups which come within the scope of application of the Law on Ethnic Groups (*Volksgruppengesetz*, Federal Law Gazette No. 396/1976) and which live and traditionally have had their home in parts of the territory of the Republic of Austria and which are composed of Austrian citizens with non-German mother tongues and with their own ethnic cultures").

25 Particularly from Article 1 of the Draft Protocol to the European Convention on Human Rights of 1993, e.g. Switzerland ("groups of individuals numerically inferior to the rest of the population of the country or of a canton, whose members are Swiss nationals, have long-standing, firm and lasting ties with Switzerland and are guided by the will to safeguard together what constitutes their common identity, in particular their culture, their traditions, their religion or their language").

Framework Convention.[26] A third group of States have simply stated that there are no national minorities in their territory.[27] While the Advisory Committee, when evaluating the States' reports on their minorities policies, has on several occasions criticised the restrictive approach taken by Member States in identifying the minorities which fall under the Convention and has asked them to reconsider their narrow interpretation of the Framework Convention's scope in consultation with the groups concerned, it has done so without itself proposing any positive definition.[28]

While the definition of the beneficiaries of minority rights raises a number of problems which have no equivalent in the protection of individual human rights, the problems do not appear insurmountable. In order to take into account the very different historical and political contexts in which minorities are placed, an open-ended definition which leaves room for the inclusion of new minorities seems desirable. However, it is hardly realistic to expect states to sign and ratify a binding legal instrument on such a delicate matter if they are unable to determine and eventually limit its scope with sufficient precision. A viable strategy

---

[26] For example Germany (Danes, Sorbians, Frisians, Sinti and Roma), Slovenia (the autochthonous Italian and Hungarian National Minorities) and Sweden (Sami, Swedish Finns, Tornedalers, Roma and Jews).

[27] The states in question are Liechtenstein, Luxembourg and Malta. See for the different declarations and reservations the website of the Council of Europe on the Convention, http://conventions.coe.int/Treaty/Commun/ListeDeclarations.asp?NT=157&CM=8&DF=08/02/05&CL=ENG&VL=1.

[28] See, e.g. the Committee's opinions on the First Cycle Report submitted by Denmark with regard to the restrictive interpretation of the Convention adopted by the Danish Government concerning its non-application to Greenlanders, Faroers and Romas, ACFC/INF/OP/I (2001)005, observations 12-23, and the report submitted by Estonia, ACFC/INF/OP/I (2002)005, observations 13-20, with regard to exclusion of the Russian minority from the Convention's scope of application. In these and in other cases the Committee has stressed that parties have a margin of appreciation in determining the personal scope of the Convention in order to take the specific circumstances prevailing in their country into account. On the other hand, it notes that this margin of appreciation must be exercised in accordance with general principles of international law and the fundamental principles set out in Article 3 of the Convention. In particular it stresses that the implementation of the Framework Convention should not be a source of "arbitrary or unjustified distinctions". The reports can be found on the website of the Council of Europe at http://www.coe.int/t/e/human_rights/minorities/2._framework_convention_(monitoring).

in addressing the definition in the relevant international instruments might therefore consist in the inclusion only in the instrument's Preamble of an open-ended definition, or alternatively in retaining a narrow definition like the one in the Draft Protocol to the ECHR in the operative part of the instrument. In both cases, however, Member States would be required to designate in an annex to the instrument at least one minority to which its provisions would apply. The State Party could add new minorities by simple notification, whereas the name of a protected minority could be withdrawn from the list only with the approval of the treaty monitoring body. If at any time a Member had not listed even a single minority in its Annex, it would automatically cease to be a party to the convention.

III. The Use of General Human Rights Instruments for the Purpose of Minority Protection: the Example of the CERD

While there are no legally binding instruments specifically designed to protect minority rights at the global level, there are several general human rights instruments which deal with some aspects of minority protection. The best known of these is Article 27 of the UNCCPR which protects the right of people belonging to ethnic, religious or linguistic minorities to enjoy and practise, in community with other members of their group, their own culture, religion and language.[29] In dealing with several individual communications under this provision the Human Rights Committee has had the opportunity to clarify its scope with regard to the minorities covered[30] and to address the difficult issue of af-

---

[29] For a detailed analysis of the interpretation and application of Article 27 see M. Nowak, *CCPR Commentary*, 2nd edition 2005, Article 27 paras. 12 et seq.; Rodley, note 13, 49 et seq.

[30] In *Lubicon Lake Band v. Canada* (Communication No. 167/1984; UN doc. A/45/40 (1990)) the Committee held that Article 27 applies to indigenous communities, too, although the applicants, like many indigenous groups, considered themselves as a people and not as a minority and therefore had brought their application under Article 1 (right to self-determination). The Committee found that historical inequities and recent developments threatening the way of life and culture of the applicants constituted a violation of Article 27 as long as they continued.

filiation of individuals with their group.[31] Other, less well known, provisions in the field include Article 30 of the Convention on the Rights of the Child which expressly extends the guarantees of Article 27 UNCCPR to children but distinguishes between ethnic, religious and linguistic minorities and "persons of indigenous origin", thus acknowledging the separate status claimed by the latter. While Article 30 of the Convention on the Rights of the Child recognizes the special status of indigenous groups in principle but does not grant their members any rights other than those enjoyed by members of ethnic, religious or linguistic minorities, ILO Convention No. 169 concerning Indigenous and Tribal Peoples in Independent Countries goes one decisive step further and defines a set of rights specifically designed to meet the special needs and demands of indigenous populations. These rights include, though the term is scrupulously avoided, a limited measure of political autonomy or self-government to be exercised through representative institutions of the relevant indigenous groups, and the rights of ownership and possession over the lands which the indigenous or tribal peoples have traditionally occupied.[32] However, the Convention has so far been ratified only by a very limited number of states.[33]

---

[31] In the case of *Lovelace v. Canada* (Communication No. 24/1977; UN doc. A/36/40 (1981) the Committee stated that an Indian woman who had been brought up on a reserve and had kept ties with her community could invoke the rights under Article 27, notwithstanding a provision of national law which deprived her of her legal status of Indian on account of her marriage to a non-Indian. In *Kitok v. Sweden* (Communication No. 197/1985; UN doc. A/43/40/ (1988), on the other hand, the Committee upheld in the last analysis national legislation which allowed the exclusion of persons whose claim for membership in an ethnic group was not accepted by the group itself from certain economic and cultural activities which, because of their central importance to the survival of the group, could only be lawfully exercised by recognised members of the group.

[32] For an overview of the Convention see R. Wolfrum, "The Protection of Indigenous Peoples in International Law", *ZaöRV* 59 (1999), 369 et seq.

[33] As of May 1, 2007, 18 countries – mainly from Latin America – had ratified the Convention; the only European countries to have done so are Denmark and – most recently – Spain.

1. The Significance of the CERD for Minority Groups

One of the general human rights instruments most relevant to the protection of minorities is the Convention on the Elimination of All Forms of Racial Discrimination to the interpretation and implementation of which Rüdiger Wolfrum has contributed significantly both as a scholar[34] and as a member – from 1990 to 2000 – of the treaty's monitoring body, the Committee on the Elimination of Racial Discrimination.[35] While the CERD was not specifically designed as a convention for the protection of minority rights, it has a number of features which are of particular relevance to the protection of minorities. To start with, the Convention defines the beneficiaries of the prohibition of racial discrimination in broad terms, by placing groups of people as well as individuals under its protection.[36] According to Article 2 para. 1 (a) CERD

---

[34] R. Wolfrum, "The Implementation of International Standards on Prevention and Elimination of Racial Discrimination", in: J. Simonides (ed.), *The Struggle against Discrimination*, 1996, 45 et seq.; id., "International Convention on the Elimination of all Forms of Racial Discrimination", in: E. Klein (ed.), *The Monitoring System of Human Rights Treaty Obligations*, 1998, 49 et seq.; id., "The Committee on the Elimination of Racial Discrimination", Max Planck UNYB 3 (1999), 489 et seq.; id., „Das Verbot der Diskriminierung von Rasse, Herkunft, Sprache oder Hautfarbe im Völkerrecht", in: R. Wolfrum (ed.), *Gleichheit und Nichtdiskriminierung im nationalen und internationalen Menschenrechtsschutz*, 2003, 215 et seq.; id., „Das Verbot der Diskriminierung gemäß den internationalen Menschenrechtsabkommen", in: C. Gaitanides/S. Kadelbach/G.C. Rodríguez Iglesias (eds.), *Europa und seine Verfassung. Festschrift für Manfred Zuleeg zum siebzigsten Geburtstag*, 2005, 385 et seq.

[35] For an analysis of the contribution of general human rights instruments at the regional level to the protection of minorities see Poulter, note 7, 254 et seq., and R. Wolfrum, „Aspekte des Schutzes von Minderheiten unter dem Europäischen Menschenrechtsschutzsystem", in: J. Bröhmer/R. Bieber/C. Calliess (eds.), *Internationale Gemeinschaft und Menschenrechte, Festschrift für Georg Ress zum 70. Geburtstag am 21. Januar 2005*, 1109 et seq., both with regard to the European system. For an analysis of the Inter-American system see J. Anaya/R. Williams, "The protection of Indigenous Peoples' rights over land and natural resources under the Inter-American System of Human Rights", Harvard Human Rights Journal 14 (2001), 33 et seq.; a review of the landmark Awas Tingni decision by the Inter-American Court of Human Rights is provided by J. Anaya/C. Grossmann, "The Case of Awas Tingni v. Nicaragua – a New Step in the International Law of Indigenous Peoples", *Ariz. J. Int'l Comp. L.* 19 (2002), 1 et seq.

[36] Thornberry, see note 1, 268 who states "that the Convention confronts the question of an „intermediate level of social reality between State and indi-

each State party undertakes "to engage in no act or practice of racial discrimination against persons, groups of persons or institutions" and to ensure that all public authorities observe this obligation. The Convention thus does not follow the approach of the other UN and regional instruments on minorities which limit the scope of their substantive obligations to individuals, at the most to individuals "in community with others", but scrupulously avoid any reference to groups as potential subjects or beneficiaries of the protected rights. In addition, the Convention conceives the grounds upon which discrimination is not permissible broadly, not limiting itself, contrary to its title, to the prohibition of distinctions and exclusions based on race. Instead it includes colour, descent, national and ethnic origin in the list of prohibited criteria (Article 1 para. 1 CERD).[37] This broad approach to the definition of racial discrimination is suitable for protecting racial, ethnic, and linguistic groups, and thus some of the core groups most commonly targeted in the debate on minority rights.[38]

Finally, the Convention understands non-discrimination as a concept which goes beyond mere formal equality and ensures to the people and groups concerned the full and effective enjoyment of their rights or, in other words, substantive equality. Articles 1(4) and 2(2) explicitly allow States to take "special measures" for the purpose of securing adequate advancement of certain racial or ethnic groups or individuals requiring such protection in order to ensure such groups or individuals equal enjoyment of human rights. These are important provisions which are of considerable relevance to minorities because they recognise in principle the legitimacy of special measures which exclusively benefit these groups while they are denied to others, i.e. the members of the majority culture. The special measures can and often will include the grant of certain specific collective rights to the racial and ethnic groups concerned. It has even been affirmed that the concept of special temporary measures is the device by which the twin principles of non-discrimination and minority protection can be fused into one principle,

---

vidual" in a more direct way than other contemporary human rights instruments, and in particular Article 27 UNCCPR.

[37] Consequently, the Committee has felt no need to try to define more precisely what is meant by the notion of "race" as a prohibited criterion for distinction in Article 1, see Wolfrum (1999), note 34, at 497.

[38] Thornberry, see note 1, 263.

that of – substantive – equality.[39] This sweeping claim has to be treated with caution, however, since the Convention expressly states that special measures must be of a temporary nature, and that they must be discontinued after their objective, i.e. the full enjoyment of the rights enjoyed by the majority by the racial or ethnic group in question, has been achieved. Articles 1(4) and 2 (2) seemingly do not call into question or undermine the "integrationist" approach of the Convention. They thus cover only one aspect of minority rights, the right of the minority group and its members effectively to integrate themselves into the dominant society if they so wish, but not the second dimension of minority rights, which is to allow the group and its members permanently to preserve their distinct identity as a separate group.[40] Nevertheless the provisions are of fundamental importance since they are based on the recognition of the need for special protection for particularly vulnerable groups.

2. The Practice of the Committee on the Elimination of Racial Discrimination

Minorities have played an important role in the different monitoring procedures used by the Committee on the Elimination of Racial Discrimination in order to secure compliance by Member States with their obligations under the Convention.[41] The situation of minorities has frequently been discussed during the reporting procedure. Just as many States deny the existence of minorities on their territory with reference to Article 27 of the UNCCPR, they also do this in reports to the Committee on the Elimination of Racial Discrimination. In response, the Committee has developed a practice of requesting from States information on the ethnic composition of their populations.[42] Inducing the States to supply specific data on the size and general economic and social situation of such populations is an important and indispensable first step in a process which may then lead to the discussion of the need for State action with regard to the groups thus identified. In its recom-

---

[39] W. MacKean, *Equality and Discrimination under International Law*, 1983, 159.

[40] See also Thornberry, note 1, 266.

[41] On these procedures see Wolfrum (1998), note 34.

[42] Thornberry, note 1, 272.

mendations, the Committee has repeatedly criticized the narrow scope of the minority legislation of Member States and recommended specific amendments to include additional categories and groups (most recently in the case of Estonia[43]). The Committee has also made good use of the provisions of Articles 1(4) and 2 (2) of the Convention. In an increasing number of cases, it has recommended or even urged State Parties to undertake special measures as provided for in Article 2 (2) of the Convention, particularly, but not exclusively, in favour of indigenous peoples (for recent examples see the concluding observations on the State Reports of Guatemala[44] and Norway[45]).

The Committee has not limited its activities to formulating recommendations and observations in the State reporting procedure. In March 2006 the Committee adopted an important decision under its early warning and urgent action procedure[46] in order to protect the land rights of the Western Shoshone people in the United States from extinction through gradual encroachment and the loss of those lands to multinational extraction industries and energy developers. In its decision, the Committee urged the State Party to halt any plans for the privatization of Western Shoshone ancestral lands, to desist from all activities intended to be conducted on those ancestral lands without consulting the tribe or nation and to stop imposing grazing fees, trespass notices, arrests and other measures on Western Shoshone people while making use of their ancestral lands.[47]

Finally, the Committee has dealt with the situation of minorities in some of its General Recommendations, most notably in General Rec-

---

[43] In its consideration of the State Report submitted by Estonia under Article 9 of the Convention (CERD/C/EST/CO/7, para. 9) the Committee recommended "that the definition of minority under the Law on Cultural Autonomy of National Minorities of 1993 be amended to include non-citizens, in particular stateless persons with long-term residence in Estonia." The concluding observations of the Committee are available at http://www.ohchr.org/english/bodies/cerd/cerds69.htm.

[44] CERD/C/GTM/CO/11, para. 12.

[45] CERD/C/NOR/CO/18, para. 17.

[46] On this procedure see Wolfrum (1999), note 34, 513 et seq.

[47] Decision 1 (68), CERD/C/USA/DEC/ 1 of 11 April 2006, available at http://www.unhchr.ch/tbs/doc.nsf/(Symbol)/CERD.C.USA.DEC.1.En?Opendocument.

ommendation No. 23 of 1997 on Indigenous Peoples[48] and General Recommendation No. 27 of 2000 on Discrimination against Roma[49]. In bygone years a wide divergence of views seems to have existed among the members of the Committee regarding the interpretation of the objectives of the Convention with regard to minorities. While some members were committed to an "integrationist approach" which holds that in the end all measures taken or recommended under the Convention, including "special measures", can have only the final aim of creating the necessary conditions for the full and effective integration of the ethnic or racial group in question into the majority society, others seemingly adopted a broader view according to which the Convention was not only compatible with, but might even require, State action which would enable the relevant minority effectively to protect its distinctiveness from mainstream society.[50]

The General Recommendations on Indigenous Peoples and on Discrimination against Roma have injected some clarity into this debate. It is clear from the Recommendation concerning Indigenous Peoples that the Committee in this context follows a particularly broad interpretation which considers the integration of indigenous groups into the dominant society as no longer the only or even the primary goal to be pursued under the Convention. In the Recommendation, the Committee in particular calls upon States parties to "recognize and respect indigenous *distinct* culture, history, language and way of life ... and to promote its preservation."[51] Moreover, States are to provide indigenous peoples with conditions allowing for sustainable economic and social development compatible with *their* cultural characteristics.[52] It also recognizes the right of indigenous peoples to their communal lands, and calls for the restitution to them of those lands when they have been taken away.[53] As Rüdiger Wolfrum has pointed out, the General Recommendation constitutes an important step towards incorporating some of the essential principles and standards concerning indigenous

---

48 Available at http://www.unhchr.ch/tbs/doc.nsf/(Symbol)/73984290dfea022b802565160056fe1c?Opendocument.

49 Available at http://www.unhchr.ch/tbs/doc.nsf/(Symbol)/11f3d6d130ab09c125694a0054932b?Opendocument.

50 Thornberry, note 1, 278 et seq.

51 General Recommendation XXIII (see note 45), para. 4 (a).

52 General Recommendation XXIII, para. 4 (c).

53 General Recommendation XXIII, para. 5.

and tribal peoples defined by ILO Convention 169, which is a decisive break with the paternalistic assimilation policies towards indigenous peoples which had informed the old ILO Convention 107, into the jurisprudence of the Committee under the CERD.[54] This matters because ILO Convention No. 169 has so far been ratified only by a handful of States,[55] while the Convention, by contrast, is the most widely supported international human rights instrument of all (as of April 2007, 173 countries had ratified the Convention).

The General Recommendation on Discrimination against Roma, on the other hand, takes a different approach. The emphasis here is clearly on the need to eliminate the many open and hidden forms of discrimination of which the Roma are victims in daily life. Accordingly, the measures discussed in this Recommendation focus on the creation of the necessary conditions for a genuine dialogue between the Roma and their environment and the need to promote tolerance and overcome prejudices and negative stereotypes.[56] The right to the maintenance of a distinct identity and culture is neither directly nor implicitly addressed.

The differences between both recommendations reflect a general trend in minority protection law. Indigenous peoples are increasingly seen as a special category of minority which, in the light of the grave injustices they have suffered and continue to suffer and in response to the particularly grave risks to which their specific "way of life" is exposed in the conditions prevailing in modern societies, are accorded specific additional rights not normally granted to minorities, like land rights. As peoples they also claim and – despite strong resistance from some states –are increasingly granted the right to self-determination, although limited to political and territorial autonomy within the concept of "internal" self-determination.[57]

---

54 Wolfrum, see note 32, 372 et seq.

55 See note 33.

56 General Recommendation XXVII, in particular paras. 5, 7 and 9.

57 Indigenous groups themselves often reject being labeled as "minorities" in their attempt to secure special legal regimes with greater legal entitlements, see J. Anaya, *Indigenous Peoples in International Law*, 2nd edition, 2004, 133 et seq.; R. Stavenhagen, "Human Rights and Peoples' Rights – the Question of Minorities", Nordic Journal of Human Rights 3 (1987), 16 et seq. (at 25). This has not prevented international human right bodies from applying general minority rights like those enshrined in Article 27 UNCCPR also to indigenous communities, see note 30 above.

IV. Indigenous Rights as an Example of Advanced Minority Protection

The trend towards the elaboration and recognition of special rights for indigenous peoples as a distinct category of minorities continues unabated. Although the UN Draft Declaration on the Rights of Indigenous Peoples still has to be adopted by the UN General Assembly,[58] consensus is slowly emerging that specific legal regimes are needed in order to satisfy the particular needs and demands of these groups. One of the more recent examples is the draft Nordic Saami Convention which is currently under consideration by the Swedish, Norwegian and Finnish governments. Its innovative features will be briefly analysed here.

The Saami are an indigenous people living in the far north of Finland, Norway, Sweden and Russia. While they enjoy special legal and even constitutional protection in some of the countries in which they live – Article 110a of the Norwegian Constitution obliges the authorities to create the necessary conditions for the Saami people to preserve and develop their culture and their way of life –attempts to develop a coherent protection regime are hampered by the fact that each of the states in which Saami live continues to apply its own national laws to the Saami population of its territory. In October 2005 a group of experts which included representatives of the Finnish, Swedish and Norwegian governments and the Saami Parliaments presented a proposal for a Nordic–Saami convention. The adoption of the Convention will allow Finland, Sweden and Norway to reach agreement on the status of the Saami, and on a range of pertinent social and cultural issues.[59]

The Preamble to the Convention recognizes the Saami people as *the* indigenous people of the three prospective member States of the Convention, i.e. of Finland, Norway and Sweden, and acknowledges the essential unity of the Saami as *one* people straddling national borders. The three States reaffirm that they have national as well as international re-

---

[58] The text of the Declaration which was adopted by the Human Rights Council on 29 June 2006 features in the Annex to Document A/HRC/1/L. 10. It is available at http://www.ohchr.org/english/issues/indigenous/declaration.htm.

[59] An – unofficial – English translation of the draft can be found at http://www.saamicouncil.net/includes/file_download.asp?deptid=2213&fileid=2097&file=Nordic%20Saami%20Convention%20(Unofficial%20 English%20 Translation).doc.

sponsibility to provide adequate conditions for the development of Saami culture and society, and explicitly recognize that the Saami people has the right to self-determination. Article 7 of the Draft Convention specifies that this obligation also covers the adoption of "special positive measures" necessary to the effective implementation of Saami rights, thus embracing a concept of "substantive equality" with regard to such rights.

The text of the Convention itself is divided into seven chapters which deal with the general rights of the Saami people, Saami governance, Saami language and culture, Saami rights to land and water, Saami livelihoods and the implementation and development of the Convention. The last chapter contains provisions on the entry into force and amendment of the Convention. The Convention is subject to ratification which is complete only after the three Saami parliaments in Finland, Norway and Sweden have approved it[60]. Amendments to the Convention have equally to be submitted to the Saami parliaments for approval.[61]

The rights laid down in the Convention are minimum rights and do not prevent the member States from granting the Saami additional or extended rights or from taking more far-reaching measures for the protection of Saami culture and society. In member States where more far-reaching rights already exist, the Convention may not be used as a legal justification for limiting those rights.[62]

The beneficiaries of the rights guaranteed by the Convention are defined in Article 4. The criteria used to determine the association of an individual with the Saami people are language, means of livelihood, political status and descent. People who are to be considered as Saami for the purposes of the Convention are those who speak the Saami language as their domestic language, have a right to pursue reindeer husbandry in Norway or Sweden, are eligible to vote in elections to the Saami parliament in their country of nationality or are children of a person who fulfils any of these requirements.

The central right guaranteed to the Saami by the Draft Convention is the right to self-determination. According to Article 3, however, this right is subject not only to the general rules and provisions of international law regarding self-determination, but also to the other provisions

---

60 Draft Nordic Saami Convention, Article 49.

61 Id., Article 51.

62 Id., Article 8.

of the Convention. Without giving a comprehensive definition of the right of self-determination, Article 3 lists the right of the Saami people to determine their own economic, social and cultural development and their right to use their natural resources for their own benefit as the key features of the right to self-determination as recognized by the Draft Convention. Since the provision does not mention the right of the Saami to determine their *political* development, it is safe to assume that self-determination under the Draft Convention does not include a right to secession. This interpretation is confirmed by Article 1 which states that the objective of the Draft Convention is to affirm and strengthen the rights of the Saami people necessary for their development, "with the smallest possible interference of national borders". Nor would such a restrictive interpretation be contrary to the prevailing concept of self-determination in international law which recognizes a right to secede as a necessary and lawful consequence of self-determination only in those cases in which the people concerned are denied any meaningful participation in the domestic political process.

The main body competent to exercise the self-determination rights is the Saami parliament, the highest representative body of the Saami in each of the participating countries the members of which are elected in general elections. The Draft Convention does not specify the matters which are to be determined by the Saami parliaments and the powers they are to be given for this purpose. It only establishes the principle that the Saami parliaments shall be given a mandate which enables them to contribute effectively to the achievement of the Saami people's right to self-determination under international law and the Convention.[63] They are granted the right to take independent decisions "on all matters where they have the mandate to do so under national or international law".[64] The Convention thus stops well short of recognizing the Saami parliaments as sovereign bodies. The same ambiguity is evident in the provision on international representation. While the member States are to promote Saami representation in international institutions and Saami participation in international meetings, this by no means implies the recognition of their right to conduct their own international relations. In keeping with this approach, the draft Convention does not, contrary to suggestions made in the literature,[65] envisage the Saami becoming

63 Id., Article 14.

64 Id., Article 15.

65 A Grahl-Madsen, *The People of the Twilight Zone – towards Sami self-government; a sovereign Sapmi; an autonomous Samieana*, 1988, 73.

party to it. The parties to the Convention will only be Finland, Norway and Sweden.

With regard to land and water rights, the Draft Convention grants the Saami the right to occupy and use the land or water areas which they have traditionally used for reindeer husbandry, hunting, fishing or in other ways to the same extent as before, regardless of whether or not they are deemed to be the owners of such areas.[66] Permits for prospecting or the extraction of natural resources in land or water areas which are either owned or have traditionally been used by the Saami for the above mentioned purposes are not to be granted by the competent state authorities without prior consultations with the Saami affected; if the prospecting or extraction would make it impossible or substantially more difficult for the Saami to continue to use the land, the permit is to be given only with the consent of both the Saami parliament and Saami people affected. In this case the Saami have the right to compensation for all damage caused by the prospecting and extraction activities.[67] Reindeer husbandry, as a central element of Saami livelihood and an important foundation of Saami culture, is to enjoy special legal protection. Taking into account the sceptical attitude hitherto displayed by Finland to the recognition of special and exclusive Saami rights with regard to reindeer husbandry, this legal protection takes different forms in the individual member States. Norway and Sweden commit themselves under the Convention to maintaining and developing reindeer husbandry as the sole right of the Saami in the Saami reindeer grazing areas, as they have previously done; Finland, on the other hand, which has hitherto known no such exclusive rights, merely undertakes to strengthen the position of Saami reindeer husbandry.[68] Customary rights to reindeer grazing across national borders are recognized, subject to special agreements which may have been concluded between Saami villages or reindeer grazing communities on the issue. The Draft Convention provides for the necessary mechanism (through arbitration committees) for the enforcement of these agreements in the case of dispute.[69]

The economic rights are complemented by linguistic and cultural rights. The relevant provisions of the draft Convention guarantee, in addition

---

[66] Id., Article 34.

[67] Id., Articles 36, 37.

[68] Id., Article 42.

[69] Id., Article 43.

to the more "traditional" rights such as the right to use, develop and pass on the Saami language to future generations[70] and the right of access to education in the Saami language within the Saami areas,[71] a number of innovative concepts such as the creation of a distinct Saami media policy which provides the Saami population with rich and multifaceted information[72] and a right of control over activities by people not of Saami origin who use elements of the Saami culture for commercial purposes. This right of control includes the right to a reasonable share of the resulting revenues.[73]

The implementation of the Nordic Saami Convention is to be monitored by a Nordic Saami Convention Committee consisting of six members, with the three member States and the three Saami parliaments appointing one member each. The Committee is to be independent in its work. It should be noted that the Committee, apart from the usual functions of such committees which consist in the submission of reports to the national governments and the elaboration of proposals for the strengthening of the Convention, is also to have the right to deliver "opinions" in response to questions from individuals and groups.[74] This mechanism, if properly implemented, may well over time develop into a fully fledged individual petition procedure.

V. Conclusion: Prospects for Minority Protection in the Future

Any future attempt to extend and improve the existing mechanisms for minority protection will have to deal with the uncertainties and ambiguities surrounding the basic concepts in this field, and particularly the concept of minorities. Upon close scrutiny, a crucial difference between minority protection and the protection of individual human rights emerges. While the individual can be made the object of an abstract legal concept without major difficulties since its essential qualities, at least for the purposes of human rights law, are readily agreed upon, the con-

70 Id., Article 23.

71 Id., Article 26.

72 Id., Article 25.

73 Id., Article 31.

74 Id., Article 45.

cept of minority is subject to a far greater degree to political and historical contingency and to cultural relativism. An open-ended definition of protected minorities would be best suited to the fluid contours of the concept, but such an approach is hardly palatable to states which fear the mushrooming of minorities vying for special rights and a greatly increased risk of serious conflict with the most vociferous minority groups. Experience with international minority protection since World War II shows that States are generally much more reluctant to consent to specific group rights and to their effective international monitoring for fear of the internal disruptions which might be caused by the controversies surrounding the implementation of those rights, a risk which appears to be far more substantial in the case of national or other minorities claiming group rights than in the case of individuals trying to enforce their entitlements under general human rights law.

In this situation, the best hope for substantial progress may lie in the conclusion of bilateral or regional agreements dealing with specific minorities. The draft Nordic Saami Convention could provide one possible model for such an approach, although the content and scope of the protected rights would have to be adapted to the special characteristics of the groups in question. In any case, the present trend in international law seems to be towards a distinction between indigenous groups and other minorities. While a greater openness among states – although it is still far from universal – towards the need for special protection of indigenous groups through the creation of specific entitlements at the international level can be observed, this flexibility apparently does not extend to the protection of minorities in general. General human rights instruments like the Convention on the Elimination of all Forms of Racial Discrimination will therefore continue to play a crucial role in the further development and protection of minority rights. This would seem to require, however, that international human rights doctrine and jurisprudence attach greater importance to the collective dimension of rights protection and its proper legal analysis than they have often done in the past.

Minority Rights as Group-Protective Rights: A Challenge for the International Law of Human Rights

*Nicola Wenzel**

The idea of minority rights was born out of the realization that individual human rights do not provide sufficient protection for members of minorities.[1] In the *Minority Schools in Albania* case, the Permanent Court of International Justice considered that minority protection included not only the maintenance of perfect equality between members of minorities and the other nationals of a State but also a second element which consists in ensuring for minorities "suitable means for the

---

* This paper is based upon a comment on Rainer Grote's presentation.

[1] For a definition of the term minority see R. Grote, "The Struggle for Minority Rights and Human Rights: Current Trends and Challenges", in this volume, 228 et seq. For the purposes of this contribution with its focus on the group-specific aspects of minority protection, the term does not encompass immigrants but includes indigenous peoples which fulfill the relevant criteria.

preservation of their racial peculiarities, their traditions and their national characteristics."[2]

The Court held that these two requirements were

> "closely interlocked, for there would be no true equality between a majority and a minority if the latter were deprived of its own institutions, and were consequently compelled to renounce that which constitutes the very essence of its being as a minority."[3]

In this famous quotation, the Permanent Court of International Justice addresses the aim as well as the *raison d'être* of minority rights. This article will build upon a further exploration of both of these aspects (I) to convey the conceptual challenges to national and international law inherent in the concept of minority rights as group-protective rights. These challenges lie in possible conflicts between group-protective rights and individual human rights (II). The ensuing reticence of States with regard to group-protective rights will be exemplified by the difficulties encountered in the adoption of the UN Draft Declaration on the Rights of Indigenous Peoples (III). Finally, ways will be explored in which to address States' legitimate concerns without altogether relinquishing the concept of group-protective rights (IV).

I. The Aim and *Raison d'être* of Minority Rights

1. The Aim of Minority Rights: Preserving the Cultural Existence of Minority Groups

The aim of minority rights is the protection of minority groups as such, the preservation of their cultural existence and their identity in the face of pressures from the dominant society to assimilate.[4] The reasons for the need to preserve the cultural existence of minority groups are manifold.[5] Only one facet will be highlighted here: the realization that mi-

---

[2] PCIJ, Ser. A/B 64 (1935), 17.

[3] *Ibid.*

[4] On the possible content of minority rights see N. Lerner, *Group Rights and Discrimination in International Law*, 2003, 39 et seq.

[5] See N. Wenzel, *Das Spannungsverhältnis zwischen Gruppenschutz und Individualschutz im Völkerrecht*, forthcoming, 21 et seq., 197 et seq., 230 et seq.

norities – the same applies to indigenous peoples – are cultural[6] groups which are constitutive of their members' identity.[7] Because of their character as so-called identifying groups[8] their continued existence is of vital importance for their members. Cultural communities give their members a sense of rootedness, of stability and the feeling of belonging to an ongoing community.[9] They define the individual's identity because it is through their cultural group that its members discern values and make choices.[10] The group provides them with a context of choice about what constitutes a meaningful and fulfilling life.

2. The *Raison d'être* of Minority Rights: The Need for Special Protection of Minority Groups

Explaining the value of cultural groups such as minorities and indigenous peoples does not yet answer the question why these groups need special protection. An alternative way of dealing with the existence of different cultural groups within a State would be to leave it to "market" forces to decide on the existence of cultural groups.[11] On the cultural marketplace, those cultural groups that provide meaningful choices to their members and therefore seem attractive would survive and others

---

6 The term culture is used here in the broad sense as defined in the preamble to the UNESCO Universal Declaration on Cultural Diversity (<http://unesdoc.unesco.org/images/0012/001271/127160m.pdf>) meaning "the set of distinctive spiritual, material, intellectual and emotional features of society or a social group" and encompassing "in addition to art and literature, lifestyles, ways of living together, value systems, traditions and beliefs." See also C.M. Cerna/J.C. Wallace, "Women and Culture, in: K.D. Askin/D.M. Koenig (eds), *Women and International Human Rights Law*, Vol. 1, 1999, 623, 624 et seq.; B. Parekh, *Rethinking Multiculturalism*, 2000, 143; R. Stavenhagen, *The Ethnic Question*, 1990, 2.

7 On constitutive groups see A. Margalit/J. Raz, "National Self-Determination", in: W. Kymlicka (ed.), *The Rights of Minority Cultures*, 1995, 79, 82 et seq.; M. Sandel, *Liberalism and the Limits of Justice*, 1982, 150.

8 M. McDonald, "Should Communities Have Rights? Reflections on Liberal Individualism", *Can.J.L.&Juris.* 4 (1991), 417, 219 et seq.

9 Parekh, see note 6, 162.

10 S. Boshammer, *Gruppen, Recht, Gerechtigkeit*, 2003, 85.

11 On this alternative approach see W. Kymlicka, *Multicultural Citizenship*, 1995, 107 et seq.

that do not attract sufficient support would disappear. In this model, the State would remain neutral and would not take sides for one group or another.[12]

This approach, however, is blind to the fact that minorities and indigenous peoples are structurally disadvantaged on the cultural marketplace.[13] Minorities and indigenous peoples are not equal players; they have to abide by majority decisions that naturally reflect the culture of the dominant society and that may be irreconcilable with their way of life.[14] The claim that the state is culturally neutral is in fact a misconception. Decisions that seem at first glance to be neutral are really culturally biased.[15] A typical example is the language used in contacts with public authorities.[16] A decision in favour of the language of the dominant society is – in most cases an unconscious – decision in favour of one aspect of the majority culture that puts the minority culture at a disadvantage. Because the original state measure is not culturally neutral but rather serves the interests of the majority culture, specific measures regulating the use of the minority language are necessary to remedy this disadvantage. The need for special protection for minority groups is thus the consequence of the disadvantages for these groups inherent in the cultural marketplace.

---

[12] Glazer speaks of "benign neglect", N. Glazer, *Ethnic Dilemmas: 1964-1982*, 1983, 183. See also N. Glazer, "Individual Rights against Group Rights", reprinted in: W. Kymlicka, *The Rights of Minority Cultures*, 1995, 123 et seq.; M. Walzer, "Pluralism: A Political Perspective", reprinted in: W. Kymlicka, *The Rights of Minority Cultures*, 1995, 139 et seq.

[13] W. Kymlicka, "Individual and Community Rights", in: J. Baker (ed.), *Group Rights*, 1994, 17, 24 et seq.; D. Sanders, "Collective Rights", *Hum.Rts.Q.* 13 (1991), 368, 373.

[14] See J. Habermas, *Die Einbeziehung des Anderen*, 1996, 173; *ibid.*, „Anerkennungskämpfe im demokratischen Rechtsstaat", in: A. Gutmann (ed.), *Charles Taylor: Multikulturalismus und die Politik der Anerkennung*, 1997, 147, 168; M. Walzer, *On Toleration*, 1997, 25.

[15] A. Addis, "Individualism, Communitarianism, and the Rights of Ethnic Minorities", *Notre Dame L.Rev.* 67 (1991), 615, 643 et seq.; A. Baumeister, "The Limits of Universalism", in: B. Haddock/P. Sutch (eds), *Multiculturalism, Identity and Rights*, 2003, 111, 115 et seq.; W. Kymlicka, *Contemporary Political Philosophy*, 2nd ed., 2002, 345 et seq.; C.H. Wellman, "Liberalism, Communitarianism, and Group Rights", *Law & Phil.* 18 (1999), 13, 39.

[16] W. Kymlicka, *Contemporary Political Philosophy*, 2nd ed., 2002, 346.

II. Minority Rights as Conceptual Challenges to National and International Law

If the idea of protecting minorities and indigenous peoples as such is pursued to its end through the recognition of far-reaching group-protective rights[17], however, it not only constitutes a conceptual challenge to the national and international legal system but also questions deep-seated beliefs and assumptions about the nature of the State.

Group-protective rights are a conceptual challenge because they empower a group. This in turn means putting that group in a dominant position *vis-à-vis* its members and enabling it to exercise power over individuals. The exercise of this power may lead to the violation of human rights. The power conferred on the group is sometimes of a social nature.[18] But the dilemma becomes particularly clear in the case of the right to autonomy.[19]

The right to autonomy is contained in article 4 of the current draft of a UN Declaration on the Rights of Indigenous Peoples[20] which provides:

> "Indigenous peoples, in exercising their right to self-determination, have the right to autonomy or self-government in matters relating to their internal and local affairs, as well as ways and means for financing their autonomous functions."

The right to autonomy is a very far-reaching right. It implies the exercise by the group of State-like power and thus places the individual

---

[17] The term "group-protective right" emphasizes the aim of the right, which is to protect the group as such. Group-protective rights include group rights (also called collective rights), i.e. rights the bearer of which is the group itself, and individual rights. i.e. rights the bearer of which is the individual member of the group. On this distinction see Wenzel, see note 5, 24 et seq.

[18] For an example see British Columbia Supreme Court, 1992 CanLII 354 (BC S.C.) – *Thomas v. Norris.*

[19] On the meaning of autonomy in the context of international law see H.-J. Heintze, "On the Legal Understanding of Autonomy", in: M. Suksi (ed.), *Autonomy*, 1998, 7 et seq.; R. Lapidoth, *Autonomy*, 1997, 29 et seq.; L.A. Rehof, "Human Rights and Self-Government for Indigenous Peoples", *Nord.J.Int'lL.* 61/62 (1992/1993), 19; D. Stahlberg, *Minderheitenschutz durch Personal- und Territorialautonomie*, 2000, 6 et seq. The PCIJ describes autonomy for minorities as a "measure of legislative, judicial, administrative and financial decentralization", PCIJ, Ser. A/B 49 (1932), 24 – *Interpretation of the Statute of Memel Territory.*

[20] UN Doc. A/HRC/1/L.3.

who is the object of measures by the group in a position equivalent to its position in case of human rights violations by States. In extreme cases, a minority group or an indigenous people may consider the encroachment on certain human rights as an integral part of its culture or as necessary for the survival of the group. There may be groups for example which consider corporal punishment as integral part of their culture. Another example, much less extreme, is a membership rule which excludes women who marry out of the group whereas male members do not lose their membership when marrying out of the group; the reason for this rule being that limited resources make such rule appear crucial for the survival of the group.[21] These examples reveal a striking dilemma. The aim of group-protective rights is the protection of a group's culture. But when practices that do not conform with human rights form an integral part of that culture, conferring group-protective rights means accepting the violation of individual human rights.

Group-protective rights and individual human rights thus seem to be irreconcilable. The possibility of conflicts with individual rights alone, however, is not a sufficient reason for not conferring group-protective rights at all.[22] There are a number of very convincing reasons for protecting minorities and indigenous peoples which have been dealt with in part above. While it is clear that respect for human rights should be ensured one way or the other States should not be allowed to use human rights as an instrument of oppression and point to certain minor human rights violations occurring within the group as an excuse for not conferring group protection at all. This does not constitute an adequate response because, if it is true that group-protective rights and individual rights are irreconcilable from a theoretical point of view, from a practical point of view they are not.[23] Rather, conflicts between individual

---

[21] A similar membership rule was at issue in a case decided by the UN Human Rights Committee (UN Doc. CCPR/C/13/D/24/1977 – *Lovelace*). See also US Supreme Court, 436 U.S. 49 (1987) – *Santa Clara Pueblo v. Martinez*.

[22] See S.J. Anaja, "Superpower Attitudes towards Indigenous Peoples and Group Rights", Proceedings of the Ninety-Third Annual Meeting of the ASIL 93 (1999), 251, 257; A. Buchanan, "The Role of Collective Rights in the Theory of Indigenous Peoples' Rights", *Transnat'lL.&Contemp.Probs.* 3 (1993), 89, 107 et seq.; K. VanderWal, "Collective Human Rights", in: J. Berting *et al.* (eds), *Human Rights in a Pluralist World*, 1990, 83, 97.

[23] For a similar approach see L. Jacobs, "Bridging the Gap between Individual and Collective Rights with the Idea of Integrity", *Can.J.L.&Juris.* 4 (1991), 375, 386; L. McDonald, "Can Collective and Individual Human Rights Coexist?", *Melb.Univ.L.Rev.*22 (1998), 310, 323 et seq.; A. Shachar, *Multicultural Ju-*

human rights and group-protective rights may be resolved on a case-by-case basis. In fact, the same approach as is used for conflicts between two individual human rights may be adopted since the conflict between group-protective rights and individual human rights is structurally no different.[24]

This approach involves balancing the group-protective right and the individual right in cases of conflict so as to ensure that both are implemented as far as possible in the specific case.[25] As a result of this balancing process core human rights such as the prohibition of torture always take precedence over the aim of group protection.[26] On the other hand, the balancing process results in States being prevented from fully imposing the individual rights contained in their Constitutions on minorities or indigenous peoples. The importance of this latter point may be demonstrated by the example of an Indian tribe in the United States that does not recognize the right to trial by jury but rather has a procedural law similar to that of Germany. Although the right to trial by jury is recognized as an important individual right in the US Constitution[27] it is highly questionable whether the United States should be able to impose on the tribe a concept of fair trial that is clearly influenced by the culture of its dominant society. The US Government has shown a certain reluctance to do so. The Indian Civil Rights Act[28] which is a

---

risdictions, 2001, 4 et seq.; V. Van Dyke, "Collective Entities and Moral Rights", reprinted in: J. Stapleton (ed.), *Group Rights*, 1995, 180, 181.

24 See A. An-Na'im, "Promises We Should All Keep in Common Cases", in: J. Cohen *et al.* (eds), *Is Multiculturalism Bad for Women?*, 1999, 59, 63; Sanders, see note 13, 383.

25 See A. Eisenberg, "The Politics of Individual and Group Difference in Canadian Jurisprudence", *Can.J.Pol.Sc.* 27 (1994), 3, 21; J. Norton, "Insular Religious Communities and the Rights of Internal Minorities", *Auck.U.L.Rev.* 9 (2001), 405, 434; Sanders, see note 13, 383 et seq.

26 This point is common ground in legal literature, see W. Kymlicka, "Universal Minority Rights?", in: Y. Morigiwa *et al.* (eds), *Universal Minority Rights?*, 2004, 13, 18.

27 See the Sixth Amendment to the US Constitution which provides, "In all criminal prosecutions, the accused shall enjoy the right to a speedy and public trial, by an impartial jury of the State and district wherein the crime shall have been committed [...]" and the Seventh Amendment, which provides, "In Suits at common law, where the value in controversy shall exceed twenty dollars, the right of trial by jury shall be preserved [...]"

28 25 U.S.C. §§ 1302 et seq.

statute that obliges Indian tribes to respect certain enumerated individual rights contains the right to trial by jury only in criminal cases but not in civil law cases. Along the same lines, the Indian Civil Rights Act contains a provision on freedom of religion but does not impose on the tribes the establishment clause of the US Constitution.[29] Balancing group-protective rights and individual human rights results in endorsing this approach. It rules out imposing the culturally-biased national human rights standards on minorities and indigenous peoples. International human rights alone can be the standard against which the action of minorities and indigenous peoples are to be measured, because they are not the expression of a particular culture but rather are universal in character.[30] Accepting that minorities and indigenous peoples do not have to abide by national human rights standards applicable in the State in which they live but only by international human rights law, however, goes hand in hand with accepting that there is no uniform human rights standard within one State, a consequence that calls into question deep-seated assumptions about the nature of the State.

A detailed analysis of the way international human rights instruments on the one hand and international group-protective instruments on the other hand accommodate the balancing approach supported here is impossible in this context.[31] But it should be clear that the conflict between group-protective rights and individual human rights does not result in a conflict of norms in the sense of conflicting obligations for States.[32] States do have positive obligations under the international hu-

---

[29] The establishment clause is contained in the First Amendment to the US Constitution. It provides; "Congress shall make no law respecting an establishment of religion." There is general agreement that the establishment clause limits governmental action that discriminates between religions and that, in particular, the government may not create an official religion. See J.A. Barron/C.T.Dienes, *First Amendment Law*, 2000, 423 et seq., 436; A.Ides/C.N. May, *Constitutional Law: Individual Rights*, 2nd ed., 2001, 382, 387.

[30] Vienna Declaration and Programme of Action (UN Doc. A/CONF.157/23, § 5): "All human rights are universal, indivisible and interdependent and interrelated. [...] While the significance of national and regional particularities and various historical, cultural and religious backgrounds must be borne in mind, it is the duty of States, regardless of their political, economic and cultural systems, to promote and protect all human rights and fundamental freedoms."

[31] For such an analysis see Wenzel, see note 5, 404 et seq., 462 et seq.

[32] For a definition of conflicts of norms in international law see N. Matz, *Wege zur Koordinierung völkerrechtlicher Verträge*, 2005, 11; J. Neumann, *Die*

man rights instruments to ensure human rights protection against groups, but limitation clauses allow them to balance individual human rights against the aim of group protection. International group-protective instruments on the other hand to a certain extent allow for interference with group-protective rights for human rights reasons.

III. The Uneasiness of States with Regard to Group-Protective Rights: The Example of the UN Draft Declaration on the Rights of Indigenous Peoples

The possibility of conflicts between group-protective rights on the one hand and individual human rights on the other hand leads to a certain reluctance of States to commit themselves to the protection of minorities and indigenous peoples[33] and is one of the reasons for the high number of soft law instruments in this area. Scepticism with regard to the recognition of group-protective rights, especially when formulated as group rights or collective rights, in a legal instrument (be it binding or not) is also one of the reasons for the numerous setbacks on the way to a United Nations Declaration on the Rights of Indigenous Peoples.

At the beginning of the movement towards a United Nations instrument for indigenous peoples in 1983 there was a study by special rapporteur Martínez Cobo on the problem of discrimination against indigenous populations, which came to the conclusion that indigenous populations were not adequately protected by the international law of human rights.[34] The working group of the Sub-Commission on Preven-

---

Koordination des WTO-Rechts mit anderen völkerrechtlichen Ordnungen, 2002, 59; J. Pauwelyn, *Conflict of Norms in Public International Law*, 2003, 175 et seq.

[33] For corresponding reservations in legal literature see B. Barry, *Culture and Equality*, 2001, 125 et seq.; S.B. Blumkin, "Protection of Minorities", in: S. Chandra (ed.), *International Protection of Minorities*, 1986, 1, 10 et seq., 38 et seq.; J. Donnelly, "Human Rights, Individual Rights and Collective Rights", in: J. Berting *et al.* (eds), *Human Rights in a Pluralist World*, 1990, 39, 46; R.E. Howard, *Human Rights and the Search for Community*, 1995, 219; Y. Tamir, "Against Collective Rights", in: L.H. Meyer *et al.*(eds), *Rights, Culture, and the Law*, 2003, 183, 186 et seq.

[34] Martínez Cobo, Study of the Problem of Discrimination against Indigenous Populations, UN Doc. E/CN.4/Sub.2/1986/7/Add.4, §§ 625 et seq.

tion of Discrimination and Protection of Minorities[35], which had commissioned the report, drafted a declaration which the Sub-Commission adopted in 1994.[36] In 1993, the United Nations General Assembly proclaimed the *International Decade of the World's Indigenous People* which aimed, *inter alia*, at the adoption of a United Nations instrument on indigenous peoples.[37] In 1995, the Human Rights Commission reacted by creating its own working group to discuss the Sub-Commission's draft. Despite several years of discussions, however, when the International Decade ended in 2004 no declaration had been adopted. A *Second International Decade of the World's Indigenous People* was proclaimed by the General Assembly in 2004.[38] In 2006, after 24 years of negotiation it looked as if the efforts had finally been successful. The new Human Rights Council[39], in its first session, adopted a modified draft for adoption by the General Assembly.[40] A foretaste of the obstacles still to be overcome, however, was the fact that the declaration was not adopted by consensus. When the draft resolution was brought before the General Assembly's 3rd Committee, a number of delegations criticized the adoption process in the Human Rights Council and demanded further consultations in order to reach consensus. The substantive criticisms put forward were essentially the lack of a definition of indigenous peoples and the implications for the territorial integrity of States of the provisions on the right to self-determination for indigenous peoples.[41] These arguments should not detract from the fact that many of these States have strong economic interests seemingly incompatible with the Declaration's provisions on the rights of indigenous

[35] On the working group and its mandate see R.L. Barsh, "Indigenous Peoples: An Emerging Subject of International Law?", *AJIL* 80 (1986), 369, 372; C.J. Iorns, "Indigenous Peoples and Self-Determination: Challenging State Sovereignty, *Case W.Res.J.Int'lL.* 24 (1992), 199, 204 et seq.; S. Pritchard, "Working Group on Indigenous Populations", in: S. Pritchard (ed.), *Indigenous Peoples, the United Nations and Human Rights*, 1998, 40 et seq.

[36] UN Doc. E/CN.4/Sub.2/1994/2/Add.1.

[37] A/RES/48/163 of 21 December 1993.

[38] A/RES/59/174 of 20 December 2004.

[39] The Human Rights Council was created by A/RES/60/251 of 3 April 2006 und succeeded to the former Human Rights Commission.

[40] UN Doc. E/CN.4/2006/79.

[41] For the reasons invoked by African States in particular see the decision by the African Union's Assembly on the UN Draft Declaration of 30 January 2007 (Assembly/AU/Dec.141 (VIII)).

peoples over the natural resources on their territories. As a result of this initiative, the 3rd Committee, instead of recommending the adoption of the draft by the General Assembly, adopted a resolution to make the General Assembly defer consideration and action on the Declaration to allow time for further consultations.[42] The General Assembly acted accordingly.[43]

The problem with this development is not just the new delay in the adoption of a UN instrument. It is also that it is unclear whether and how the new consultation process within the General Assembly will involve representatives of indigenous peoples. The active participation of indigenous peoples in the drafting process within the Human Rights Council and its predecessor, the Human Rights Committee, however, was one of the main achievements of this process.[44]

IV. Addressing States' Concerns

In their latest statements on the Draft, delegations do not explicitly mention concerns about the concept of group-protective rights, although the fear of possible conflicts between collective rights and individual human rights and uncertainty as to the legal implications of the recognition of group rights in a legal instrument regularly emerged in the debate.[45] The only option is to address these concerns openly and clearly in the text of the UN instrument itself. This implies first of all

---

42 UN Doc. A/C.3/61/L.57/Rev.1.

43 UN Doc. A/RES/61/178.

44 Speaking more generally, the credibility of the Human Rights Council is itself in jeopardy if discussions on texts already adopted by the Council are reopened in the General Assembly on the grounds that the Human Rights Council is not sufficiently representative. The controversy around the Declaration on the Rights of Indigenous Peoples is a point of crystallization for the tensions resulting from the search for a new equilibrium in the relations between the Human Rights Council and the General Assembly.

45 See for example the reservations expressed by the United States with regard to the recognition of collective rights in the UN Draft Declaration, UN Doc. E/CN.4/Sub.2/1993/29, § 68. J. Corntassel, "Partnership in Action? Indigenous Political Mobilization and Co-optation during the First UN Indigenous Decade (1995-2004)", *Hum.Rts.Q.* 29 (2007), 137, 151 speaks of "ongoing state resistance to the language of the Draft Declaration relating to the recognition of collective rights [...]".

acknowledging that conflicts between group-protective rights and individual human rights may arise. Then, a normative solution to the problem has to be developed along the lines set out above and anchored in the text of the declaration. The main challenge is to allow for a balance while preventing the use by States of human rights as an instrument of oppression. A solution for indigenous peoples exercising territorial autonomy may be to absolve States from their human rights responsibility with regard to acts of the autonomous group and instead to bind the group itself to international human rights by letting it become a party to international human rights instruments.[46]

---

46 For details see Wenzel, see note 5, 485 et seq.

List of Authors

Benzing, Markus

Research Fellow, Max Planck Institute for Comparative Public Law and International Law; Doctoral Candidate, University of Heidelberg

Grote, Rainer

Privatdozent, Dr. iur., LL.M., Senior Research Fellow, Max Planck Institute for Comparative Public Law and International Law, Heidelberg

Hestermeyer, Holger

Dr., LL.M. (Berkeley), Senior Research Fellow, Max Planck Institute for Comparative Public Law and International Law, Heidelberg

Kaiser, Karen

Dr. iur., Senior Research Fellow, Max Planck Institute for Public International and Comparative Law, Heidelberg

Köbele, Michael

LL.M. (Michigan); Postgraduate Diploma in Competition Law (King's College); Attorney-at-law (Frankfurt, Germany; Brussels E-List, Belgium); Associate, Latham & Watkins LLP (Brussels, Belgium)

König, Doris

Professor of Public Law, International and European Law, Bucerius Law School – Hochschule für Rechtswissenschaft, Hamburg

Matz-Lück, Nele

Dr. iur., LL.M. (University of Wales, Aberystwyth), Senior Research Fellow, Max Planck Institute for Comparative Public Law and International Law, Heidelberg

Röben, Volker

Professor, University of Swansea, Wales

Stoll, Tobias

Prof. Dr. iur., Institute for International Law and European Law, Georg-August-University Göttingen

Vöneky, Silja

Head of an Independent Junior Research Group at the Max Planck Institute for Comparative Public Law and International Law, Heidelberg

Wenzel, Nicola

Dr. iur., LL.M., Senior Research Fellow, Max Planck Institute for Comparative Public Law and International Law, Heidelberg

Max-Planck-Institut für ausländisches öffentliches Recht und Völkerrecht

Beiträge zum ausländischen öffentlichen Recht und Völkerrecht

Hrsg.: A. von Bogdandy, R. Wolfrum

Bde. 27–59 erschienen im Carl Heymanns Verlag KG Köln, Berlin (Bestellung an: Max-Planck-Institut für Völkerrecht, Im Neuenheimer Feld 535, 69120 Heidelberg); ab Band 60 im Springer Berlin, Heidelberg, New York, London, Paris, Tokyo, Hong Kong, Barcelona

---

193 Doris *König*, Peter-Tobias *Stoll*, Volker *Röben*, Nele *Matz-Lück* (eds.): **International Law Today: New Challenges and the Need for Reform?** 2008. VIII, 260 Seiten. Geb. € 69,95

191 Nicola *Wenzel*: **Das Spannungsverhältnis zwischen Gruppenschutz und Individualschutz im Völkerrecht.** 2008. XXXI, 646 Seiten. Geb. € 99,95

190 Winfried *Brugger*, Michael *Karayanni* (eds.): **Religion in the Public Sphere: A Comparative Analysis of German, Israeli, American and International Law.** 2007. XVI, 467 Seiten. Geb. € 89,95 zzgl. landesüblicher MwSt.

189 Eyal *Benvenisti*, Chaim *Gans*, Sari *Hanafi* (eds.): **Israel and the Palestinian Refugees.** 2007. VIII, 502 Seiten. Geb. € 94,95 zzgl. landesüblicher MwSt.

188 Eibe *Riedel*, Rüdiger *Wolfrum* (eds.): **Recent Trends in German and European Constitutional Law.** 2006. VII, 289 Seiten. Geb. € 74,95 zzgl. landesüblicher MwSt.

187 Marcel *Kau*: **United States Supreme Court und Bundesverfassungsgericht.** 2007. XXV, 538 Seiten. Geb. € 99,95 zzgl. landesüblicher MwSt.

186 Philipp *Dann*, Michał *Rynkowski* (eds.): **The Unity of the European Constitution.** 2006. IX, 394 Seiten. Geb. € 79,95 zzgl. landesüblicher MwSt.

185 Pál *Sonnevend*: **Eigentumsschutz und Sozialversicherung.** 2008. XVIII, 278 Seiten. Geb. € 74,95

184 Jürgen *Bast*: **Grundbegriffe der Handlungsformen der EU.** 2006. XXI, 485 Seiten. Geb. € 94,95

183 Uwe *Säuberlich*: **Die außervertragliche Haftung im Gemeinschaftsrecht.** 2005. XV, 314 Seiten. Geb. € 74,95

182 Florian *von Alemann*: **Die Handlungsform der interinstitutionellen Vereinbarung.** 2006. XVI, 518 Seiten. Geb. € 94,95

181 Susanne *Förster*: **Internationale Haftungsregeln für schädliche Folgewirkungen gentechnisch veränderter Organismen.** 2007. XXXVI, 421 Seiten. Geb. € 84,95

180 Jeanine *Bucherer*: **Die Vereinbarkeit von Militärgerichten mit dem Recht auf ein faires Verfahren gemäß Art. 6 Abs. 1 EMRK, Art. 8 Abs. 1 AMRK und Art. 14 Abs. 1 des UN Paktes über bürgerliche und politische Rechte.** 2005. XVIII, 307 Seiten. Geb. € 74,95

179 Annette *Simon*: **UN-Schutzzonen – Ein Schutzinstrument für verfolgte Personen?** 2005. XXI, 322 Seiten. Geb. € 74,95

178 Petra *Minnerop*: **Paria-Staaten im Völkerrecht?** 2004. XXIII, 579 Seiten. Geb. € 99,95

177 Rüdiger *Wolfrum*, Volker *Röben* (eds.): **Developments of International Law in Treaty Making**. 2005. VIII, 632 Seiten. Geb. € 99,95 zzgl. landesüblicher MwSt.

176 Christiane *Höhn*: **Zwischen Menschenrechten und Konfliktprävention. Der Minderheitenschutz im Rahmen der Organisation für Sicherheit und Zusammenarbeit in Europa (OSZE).** 2005. XX, 418 Seiten. Geb. € 84,95

175 Nele *Matz*: **Wege zur Koordinierung völkerrechtlicher Verträge. Völkervertragsrechtliche und institutionelle Ansätze.** 2005. XXIV, 423 Seiten. Geb. € 84,95

174 Jochen Abr. *Frowein*: **Völkerrecht – Menschenrechte – Verfassungsfragen Deutschlands und Europas. Ausgewählte Schriften.** Hrsg. von Matthias *Hartwig*, Georg *Nolte*, Stefan *Oeter*, Christian *Walter*. 2004. VIII, 732 Seiten. Geb. € 119,95

173 Oliver *Dörr* (Hrsg.): **Ein Rechtslehrer in Berlin. Symposium für Albrecht Randelzhofer.** 2004. VII, 117 Seiten. Geb. € 54,95

172 Lars-Jörgen *Geburtig*: **Konkurrentenrechtsschutz aus Art. 88 Abs. 3 Satz 3 EGV. Am Beispiel von Steuervergünstigungen.** 2004. XVII, 412 Seiten (4 Seiten English Summary). Geb. € 84,95

171 Markus *Böckenförde*: **Grüne Gentechnik und Welthandel. Das Biosafety-Protokoll und seine Auswirkungen auf das Regime der WTO.** 2004. XXIX, 620 Seiten. Geb. € 99,95

170 Anja *v. Hahn*: **Traditionelles Wissen indigener und lokaler Gemeinschaften zwischen geistigen Eigentumsrechten und der public domain.** 2004. XXV, 415 Seiten. Geb. 84,95

169 Christian *Walter*, Silja *Vöneky*, Volker *Röben*, Frank *Schorkopf* (eds.): **Terrorism as a Challenge for National and International Law: Security versus Liberty?** 2004. XI, 1484 Seiten. Geb. € 169,95 zzgl. landesüblicher MwSt.

168 Kathrin *Osteneck*: **Die Umsetzung von UN-Wirtschaftssanktionen durch die Europäische Gemeinschaft.** 2004. XXXIX, 579 Seiten. Geb. € 99,95

167 Stephan *Sina*: **Der völkerrechtliche Status des Westjordanlandes und des Gaza-Streifens nach den Osloer Verträgen.** 2004. XXI, 410 Seiten. Geb. € 84,95

166 Philipp *Dann*: **Parlamente im Exekutivföderalismus.** 2004. XXIII, 474 Seiten. Geb. € 89,95

165 Rüdiger *Wolfrum* (Hrsg.): **Gleichheit und Nichtdiskriminierung im nationalen und internationalen Menschenrechtsschutz.** 2003. VIII, 299 Seiten. Geb. € 74,95

164 Rüdiger *Wolfrum*, Nele *Matz*: **Conflicts in International Environmental Law.** 2003. XI, 213 Seiten. Geb. € 64,95 zzgl. landesüblicher MwSt.

163 Adam *Bodnar*, Michał *Kowalski*, Karen *Raible*, Frank *Schorkopf* (eds.): **The Emerging Constitutional Law of the European Union.** 2003. IX, 595 Seiten. Geb. € 99,95 zzgl. landesüblicher MwSt.

162 Jochen Abr. *Frowein*, Klaus *Scharioth*, Ingo *Winkelmann*, Rüdiger *Wolfrum* (Hrsg.): **Verhandeln für den Frieden/Negotiating for Peace. Liber Amicorum Tono Eitel.** 2003. XIII, 866 Seiten. Geb. € 129,95

161 Michaela *Fries*: **Die Bedeutung von Artikel 5 (f) der Rassendiskriminierungskonvention im deutschen Recht.** 2003. XIX, 429 Seiten. Geb. € 84,95

160 Helen *Keller*: **Rezeption des Völkerrechts.** 2003. XXXV, 855 Seiten. Geb. € 129,95

159 Cordula *Dröge*: **Positive Verpflichtungen der Staaten in der Europäischen Menschenrechtskonvention.** 2003. XX, 432 Seiten. Geb. € 89,95

158 Dagmar *Richter*: **Sprachenordnung und Minderheitenschutz im schweizerischen Bundesstaat.** 2005. LIV, 1315 Seiten. Geb. € 179,95

157 Thomas *Giegerich*: **Europäische Verfassung und deutsche Verfassung im transnationalen Konstitutionalisierungsprozeß: Wechselseitige Rezeption, konstitutionelle Evolution und föderale Verflechtung.** 2003. LXV, 1534 Seiten. Geb. € 199,95

156 Julia *Sommer*: **Verwaltungskooperation am Beispiel administrativer Informationsverfahren im Europäischen Umweltrecht.** 2003. XXX, 891 Seiten. Geb. € 129,95

155 Frank *Schorkopf*: **Die Maßnahmen der XIV EU-Mitgliedstaaten gegen Österreich – Möglichkeiten und Grenzen einer „streitbaren Demokratie" auf europäischer Ebene.** 2002. XIII, 217 Seiten. Geb. € 64,95

154 Hanri *Mostert*: **The Constitutional Protection and Regulation of Property and its Influence on the Reform of Private Law and Landownership in South Africa and Germany.** 2002. XXV, 643 Seiten. Geb. € 99,95 zzgl. landesüblicher MwSt.

153 Stefan *Ohlhoff*: **Methoden der Konfliktbewältigung bei grenzüberschreitenden Umweltproblemen im Wandel.** 2003. XXX, 651 Seiten. Geb. € 99,95

152 Hans-Joachim *Cremer*, Thomas *Giegerich*, Dagmar *Richter*, Andreas *Zimmermann* (Hrsg.): **Tradition und Weltoffenheit des Rechts. Festschrift für Helmut Steinberger.** 2002. XVI, 1483 Seiten. Geb. € 199,–

Printing: Krips bv, Meppel, The Netherlands
Binding: Stürtz, Würzburg, Germany